Changing Earth and Human Activity

elevate science
MODULES

SAVVAS
LEARNING COMPANY

AUTHORS

You're an author!

As you write in this science book, your answers and personal discoveries will be recorded for you to keep, making this book unique to you. That is why you are one of the primary authors of this book.

In the space below, print your name, school, town, and state. Then write a short autobiography that includes your interests and accomplishments.

YOUR NAME ....

SCHOOL ....

TOWN, STATE ....

AUTOBIOGRAPHY ....

....

Your Photo

Savvas Learning Company LLC, 15 East Midland Avenue, Paramus, NJ 07652

The cover photo shows the Langkawi Sky Bridge, a cable bridge over the tropical rainforest.

Front cover: Bridge, 35007/E+/Getty Images; Back cover: Science Doodle, LHF Graphics/Shutterstock.

SAVVAS LEARNING COMPANY

ISBN-13: 978-1-418-29161-7
ISBN-10: 1-418-29161-7
4 20

Program Authors

ZIPPORAH MILLER, Ed.D.

Coordinator for K-12 Science Programs, Anne Arundel County Public Schools

Dr. Zipporah Miller currently serves as the Senior Manager for Organizational Learning with the Anne Arundel County Public School System. Prior to that she served as the K-12 Coordinator for science in Anne Arundel County. She conducts national training to science stakeholders on the Next Generation Science Standards. Dr. Miller also served as the Associate Executive Director for Professional Development Programs and conferences at the National Science Teachers Association (NSTA) and served as a reviewer during the development of Next Generation Science Standards. Dr. Miller holds a doctoral degree from the University of Maryland College Park, a master's degree in school administration and supervision from Bowie State University and a bachelor's degree from Chadron State College.

MICHAEL J. PADILLA, Ph.D.

Professor Emeritus, Eugene P. Moore School of Education, Clemson University, Clemson, South Carolina

Michael J. Padilla taught science in middle and secondary schools, has more than 30 years of experience educating middle-school science teachers, and served as one of the writers of the 1996 U.S. National Science Education Standards. In recent years Mike has focused on teaching science to English Language Learners. His extensive experience as Principal Investigator on numerous National Science Foundation and U.S. Department of Education grants resulted in more than $35 million in funding to improve science education. He served as president of the National Science Teachers Association, the world's largest science teaching organization, in 2005–6.

MICHAEL E. WYSESSION, Ph.D

Professor of Earth and Planetary Sciences, Washington University, St. Louis, Missouri

Author of more than 100 science and science education publications, Dr. Wysession was awarded the prestigious National Science Foundation Presidential Faculty Fellowship and Packard Foundation Fellowship for his research in geophysics, primarily focused on using seismic tomography to determine the forces driving plate tectonics. Dr. Wysession is also a leader in geoscience literacy and education; he is the chair of the Earth Science Literacy Initiative, the author of several popular video lectures on geology in the *Great Courses* series, and a lead writer of the *Next Generation Science Standards**.

---

*Next Generation Science Standards is a registered trademark of Achieve. Neither Achieve nor the lead states and partners that developed the Next Generation Science Standards were involved in the production of this product, and do not endorse it. NGSS Lead States. 2013. *Next Generation Science Standards: For States, By States.* Washington, DC: The National Academies Press.

REVIEWERS

Program Consultants

Carol Baker
Science Curriculum

Dr. Carol K. Baker is superintendent for Lyons Elementary K-8 School District in Lyons, Illinois. Prior to this, she was Director of Curriculum for Science and Music in Oak Lawn, Illinois. Before this she taught Physics and Earth Science for 18 years. In the recent past, Dr. Baker also wrote assessment questions for ACT (EXPLORE and PLAN), was elected president of the Illinois Science Teachers Association from 2011–2013, and served as a member of the Museum of Science and Industry (Chicago) advisory board. She is a writer of the Next Generation Science Standards. Dr. Baker received her B.S. in Physics and a science teaching certification. She completed her master's of Educational Administration (K-12) and earned her doctorate in Educational Leadership.

Jim Cummins
ELL

Dr. Cummins's research focuses on literacy development in multilingual schools and the role technology plays in learning across the curriculum. *Elevate Science* incorporates research-based principles for integrating language with the teaching of academic content based on Dr. Cummins's work.

Elfrieda Hiebert
Literacy

Dr. Hiebert, a former primary-school teacher, is President and CEO of TextProject, a non-profit aimed at providing open-access resources for instruction of beginning and struggling readers, She is also a research associate at the University of California Santa Cruz. Her research addresses how fluency, vocabulary, and knowledge can be fostered through appropriate texts, and her contributions have been recognized through awards such as the Oscar Causey Award for Outstanding Contributions to Reading Research (Literacy Research Association, 2015), Research to Practice award (American Educational Research Association, 2013), and the William S. Gray Citation of Merit Award for Outstanding Contributions to Reading Research (International Reading Association, 2008).

Content Reviewers

Alex Blom, Ph.D.
Associate Professor
Department Of Physical Sciences
Alverno College
Milwaukee, Wisconsin

Joy Branlund, Ph.D.
Department of Physical Science
Southwestern Illinois College
Granite City, Illinois

Judy Calhoun
Associate Professor
Physical Sciences
Alverno College
Milwaukee, Wisconsin

Stefan Debbert
Associate Professor of Chemistry
Lawrence University
Appleton, Wisconsin

Diane Doser
Professor
Department of Geological Sciences
University of Texas at El Paso
El Paso, Texas

Rick Duhrkopf, Ph.D.
Department of Biology
Baylor University
Waco, Texas

Jennifer Liang
University of Minnesota Duluth
Duluth, Minnesota

Heather Mernitz, Ph.D.
Associate Professor of Physical Sciences
Alverno College
Milwaukee, Wisconsin

Joseph McCullough, Ph.D.
Cabrillo College
Aptos, California

Katie M. Nemeth, Ph.D.
Assistant Professor
College of Science and Engineering
University of Minnesota Duluth
Duluth, Minnesota

Maik Pertermann
Department of Geology
Western Wyoming Community College
Rock Springs, Wyoming

Scott Rochette
Department of the Earth Sciences
The College at Brockport State University of New York
Brockport, New York

David Schuster
Washington University in St Louis
St. Louis, Missouri

Shannon Stevenson
Department of Biology
University of Minnesota Duluth
Duluth, Minnesota

Paul Stoddard, Ph.D.
Department of Geology and Environmental Geosciences
Northern Illinois University
DeKalb, Illinois

Nancy Taylor
American Public University
Charles Town, West Virginia

Teacher Reviewers

Jennifer Bennett, M.A.
Memorial Middle School
Tampa, Florida

Sonia Blackstone
Lake County Schools
Howey In the Hills, Florida

Teresa Bode
Roosevelt Elementary
Tampa, Florida

Tyler C. Britt, Ed.S.
Curriculum & Instructional Practice Coordinator
Raytown Quality Schools
Raytown, Missouri

A. Colleen Campos
Grandview High School
Aurora, Colorado

Ronald Davis
Riverview Elementary
Riverview, Florida

Coleen Doulk
Challenger School
Spring Hill, Florida

Mary D. Dube
Burnett Middle School
Seffner, Florida

Sandra Galpin
Adams Middle School
Tampa, Florida

Margaret Henry
Lebanon Junior High School
Lebanon, Ohio

Christina Hill
Beth Shields Middle School
Ruskin, Florida

Judy Johnis
Gorden Burnett Middle School
Seffner, Florida

Karen Y. Johnson
Beth Shields Middle School
Ruskin, Florida

Jane Kemp
Lockhart Elementary School
Tampa, Florida

Denise Kuhling
Adams Middle School
Tampa, Florida

Esther Leonard, M.Ed. and L.M.T.
Gifted and talented Implementation Specialist
San Antonio Independent School District
San Antonio, Texas

Kelly Maharaj
Challenger K–8 School of Science and Mathematics
Spring Hill, Florida

Kevin J. Maser, Ed.D.
H. Frank Carey Jr/Sr High School
Franklin Square, New York

Angie L. Matamoros, Ph.D.
ALM Science Consultant
Weston, Florida

Corey Mayle
Brogden Middle School
Durham, North Carolina

Keith McCarthy
George Washington Middle School
Wayne, New Jersey

Yolanda O. Peña
John F. Kennedy Junior High School
West Valley City, Utah

Kathleen M. Poe
Jacksonville Beach Elementary School
Jacksonville Beach, Florida

Wendy Rauld
Monroe Middle School
Tampa, Florida

Anne Rice
Woodland Middle School
Gurnee, Illinois

Bryna Selig
Gaithersburg Middle School
Gaithersburg, Maryland

Pat (Patricia) Shane, Ph.D.
STEM & ELA Education Consultant
Chapel Hill, North Carolina

Diana Shelton
Burnett Middle School
Seffner, Florida

Nakia Sturrup
Jennings Middle School
Seffner, Florida

Melissa Triebwasser
Walden Lake Elementary
Plant City, Florida

Michele Bubley Wiehagen
Science Coach
Miles Elementary School
Tampa, Florida

Pauline Wilcox
Instructional Science Coach
Fox Chapel Middle School
Spring Hill, Florida

Safety Reviewers

Douglas Mandt, M.S.
Science Education Consultant
Edgewood, Washington

Juliana Textley, Ph.D.
Author, NSTA books on school science safety
Adjunct Professor
Lesley University
Cambridge, Massachusetts

TOPIC 1

Earth's Surface Systems xii

The Essential Question **What processes change Earth's surface?**

Quest KICKOFF **Ingenious Island** 2

uConnect Lab How Does Gravity Affect Materials on a Slope? 3A

MS-ESS2-2, MS-ESS3-2

LESSON 1 Weathering and Soil 4

Literacy Connection Write Explanatory Texts 7

Math Toolbox Reason Quantitatively 8

Quest CHECK-IN Breaking It Down 12

uEngineer It! STEM Ground Shifting Advances: Maps Help Predict 13

LESSON 2 Erosion and Deposition 14

Literacy Connection Integrate With Visuals 15

Math Toolbox Analyze Quantitative Relationships 17

Quest CHECK-INS Ingenious Island: Part I; Changing Landscapes 20

Career Civil Engineer 21

LESSON 3 Water Erosion 22

Literacy Connection Cite Textual Evidence 23

Quest CHECK-IN Ingenious Island: Part II 31

Case Study Buyer Beware! 32

LESSON 4 Glacial and Wave Erosion 34

Math Toolbox Reason Abstractly 36

Literacy Connection Write Informative Texts 41

Quest CHECK-IN Breaking Waves 43

Review and Assess 44

Evidence-Based Assessment.......................................46

Quest FINDINGS Reflect on Your Ingenious Island 47

uDemonstrate Materials on a Slope 48

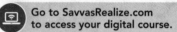

Go to SavvasRealize.com to access your digital course.

VIDEO
- Civil Engineer

INTERACTIVITY
- Colors of the Sand
- Dating Using Weathering Rates
- Classify the Force of Weathering
- Predicting Disasters
- Material Slope Angle
- Changing Landscapes
- Karst Topography
- Carving a Canyon
- Mammoth Caves
- Effects of Glaciers
- Glacial Ice
- Coastline Management

VIRTUAL LAB
- Save the Town

ASSESSMENT

eTEXT

HANDS-ON LABS

uConnect How Does Gravity Affect Materials on a Slope?

uInvestigate
- Freezing and Thawing
- Small, Medium, and Large
- Raindrops Falling
- Changing Coastlines

uDemonstrate Materials on a Slope

TOPIC 2

Distribution of Natural Resources

Distribution of Natural Resources 52

The Essential Question How is the distribution of natural resources the result of geological processes?

Quest KICKOFF Predicting Boom or Bust 54

uConnect Lab What's in a Piece of Coal? 55A

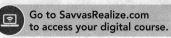

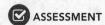

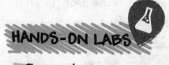

MS-ESS3-1, MS-ESS3-3, MS-ESS3-4

LESSON 1 Nonrenewable Energy Resources 56
- **Math Toolbox** Analyze Relationships 62
- **Literacy Connection** Cite Textual Evidence 63
- **Quest CHECK-IN** Surviving on Fossil Fuels 65

LESSON 2 Renewable Energy Resources 66
- **Math Toolbox** Represent Quantitative Relationships 70
- **Literacy Connection** Draw Evidence 71
- **Quest CHECK-IN** Renewable Energy 72
- **uEngineer It! STEM** Micro-Hydro Power 73

LESSON 3 Mineral Resources 74
- **Literacy Connection** Determine Meaning 76
- **Quest CHECK-IN** Surviving on Minerals 81
- **Case Study** Phosphorus Fiasco 82

LESSON 4 Water Resources 84
- **Math Toolbox** Draw Comparative Inferences 86
- **Literacy Connection** Support Author's Claim 88
- **Quest CHECK-IN** Surviving on Water 90
- **It's All Connected** The Pseudoscience of Water Dowsing ... 91

Review and Assess 92
- Evidence-Based Assessment 94
- **Quest FINDINGS** Reflect on Boomtowns 95
- **uDemonstrate** To Drill or Not to Drill 96

Go to SavvasRealize.com to access your digital course.

VIDEO
- Geophysicist

INTERACTIVITY
- Distribution of Fossil Fuels
- Using Renewable Resources
- Biogas Farming
- Distribution of Minerals
- Distribution of Water Resources
- Wetland Restoration
- Water Worth

VIRTUAL LAB
- Go with the Flow (Through an Aquifer)

ASSESSMENT

eTEXT

HANDS-ON LABS

uConnect What's in a Piece of Coal?

uInvestigate
- Fossil Fuels
- The Power of Wind
- Cool Crystals
- An Artesian Well

uDemonstrate To Drill or Not to Drill

TOPIC 3

Human Impacts on the Environment

Human Impacts on the Environment 100

The Essential Question: How does human activity impact Earth's systems?

Quest KICKOFF Trash Backlash 102

uConnect Lab Finding a Solution for Your Pollution 103A

MS-ESS3-4

LESSON 1 Population Growth and Resource Consumption 104

Math Toolbox Draw Comparative Inferences 107

Literacy Connection Determine Conclusions 109

Quest CHECK-IN More Trash, Less Space 111

LESSON 2 Air Pollution 112

Literacy Connection Cite Textual Evidence 116

Math Toolbox Analyze Quantitative Relationships 118

Quest CHECK-IN Trash vs. Water 120

Global to Local Working Together to Reduce Air Pollution 121

LESSON 3 Impacts on Land 122

Math Toolbox Analyze Proportional Relationships 127

Literacy Connection Cite Textual Evidence 129

Quest CHECK-IN Life of a Landfill 133

Case Study Nothing Goes to Waste 134

LESSON 4 Water Pollution 136

Literacy Connection Draw Evidence 139

Math Toolbox Analyze Proportional Relationships 141

Quest CHECK-IN Reducing Waste 144

uEngineer It! STEM From Wastewater to Tap Water 145

Review and Assess 146

Evidence-Based Assessment 148

Quest FINDINGS Reflect on Trash Backlash 149

uDemonstrate Washing Away 150

Science and Engineering Practices Handbook 154

Appendices, Glossary, Index 166

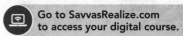

Go to SavvasRealize.com to access your digital course.

VIDEO
- Water Engineer

INTERACTIVITY
- Modern Life
- Human Population Growth
- Sources of Resources
- Damage From the Skies
- Sources and Solutions of Air Pollution
- Farming Lessons
- Ride the Light Rail
- Water Cycle Interrupted
- Mutation Mystery
- Wetland Restoration
- Research Water Pollution

VIRTUAL LAB
- Electricity Usage

ASSESSMENT

eTEXT

HANDS-ON LABS

uConnect Finding a Solution for Your Pollution

uInvestigate
- Doubling Time
- It's All in the Air
- Mining Matters
- Getting Clean

uDemonstrate
Washing Away

Go to SavvasRealize.com to access your digital course.

Elevate Science combines the best science narrative with a robust online program. Throughout the lessons, digital support is presented at point of use to enhance your learning experience.

Online Resources

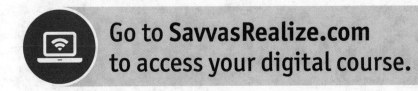

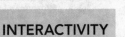

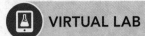

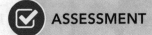

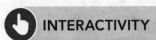

Savvas Realize™ is your online science class. This digital-learning environment includes:

- Student eTEXT
- Instructor eTEXT
- Project-Based Learning
- Virtual Labs
- Interactivities
- Videos
- Assessments
- Study Tools
- and more!

Digital Features

VIDEO

INTERACTIVITY

VIRTUAL LAB

ASSESSMENT

eTEXT

APP

Keep an eye out for these **icons**, which indicate the different ways your textbook is enhanced online.

Digital activities are located throughout the narrative to deepen your understanding of scientific concepts.

INTERACTIVITY

Interpret models of relationships in various ecosystems.

Elevate your thinking!

Elevate Science takes science to a whole new level and lets you take ownership of your learning. Explore science in the world around you. Investigate how things work. Think critically and solve problems! *Elevate Science* helps you think like a scientist, so you're ready for a world of discoveries.

Explore Your World

Explore real-life scenarios with engaging Quests that dig into science topics around the world. You can:

- Solve real-world problems
- Apply skills and knowledge
- Communicate solutions

Quest KICKOFF

What do you think is causing Pleasant Pond to turn green?

In 2016, algal blooms turned bodies of water green and slimy in Florida, Utah, California, and 17 other states. These blooms put people and ecosystems in danger. Scientists, such as limnologists, are working to predict and prevent future algal blooms. In this problem-based Quest activity, you will investigate an algal bloom at a lake and determine its cause. In labs and digital activities, you will apply what you learn in each lesson to help you gather evidence to solve the mystery. With enough evidence, you will be able to identify what you believe is the cause of the algal bloom and present a solution in the Findings activity.

Make Connections

Elevate Science connects science to other subjects and shows you how to better understand the world through:

- Mathematics
- Reading and Writing
- Literacy

Math Toolbox

Graphing Population Changes

Ohio's Deer Population

Changes in a population over time, such as white-tailed deer in Ohio, can be displayed in a graph.

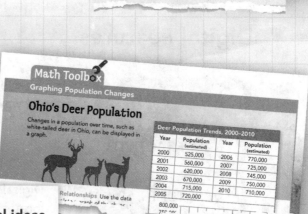

Deer Population Trends, 2000–2010

Year	Population (estimated)	Year	Population (estimated)
2000	525,000	2006	770,000
2001	560,000	2007	725,000
2002	620,000	2008	745,000
2003	670,000	2009	750,000
2004	715,000	2010	710,000
2005	720,000		

Relationships Use the data

800,000

READING CHECK **Determine Central ideas**
What adaptations might the giraffe have that help it survive in its environment?

Academic Vocabulary

Relate the term *decomposer* to the verb *compose*. What does it mean to compose something?

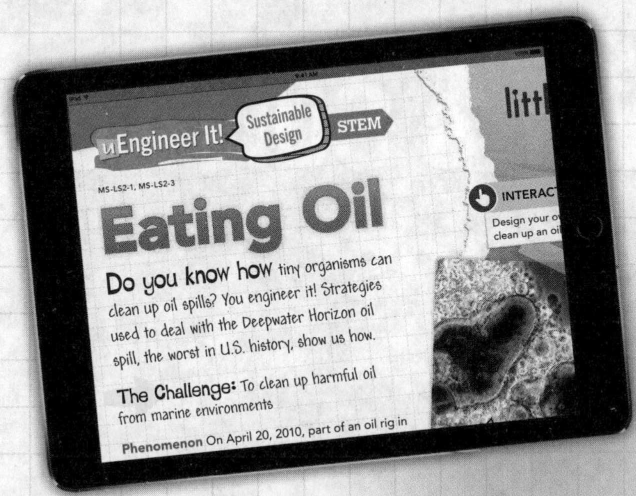

uEngineer It!
Sustainable Design
STEM
MS-LS2-1, MS-LS2-3
Eating Oil
Do you know how tiny organisms can clean up oil spills? You engineer it! Strategies used to deal with the Deepwater Horizon oil spill, the worst in U.S. history, show us how.
The Challenge: To clean up harmful oil from marine environments
Phenomenon On April 20, 2010, part of an oil rig in

Build Skills for the Future

- Master the Engineering Design Process
- Apply critical thinking and analytical skills
- Learn about STEM careers

Focus on Inquiry

Case studies put you in the shoes of a scientist to solve real-world mysteries using real data. You will be able to:

- Analyze Data
- Test a hypothesis
- Solve the Case

Case Study
MS-LS2-1
THE CASE OF THE DISAPPEARING
Cerulean Warbler
The cerulean warbler is a small, migratory songbird named for its blue color. Cerulean warblers breed in eastern North America during the spring and summer. The warblers spend the winter months in the Andes Mountains of Colombia, Venezuela, Ecuador, and Peru in northern part of South America.

Enter the Lab

Hands-on experiments and virtual labs help you test ideas and show what you know in performance-based assessments. Scaffolded labs include:

- STEM Labs
- Design Your Own
- Open-ended Labs

Alike and Different: Living Things
Click the pictures.
Compare how living things and their parents are alike and different.
Write your answer below.
Type your answer here.

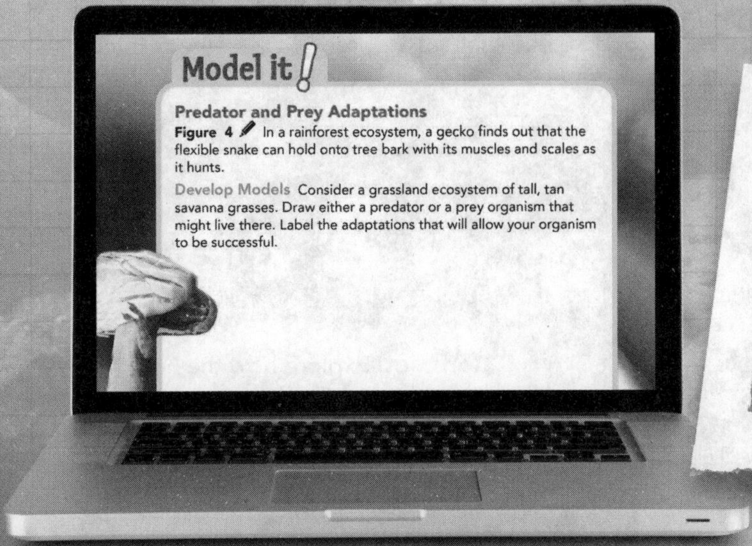

Model it!
Predator and Prey Adaptations
Figure 4 In a rainforest ecosystem, a gecko finds out that the flexible snake can hold onto tree bark with its muscles and scales as it hunts.
Develop Models Consider a grassland ecosystem of tall, tan savanna grasses. Draw either a predator or a prey organism that might live there. Label the adaptations that will allow your organism to be successful.

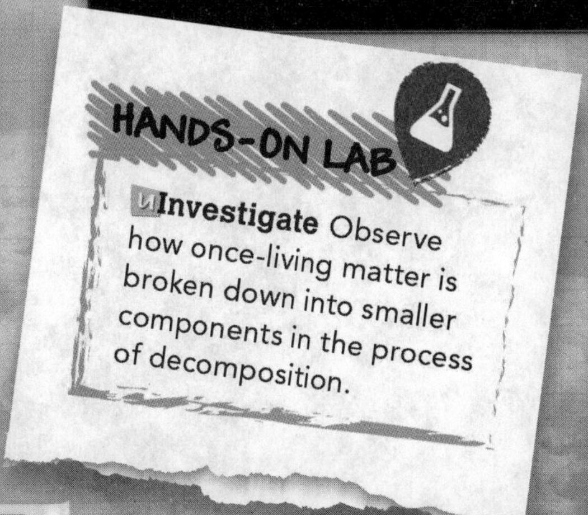

HANDS-ON LAB
uInvestigate Observe how once-living matter is broken down into smaller components in the process of decomposition.

TOPIC 1

Earth's Surface Systems

How did this rock get its strange shape?

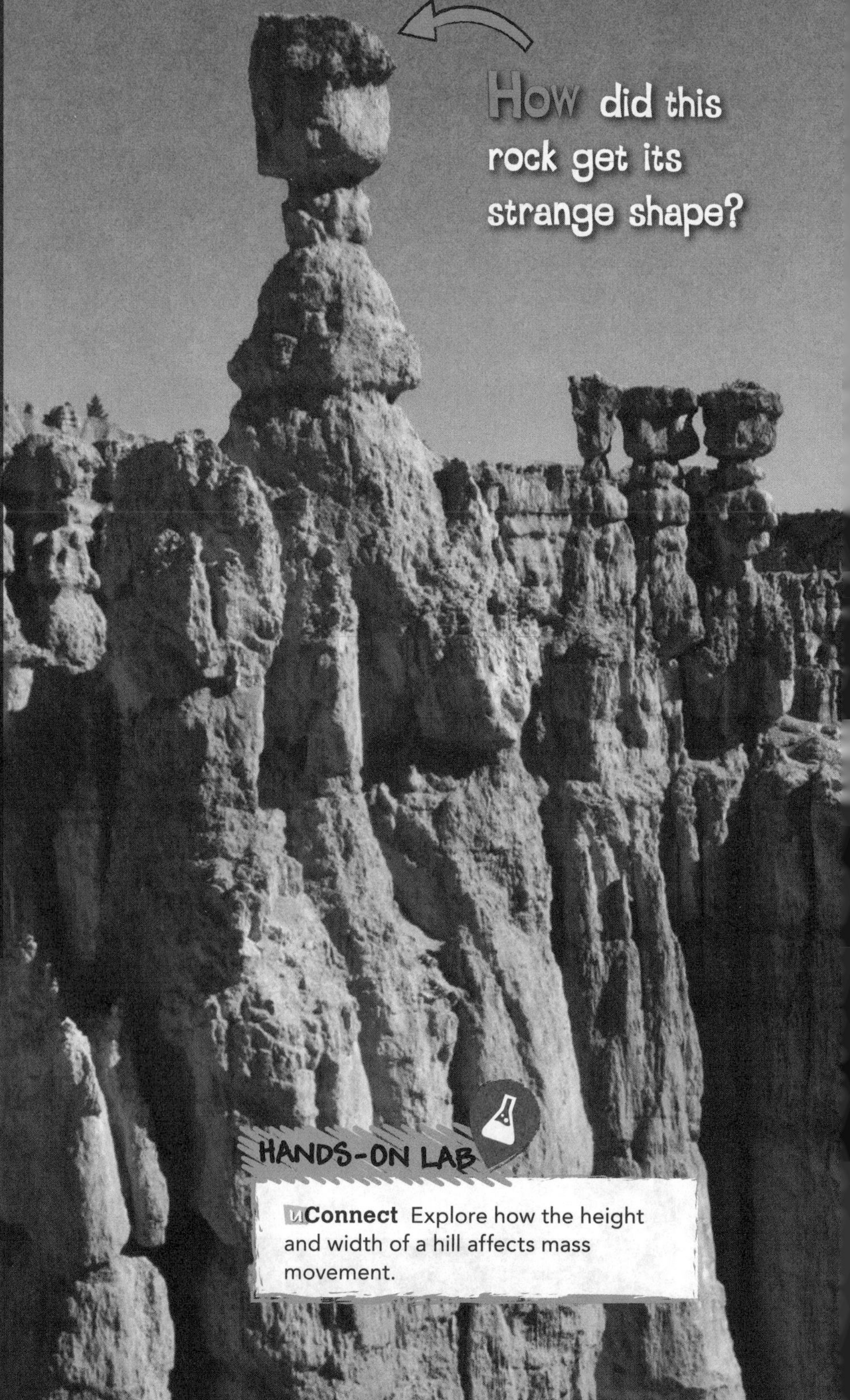

LESSON 1
Weathering and Soil
uInvestigate Lab: Freezing and Thawing

uEngineer It! STEM **Ground Shifting Advances**

LESSON 2
Erosion and Deposition
uInvestigate Lab: Small, Medium, and Large

LESSON 3
Water Erosion
uInvestigate Lab: Raindrops Falling

LESSON 4
Glacial and Wave Erosion
uInvestigate Lab: Changing Coastlines

NGSS PERFORMANCE EXPECTATIONS

MS-ESS2-2 Construct an explanation based on evidence for how geoscience processes have changed Earth's surface at varying time and spatial scales.

MS-ESS3-2 Analyze and interpret data on natural hazards to forecast future catastrophic events and inform the development of technologies to mitigate their effects.

HANDS-ON LAB

uConnect Explore how the height and width of a hill affects mass movement.

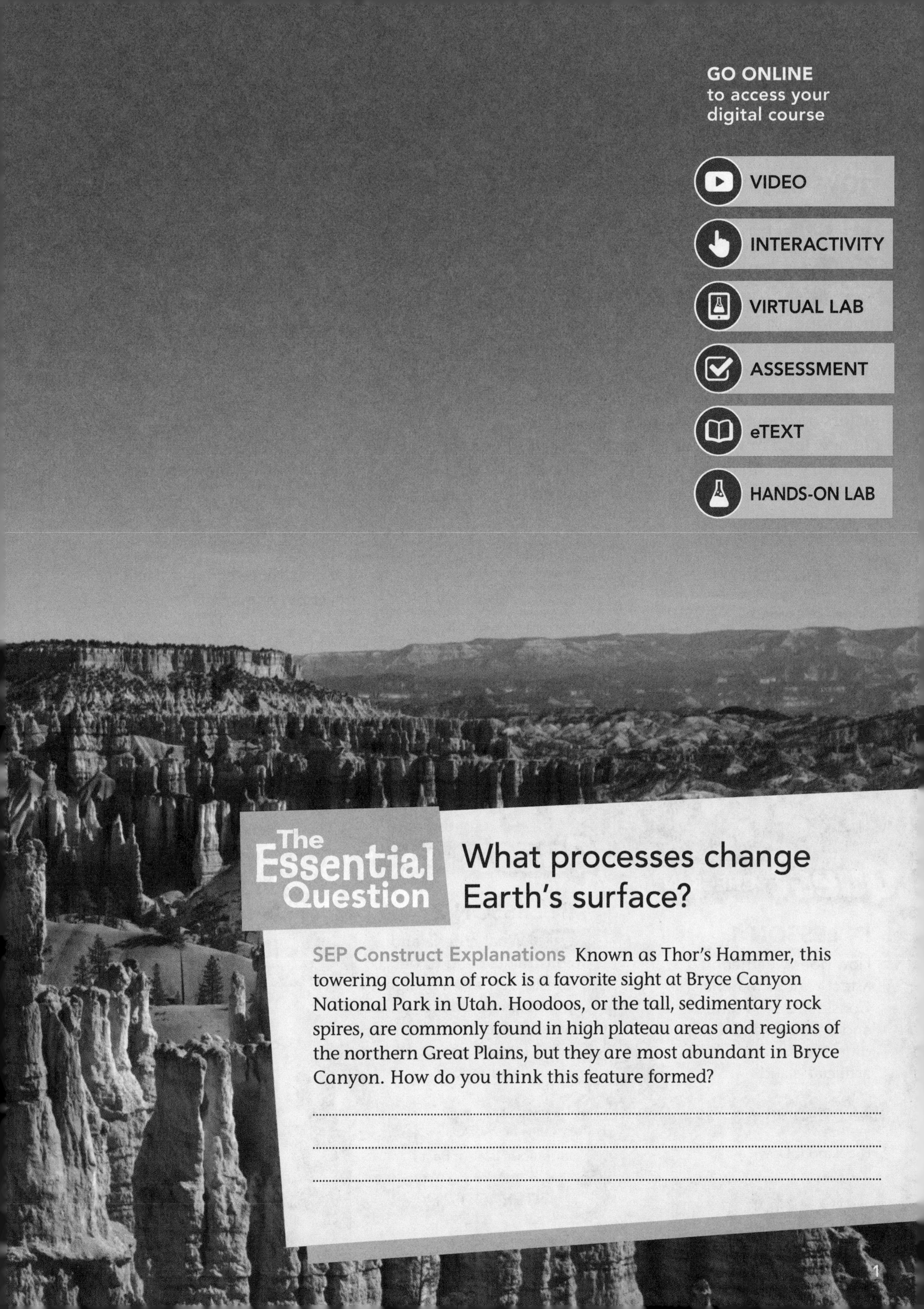

GO ONLINE
to access your digital course

- VIDEO
- INTERACTIVITY
- VIRTUAL LAB
- ASSESSMENT
- eTEXT
- HANDS-ON LAB

The Essential Question

What processes change Earth's surface?

SEP Construct Explanations Known as Thor's Hammer, this towering column of rock is a favorite sight at Bryce Canyon National Park in Utah. Hoodoos, or the tall, sedimentary rock spires, are commonly found in high plateau areas and regions of the northern Great Plains, but they are most abundant in Bryce Canyon. How do you think this feature formed?

....

....

....

Quest KICKOFF

How can I design and build an artificial island?

STEM **Phenomenon** One way to expand a city surrounded by water is to make more land. In New York City, the area of lower Manhattan known as Battery Park City was created by civil engineers using soil and rock excavated during the construction of new skyscrapers. But what factors do engineers need to consider when they create new land in water? In this problem-based Quest activity, you will design an artificial island that can withstand nature's forces and that has minimal environmental impact.

INTERACTIVITY

Ingenious Island

MS-ESS2-2 Construct an explanation based on evidence for how geoscience processes have changed Earth's surface at varying time and spatial scales.
MS-ESS3-2 Analyze and interpret data on natural hazards to forecast future catastrophic events and inform the development of technologies to mitigate their effects.

NBC LEARN VIDEO

After watching the Quest Kickoff video about how coastal engineers study and reduce coastal erosion, complete the 3-2-1 activity.

3 ways that water changes land

....

....

....

2 ways that wind changes land

....

....

1 way that those changes could be prevented or minimized

....

....

Quest CHECK-IN

IN LESSON 1

How does weathering affect various materials? Consider the benefits and drawbacks of using different materials for an artificial island.

HANDS-ON LAB

Breaking It Down

Quest CHECK-INS

IN LESSON 2

STEM What criteria and constraints need to be considered when designing your island model to resist erosion over periods of time? Design and build your island model.

HANDS-ON LAB

Ingenious Island: Part I

INTERACTIVITY

Changing Landscapes

Quest CHECK-IN

IN LESSON 3

STEM How resistant is your island model to erosion? Test the effects of the agents of erosion on your model and make improvements.

HANDS-ON LAB

Ingenious Island: Part II

Beachfront properties line one of the "branches" of the Palm Jumeirah in the United Arab Emirates. The palm-shaped artificial island extends into the Persian Gulf off the coast of Dubai. It provides miles of additional shoreline for homes and elaborate hotels.

Quest CHECK-IN

IN LESSON 4

How can wave erosion impact the location of your artificial island? Adjust your design as needed to account for wave erosion.

INTERACTIVITY

Breaking Waves

Quest FINDINGS

Complete the Quest!

Present your island model and explain how your design decisions relate to the forces that change Earth's surface.

INTERACTIVITY

Reflect on Your Ingenious Island

uConnect Lab

MS-ESS3-2

How Does Gravity Affect Materials On A Slope?

How can you collect and **analyze data** to help determine if earth material will move downslope and pose a hazard?

Materials

(per group)

- large plastic cup
- cardboard
- beaker
- piece of paper on clipboard
- dry sand
- dry pea gravel
- dry potting soil
- protractor
- paper
- empty container for materials

Safety

Be sure to follow all safety procedures provided by your teacher. The Safety Appendix of your textbook provides more details about the safety icons.

Background

Phenomenon You are a park ranger at Yellowstone National Park and have been asked to scout the park for high-risk areas where debris may move down a slope due to gravity. Identifying these areas can help limit damage to structures and prevent injuries to people. Before you identify high-risk areas, you want to collect and analyze data on different types of ground materials and how steep an incline made of that material can be before it starts to slide down a slope. The angle of the slope just before material starts to move is known as the angle of repose.

Plan an Investigation

☐ 1. **Plan an Investigation** Use the materials provided to plan an investigation to determine the angle of repose of dry gravel, soil, and sand.

☐ 2. Consider the following questions before you begin:
- What variables do you need to control?
- What data will you collect?
- How many trials will you conduct?

☐ 3. On a piece of paper write your procedure. Have your teacher approve your plan before you begin.

Observations

HANDS-ON LAB

Connect Go online for a downloadable worksheet of this lab.

Analyze and Interpret Data

1. **SEP Analyze Data** Which material had the highest angle of repose? Which had the lowest?

2. **CCC Cause and Effect** Observe the list of slopes around Yellowstone National Park. On which slopes should signs be placed warning of landslide danger?

	Angle	Type of Material	Should a Sign be Placed?
Slope A	45 degrees	sand	
Slope B	20 degrees	soil	
Slope C	50 degrees	gravel	

3. **SEP Explain Phenomena** Antlions are a type of insect that build a cone-shaped hole in sandy soil and lie beneath it in the center. When ants or other insects walk into the cone, they slide down and into the grasp of the waiting antlion. Use what you learned in the lab to explain how antlions capture prey.

LESSON 1

Weathering and Soil

Guiding Questions

- How does erosion change Earth's surface?
- How does weathering change Earth's surface?
- How does soil form?

Connections

Literacy Write Explanatory Texts

Math Reason Quantitatively

MS-ESS2-2

HANDS-ON LAB

uInvestigate Look at how ice helps to break down rock.

Vocabulary

uniformitarianism
erosion
mechanical weathering
chemical weathering
soil
humus

Academic Vocabulary

principle
component

Connect It!

The Wave is a stunning dip in Earth's surface. Draw an arrow showing where the material originally covering the Wave would have begun.

SEP Construct Explanations What processes have broken apart and carried off the many layers of solid rock that covered the Wave for millions of years?

....

....

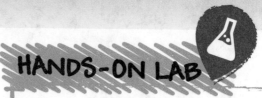

Breaking Down Earth's Surface

Even the hardest rocks wear down over time on Earth's surface. Natural processes, such as the one that produced the Wave in **Figure 1**, break down rocks and carry the pieces away. Geologists make inferences about what processes shaped Earth's surface in the past based on the **principle** of **uniformitarianism** (yoon uh form uh TAYR ee un iz um). This principle states that the geologic processes that operate today also operated in the past. Scientists infer that ancient landforms and features formed through the same processes they observe today and will continue to do so in the future.

The processes of weathering and **erosion** (ee ROH zhun) work together to change Earth's surface by wearing down and carrying away rock particles. The process of weathering breaks down rock and other substances. Heat, cold, water, ice, and gases all contribute to weathering. Erosion involves the removal of rock particles by wind, water, ice, or gravity.

Weathering and erosion work continuously to reshape Earth's surface. The same processes that wear down mountains also cause bicycles to rust, paint to peel, and sidewalks to crack. Weathering and erosion can take millions of years to break down and wear away huge mountains, or they can take seconds to carry rock away in an avalanche. These processes started changing Earth's surface billions of years ago and they continue to do so.

Academic Vocabulary

Describe another principle you follow in science or in your everyday life.

....

....

....

Determine Meaning

How has weathering or erosion affected you? In your science notebook, describe an example of weathering or erosion you observed and any impact it had on you or your community.

Riding the Rock Wave

Figure 1 Known as the Wave, this sandstone dip in Earth's surface in Northern Arizona was buried beneath solid rock for millions of years.

Mechanical Weathering

Figure 2 Label each photo with an agent of mechanical weathering.

CCC Stability and Change How might more than one agent of mechanical weathering operate in the same place?

HANDS-ON LAB

Investigate Look at how ice helps to break down rock.

Weathering Earth's Surface

The type of weathering in which rock is physically broken into smaller pieces is called **mechanical weathering**. A second type of weathering, called chemical weathering, also breaks down rock. **Chemical weathering** is the process that breaks down rock through chemical changes.

Mechanical Weathering Rocks that are cracked or split in layers have undergone mechanical weathering. Mechanical weathering usually happens gradually, over very long periods of time. Mechanical weathering, as part of erosion, can eventually wear away whole mountains.

The natural agents of mechanical weathering include freezing and thawing, release of pressure, plant growth, actions of animals, and abrasion, as shown in **Figure 2**. Abrasion (uh BRAY zhun) refers to the wearing away of rock by rock particles carried by water, ice, wind, or gravity. Human activities, such as mining and farming, also cause mechanical weathering.

Through mechanical weathering, Earth systems interact and shape the surface. For example, the geosphere (rocks) interacts with the hydrosphere (water, ice) during frost wedging. Frost wedging occurs when water seeps into cracks in rocks and expands as it freezes. Wedges of ice in rocks widen and deepen cracks. When the ice melts, water seeps deeper into the cracks. With repeated freezing and thawing, the cracks slowly expand until pieces of rock break off.

Chemical Weathering Chemical weathering often produces new minerals as it breaks down rock. For example, granite is made up of several minerals, including feldspars. Chemical weathering causes the feldspar to eventually change to clay minerals.

Water, oxygen, carbon dioxide, living organisms, and acid rain cause chemical weathering. Water weathers some rock by dissolving it. Water also carries other substances, including oxygen, carbon dioxide, and other chemicals, that dissolve or break down rock.

The oxygen and carbon dioxide gases in the atmosphere cause chemical weathering. Rust forms when iron combines with oxygen in the presence of water. Rusting makes rock soft and crumbly and gives it a red or brown color. When carbon dioxide dissolves in water, carbonic acid forms. This weak acid easily weathers certain types of rock, such as marble and limestone.

As a plant's roots grow, they produce weak acids that gradually dissolve rock. Lichens—plantlike organisms that grow on rocks—also produce weak acids.

Humans escalate chemical weathering by burning fossil fuels. This pollutes the air and results in rainwater that is more strongly acidic. Acid rain causes very rapid chemical weathering of rock.

READING CHECK **Summarize Text** How are the agents of weathering similar and different?

Literacy Connection

Write Explanatory Texts
An ancient marble statue is moved from a rural location to a highly polluted city. Explain how the move might affect the statue and why you think so.

INTERACTIVITY

Find out how weathering rates help with dating.

Rate of Weathering

Rate of Weathering In historic cemeteries, slate tombstones from the 1700s are less weathered than marble tombstones from the 1800s. Why? Some kinds of rocks weather more rapidly than others. The rate at which weathering occurs is determined by the type of rock and the climate.

Type of Rock Rocks wear down slowly if they are made of minerals that do not dissolve easily. Rocks weather faster if they are made of minerals that dissolve easily.

Some rocks weather more easily because they are permeable. A permeable (PUR mee uh bul) material is full of tiny air spaces. The spaces increase the surface area. As water seeps through the spaces in the rock, it carries chemicals that dissolve the rock and removes material broken down by weathering.

Climate Climate is the average weather conditions in an area. Weathering occurs faster in wet climates. Rainfall causes chemical changes. Freezing and thawing cause mechanical changes in cold and wet climates.

Chemical reactions occur faster at higher temperatures. That is why chemical weathering occurs more quickly where the climate is both hot and wet. Human activities, such as those that produce acid rain, also increase the rate of weathering.

Math Toolbox

Comparing Weathered Limestone

The data table shows how much rock was broken down by weathering for two identical pieces of limestone in two different locations.

1. **Construct Graphs** Use the data to make a double-line graph. Decide how to make each line look different. Be sure to provide a title and label the axes and each graph line.
2. **SEP Use Mathematics** Compare the slopes of each line.

....

....

3. **Reason Quantitatively** As time increases, the limestone thickness (increases/decreases).
4. **SEP Analyze Data** Limestone A weathered at a (slower/faster) rate than Limestone B.

Weathering Rates of Limestone

Time (years)	Thickness of Limestone Lost (mm)	
	Limestone A	Limestone B
200	1.75	0.80
400	3.50	1.60
600	5.25	2.40
800	7.00	3.20
1,000	8.75	4.00

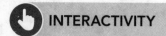

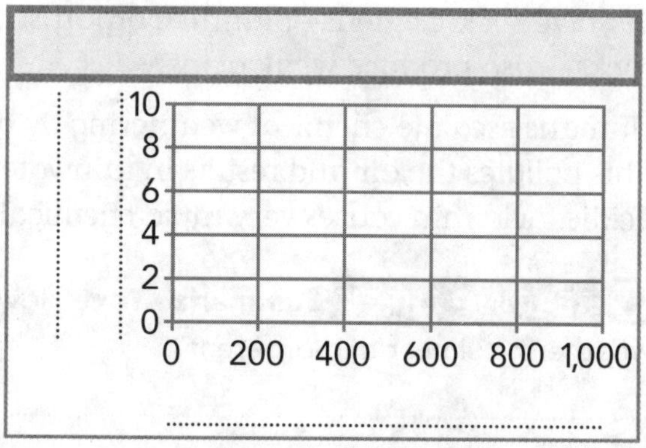

Gravel
2 mm
& larger

Sand
Less than
2 mm

Silt
Less than
0.05 mm

Clay
Less than
0.002 mm

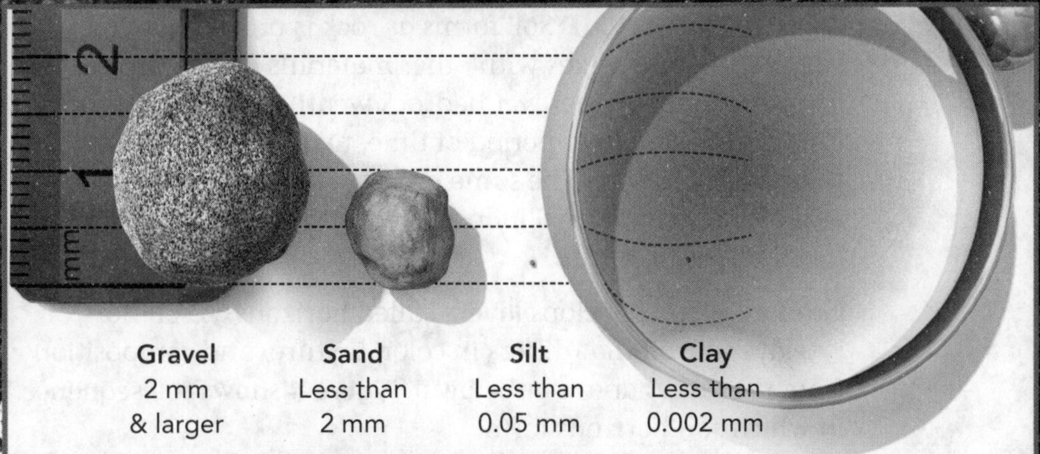

Source: Michigan Technological University

Forming Soil

Have you ever wondered how plants grow on rocks? Plants can grow only when soil begins to form in the cracks. **Soil** is the loose, weathered material on Earth's surface in which plants grow.

Soil Composition Soil is a mixture of rock particles, minerals, decayed organic material, water, and air. The main **components** of soil come from bedrock. Bedrock is the solid layer of rock beneath the soil. Once bedrock is exposed to air, water, and living things, it gradually weathers into smaller and smaller particles.

The particles of rock in soil are classified by size as gravel, sand, silt, and clay. **Figure 3** shows the relative sizes of these particles. A soil's texture depends on the size of the soil particles.

The decayed organic material in soil is called humus. **Humus** (HYOO mus) is a dark-colored substance that forms as plant and animal remains decay. Humus helps to create spaces in soil that are then filled by air and water. It contains nutrients that plants need.

☑ READING CHECK **Write Explanatory Texts** Explain how you might determine the rate of weathering on a sample of rock.

...

...

...

...

...

Soil Particle Size

Figure 3 ✏ The rock particles shown here have been enlarged. On the graph, mark the size of a 1.5-mm particle with an X.

Classify Explain how you would classify that size particle and why.

...

...

...

Academic Vocabulary

What are the similarities between components of a computer and the components of soil?

...

...

...

...

...

👆 **INTERACTIVITY**

Learn how minerals affect the colors of sand.

INTERACTIVITY

Identify different types of weathering.

Soil Formation

Soil Formation Soil forms as rock is broken down by weathering and mixes with other materials on the surface. Soil forms constantly wherever bedrock weathers. Soil formation continues over a long period of time, taking hundreds to thousands of years. The same process that forms soil today was also taking place billions of years ago and will continue to form soil in the future.

Gradually, soil develops layers called horizons. A soil horizon is a layer of soil that differs in color, texture, and composition from the layers above or below it. **Figure 4** shows the sequence in which soil horizons form.

Soil and Organisms Recall that organisms are part of Earth's biosphere. Many organisms live in soil and interact with the geosphere. Some soil organisms aid in the formation of humus, which makes soil rich in the nutrients that plants need. Other soil organisms mix the soil and make spaces in it for air and water.

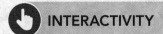

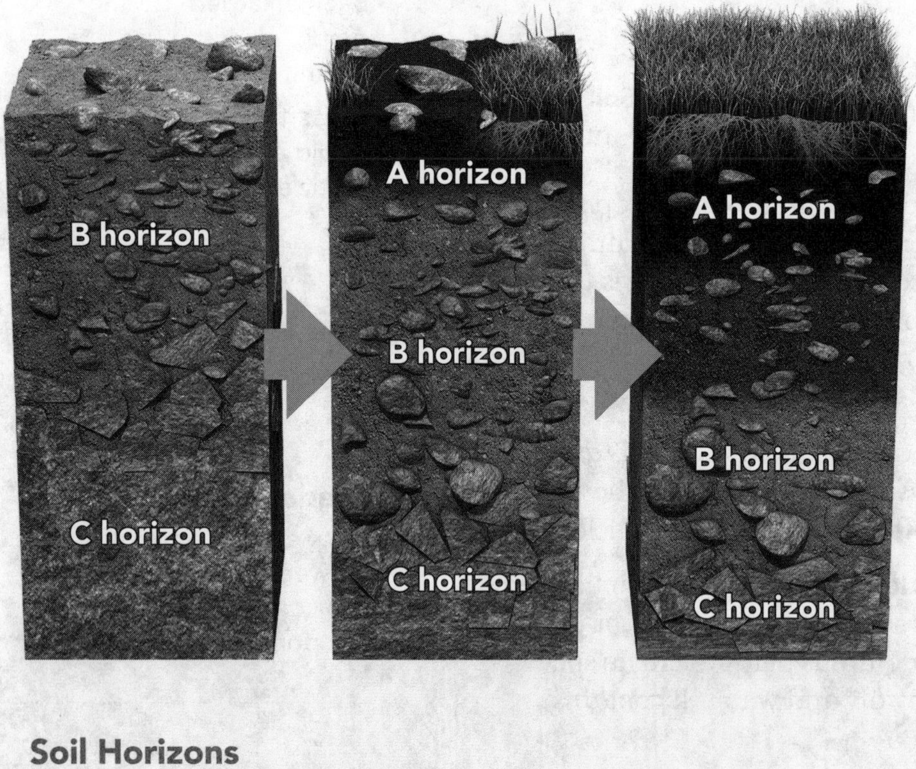

A horizon
The A horizon is made up of topsoil, a crumbly, dark brown soil that is a mixture of humus, clay, and minerals. Topsoil forms as plants add organic material to the soil, and plant roots weather pieces of rock.

B horizon
The B horizon, often called subsoil, usually consists of clay and other particles of rock, but little humus. It forms as rainwater washes these materials down from the A horizon.

C horizon
The C horizon forms as bedrock begins to weather. The rock breaks up into small particles.

Soil Horizons

Figure 4 Soil horizons form in three main steps.

1. SEP Use Models Underline the soil horizon that contains the most organic matter.
2. SEP Construct Explanations In what climates would you expect soil to form fastest? Why?

....

....

Forming Humus Dead leaves, roots, and other plant materials contribute most of the organic remains that form humus. Humus forms in a process called decomposition carried out by a combination of decomposers including fungi, bacteria, worms, and other organisms. Decomposers break down the remains of dead organisms into smaller pieces through the process of chemical digestion. This material then mixes with the soil as nutrient-rich humus where it can be used by living plants.

Mixing the Soil Earthworms and burrowing mammals mix humus with air and other materials in soil, as shown in **Figure 5**. As earthworms eat their way through the soil, they carry humus down to the subsoil and from the subsoil up to the surface. These organisms increase the soil's fertility by dispersing organic matter throughout the soil. Mammals such as mice, moles, and prairie dogs break up hard, compacted soil and mix humus with it. Animal wastes contribute nutrients to the soil as well.

READING CHECK **Integrate With Visuals** Review the information and illustrations in **Figure 4**. How is weathering related to soil formation?

....

....

....

Organisms Impact Soil

Figure 5 Earthworms and chipmunks break up hard, compacted soil, making it easier for air and water to enter the soil.

1. SEP Synthesize Information Besides breaking up and mixing soil, the (earthworm/chipmunk) is also a decomposer.
2. CCC Systems As these organisms change the soil, which Earth systems are interacting?

....

....

Model It!

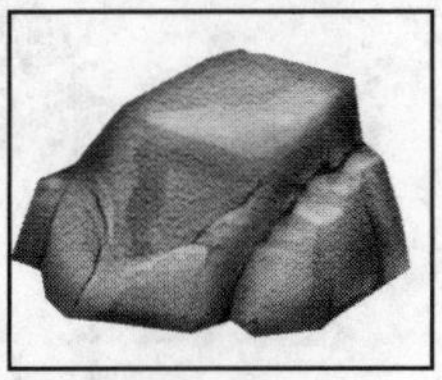

Bedrock

→ [ ] → [ ] → [ ] →

....

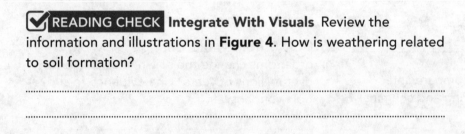

Topsoil

From Rock to Soil

Figure 6 The illustrations show bedrock and topsoil rich in humus.

1. SEP Develop Models In the empty boxes, draw the processes that help to change the bedrock into soil. Label the processes in each drawing. Include at least two processes that involve organisms.
2. SEP Use Models The topsoil represents the (A/B/C) horizon.

LESSON 1 Check

MS-ESS2-2

1. **CCC Cause and Effect** How does erosion affect Earth's surface?

2. **SEP Construct Explanations** Explain how water can wear down Earth's surface at scales that are large and small in size, or short and long in duration.

3. **Compare and Contrast** Compare and contrast mechanical weathering and chemical weathering.

4. **SEP Evaluate Information** A community group needs advice on choosing rock for a city park monument that will last a long time. Explain the factors that would likely affect how long the monument lasts.

5. **CCC Stability and Change** How did organisms change the soil in North America over millions of years? Cite evidence to support your answer.

Quest CHECK-IN

In this lesson, you learned how weathering and erosion change Earth's surface. You also discovered how soil forms.

SEP Use Models How can modeling the effects of weathering on different materials help you to design your island?

HANDS-ON LAB

Breaking It Down

Investigate what constraints need to be considered when designing an island to resist long-term erosion.

uEngineer It! Defining the Problem STEM

MS-ESS2-2, MS-ESS3-2

GROUND SHIFTING ADVANCES: Maps Help Predict

INTERACTIVITY

Learn about the causes of landslides and predict where they might occur.

Do you know what happens after heavy rains or earthquakes in California? There are landslides. Engineers look for patterns to determine how and where they can happen.

The Challenge: To protect highways and towns from landslides.

Landslides destroy roadways, cut people off from access to vital services, and disrupt local economies.

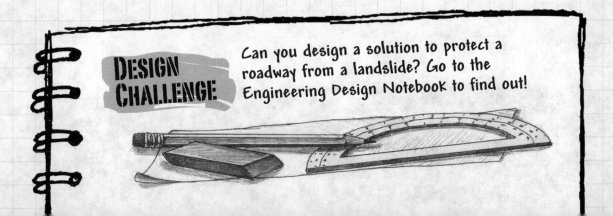

Phenomenon Evaluating hazards is one way to prepare for natural disasters. In the early 1970s, the California Geological Survey (CGS) began drawing up "Geology for Planning" maps. Its goal was to create maps showing areas all over the state where natural hazards, such as wildfires and landslides, were most likely to occur. Engineers and city planners could then use the maps to prepare for, or possibly prevent, natural disasters.

In 1997, the Caltrans Highway Corridor Mapping project began. Caltrans stands for California Department of Transportation. Caltrans engineers set out to map all known sites of landslides, as well as unstable slopes along the major interstate highways. Most of the landslide sites were along highways that wind through California's mountains. Using these maps, engineers have installed sensitive monitoring equipment to help predict future landslides.

DESIGN CHALLENGE

Can you design a solution to protect a roadway from a landslide? Go to the Engineering Design Notebook to find out!

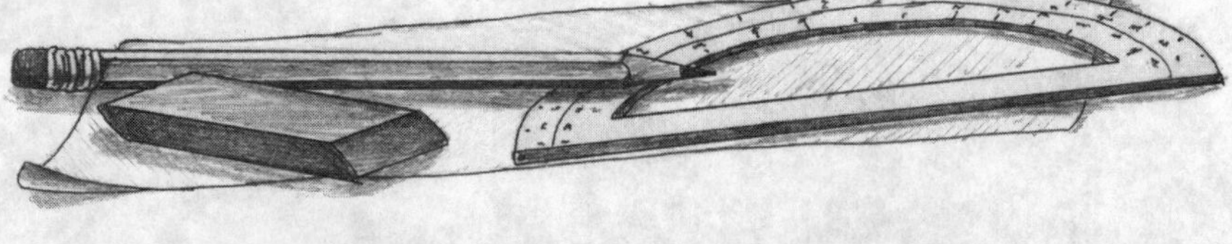

LESSON

2 Erosion and Deposition

Guiding Questions

- What processes change Earth's surface?
- How does mass movement change Earth's surface?
- How does wind change Earth's surface?

Connections

Literacy Integrate With Visuals

Math Analyze Quantitative Relationships

MS-ESS2-2, MS-ESS3-2

HANDS-ON LAB

uInvestigate Examine how particle size affects erosion and deposition.

Vocabulary

sediment
deposition
mass movement
deflation
sand dune
loess

Academic Vocabulary

similar
significant

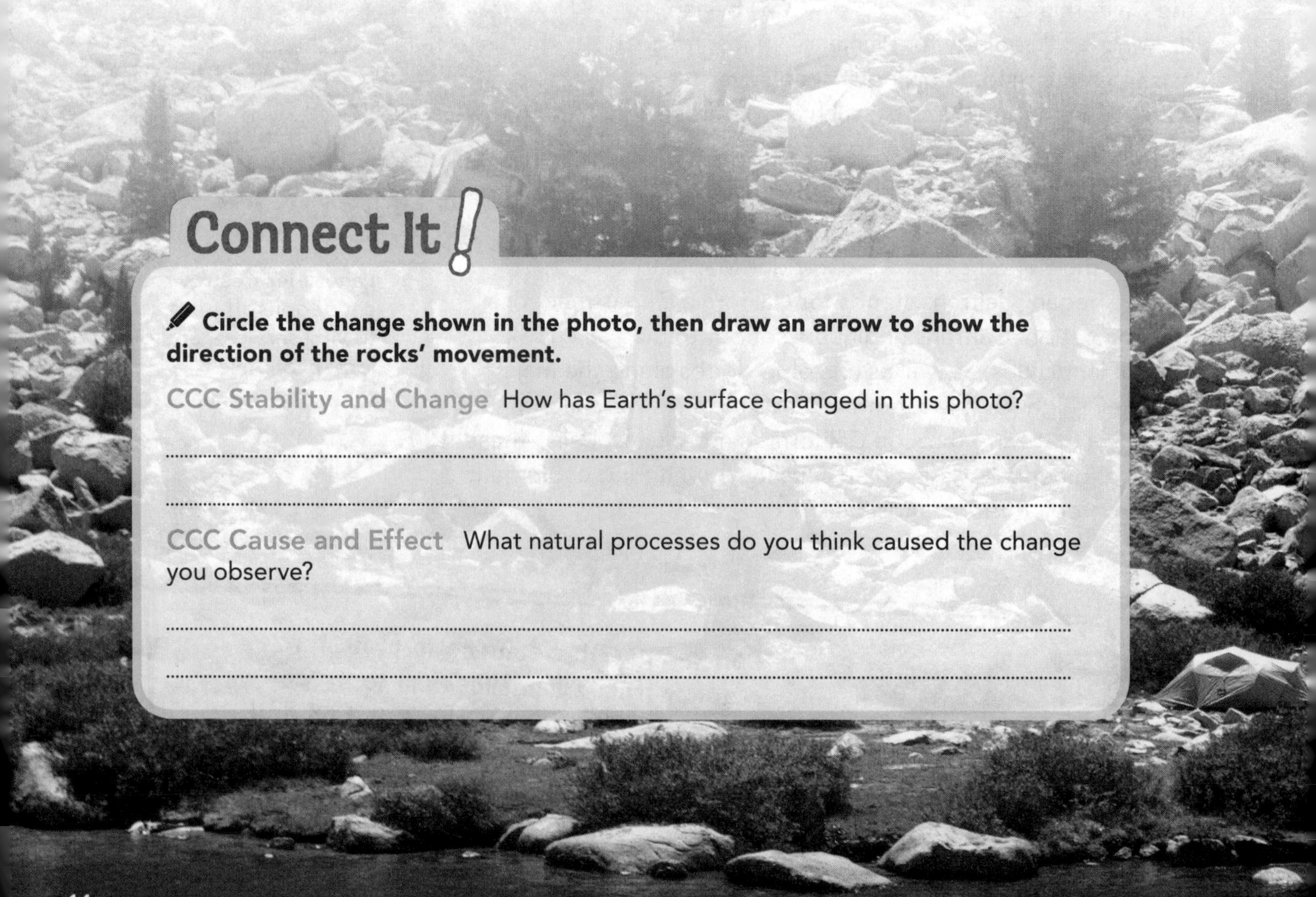

Connect It!

Circle the change shown in the photo, then draw an arrow to show the direction of the rocks' movement.

CCC Stability and Change How has Earth's surface changed in this photo?

....

....

CCC Cause and Effect What natural processes do you think caused the change you observe?

....

....

Changing Earth's Surface

Have you ever watched water carry away bits of gravel and soil during a rainstorm? If so, you observed erosion. Recall that erosion is a process that moves weathered rock from its original location. Gravity, water, ice, and wind are all agents of erosion.

The process of erosion moves material called **sediment**. Sediment may consist of pieces of rock or soil, or the remains of plants and animals.

Deposition occurs where the agents of erosion deposit, or lay down, sediment. Like erosion, deposition changes the shape of Earth's surface. You may have watched an ant carry away bits of soil and then put the soil down in a different location to build an ant hill. The ant's activity is **similar** to erosion and deposition, which involves picking up, carrying away, and putting down sediment in a different place.

Weathering, erosion, transportation, and deposition act together in a continuous cycle that wears down and builds up Earth's surface. As erosion wears down a mountain in one place, deposition builds up a new landform in another place. Some changes happen over a large area, while others occur in a small space. Some happen slowly over thousands or millions of years, and others take only a few minutes or seconds, such as the rockslide shown in **Figure 1**. No matter how large or fast the changes, the cycle of erosion and deposition is continuous. The same changes that shaped Earth's surface in the past still shape it today and will continue to shape it in the future.

Academic Vocabulary

Using two things you can observe right now, write a sentence describing how they are similar.

Literacy Connection

Integrate With Visuals

In the third paragraph of the text, underline a statement that is supported by evidence in the photograph.

Moving Rock

Figure 1 The sudden change in the appearance of this hillside was caused by the natural movement of rock.

INTERACTIVITY

Explore the ways slope influences mass movement.

Mass Movement

If you place a ball at the top of a hill, with a slight push the ball will roll down the hill. Gravity pulls the ball downward. Gravity is also the force that moves rock and other materials downhill.

Gravity causes **mass movement**, one of several processes that move sediment downhill. Mass movement can be rapid or slow. Erosion and deposition both take place during a mass movement event. The different types of mass movement include landslides, mudflows, slumps, and creep (**Figure 2**).

A mass movement may be caused by a natural disaster, such as a flood, earthquake, or hurricane. Natural disasters can dramatically and suddenly change Earth's surface. Scientists make maps of past mass movements in a region to better understand their hazards. Such maps help scientists to identify patterns and predict where future mass movement is likely to occur in order to prevent human casualties.

READING CHECK **Integrate With Visuals** Read and think about the information relating to different kinds of mass movement. Which type of mass movement do you think is least dangerous? Why?

....

....

Mass Movement

Figure 2 Different types of mass movement have different characteristics.

1. SEP Develop Models Draw arrows on each image of mass movement to show the direction that material moves.
2. CCC Patterns What pattern(s) can you identify among the types of mass movement?

....

....

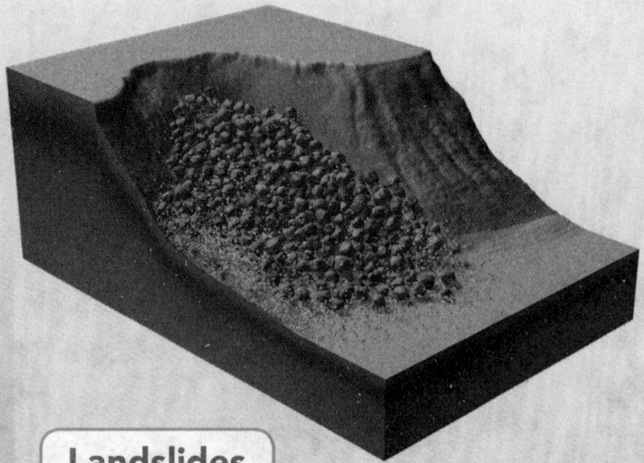

Landslides

A landslide occurs when rock and soil slide quickly down a steep slope. Some landslides contain huge masses of rock, while others contain only small amounts of rock and soil. Often caused by earthquakes, landslides occur where road builders have cut highways through hills or mountains, leaving behind unstable slopes.

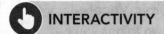

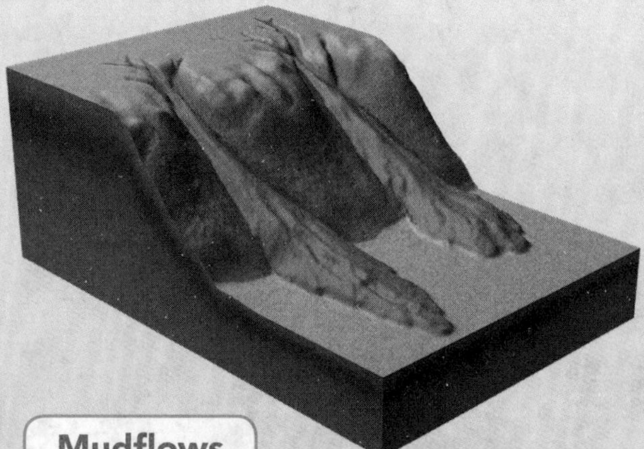

Mudflows

A mudflow is the rapid downhill movement of a mixture of water, rock, and soil. Mudflows often occur after heavy rains in a normally dry area. In clay-rich soils with a high water content, mudflows may occur even on very gentle slopes. Under certain conditions, clay-rich soil suddenly behaves as a liquid and begins to flow.

Math Toolbox

Major Landslides and Mudflows

Landslides and mudflows are a problem in all 50 states and all around the world. Annually in the United States, landslides cause $1 billion to $2 billion in damage and about 25 deaths. But some catastrophic mass movements in other countries have killed more than 100,000 people.

1. **CCC Scale, Proportion, and Quantity** What proportion of the landslides were caused by earthquakes?

....

2. **Analyze Quantitative Relationships** Which process caused the most landslides? Which caused the fewest landslides?

....

Major Landslides and Mudflows of the 20th Century

Year	Location	Cause
1919	Java, Indonesia	volcanic eruption
1920	Ningxia, China	earthquake
1933	Sichuan, China	earthquake
1949	Tadzhikistan	earthquake
1958	Japan	heavy rains
1970	Peru	earthquake
1980	Washington, USA	earthquakes
1983	Utah, USA	heavy rain and snowmelt
1985	Colombia	volcano
1998	Central America	hurricane rains

Slumps

In a slump, a mass of rock and soil suddenly slips down a slope. Unlike a landslide, the material in a slump moves down in one large mass. It looks as if someone pulled the bottom out from under part of the slope. A slump often occurs when water soaks the bottom of clay-rich soil.

Creep

Creep is the very slow downhill movement of rock and soil. It can even occur on gentle slopes. Creep often results from the freezing and thawing of water in cracked layers of rock beneath the soil. Even though it occurs slowly, you can see the effects of creep in vertical objects such as telephone poles and tree trunks. Creep may tilt these objects at unusual angles.

Erosion and Deposition by Wind

HANDS-ON LAB

Investigate Examine how particle size affects erosion and deposition.

Recall that wind, or moving air, is an agent of erosion and deposition. Through these processes, wind wears down and builds up Earth's surface.

Academic Vocabulary

Describe a significant change in weather from the winter to the summer.

....

....

....

Wind Erosion

Wind can be a **significant** agent in shaping the land in areas where there are few plants to hold the soil in place. In a sandstorm, strong winds pick up large amounts of sediment and loose soil and transport it to new locations.

Deflation Wind causes erosion mainly by **deflation**, the process by which wind removes surface materials. You can see the process of deflation in **Figure 3**. When wind blows over the land, it picks up the smallest particles of sediment, such as clay and silt. Stronger, faster winds pick up larger particles. Slightly larger particles, such as sand, might skip or bounce for a short distance. Strong winds can roll even larger and heavier sediment particles. In deserts, deflation can create an area called desert pavement where smaller sediments are blown away, and larger rock fragments are left behind.

Abrasion Wind, water, and ice carry particles that rub or scrape against exposed rock. As particles move against the rock, friction wears away the rock by the process of abrasion.

Wind Erosion and Deflation

Figure 3 Wind causes deflation by moving surface particles in three ways.

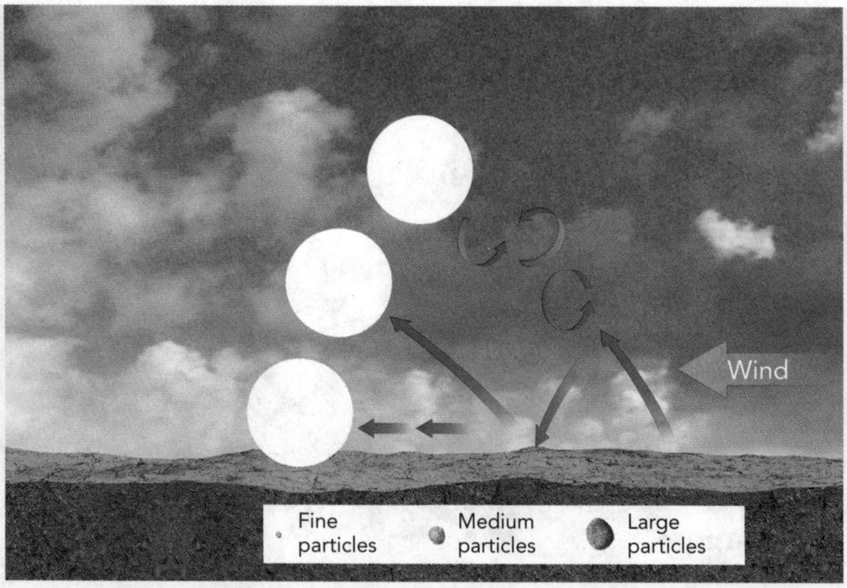

1. Claim In each circle, draw the size of particles that would be moved by the wind.
2. Evidence How does a particle's size affect how high and far it travels?

   ....

   ....

   ....

3. Reasoning Complete each sentence to the right with one of the following words: Fine, Medium, Large.

.... particles are carried through the air.

.... particles skip or bounce.

.... particles slide or roll.

Wind Deposition All the sediment picked up by wind eventually falls to the ground. This happens when the wind slows down or encounters an obstacle. Wind deposition may form sand dunes and loess deposits.

Sand Dunes When wind meets an obstacle, such as a clump of grass, the result is usually a deposit of windblown sand called a **sand dune**. **Figure 4** shows how wind direction can form different dunes. The shape and size of sand dunes is determined by the direction of the wind, the amount of sand, and the presence of plants. This same process changed Earth's surface billions of years ago, just as it does today. You can predict how wind deposition will affect the surface in the future. You can see sand dunes on beaches and in deserts where wind-blown sediment builds up. Sand dunes also move over time because the sand shifts with the wind from one side of the dune to the other. Sometimes plants begin growing on a dune, and the roots help to anchor the dune in one place.

Loess Deposits The wind drops sediment that is finer than sand but coarser than clay far from its source. This fine, wind-deposited sediment is **loess** (LOH es). There are large loess deposits in central China and in states such as Nebraska, South Dakota, Iowa, Missouri, and Illinois. Loess helps to form soil rich in nutrients. Many areas with thick loess deposits are valuable farmlands.

READING CHECK **Cite Textual Evidence** What factors affect wind erosion and deposition?

....

....

Question It!

Moving Sand Dunes

Sand dunes keep drifting and covering a nearby, busy parking lot.

SEP Define Problems State the problem that needs to be solved in the form of a question.

....

....

SEP Design Solutions Describe two possible solutions to the problem. Explain why each would solve the problem.

....

....

....

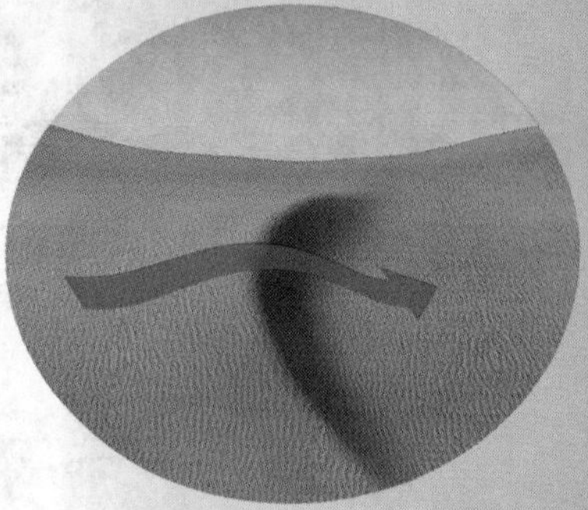

Crescent-shaped dune

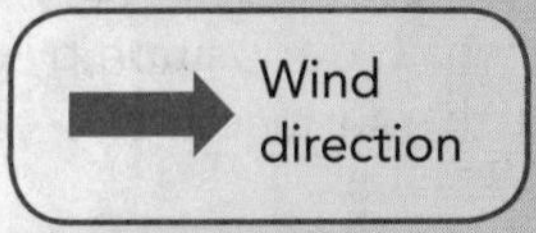

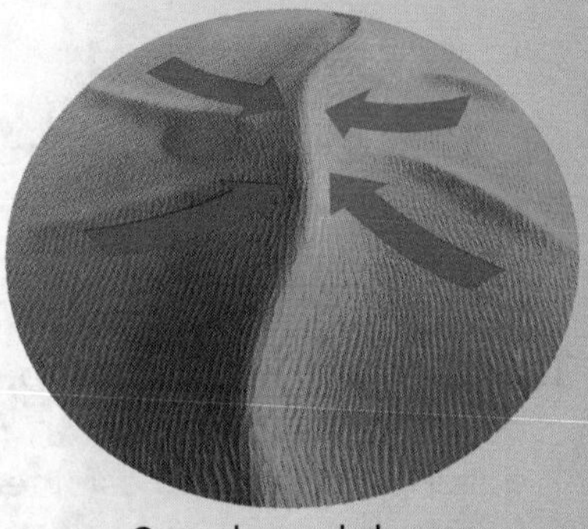

Star-shaped dunes

Dune Formation

Figure 4 Sand dunes form and change shape as the wind deposits sand.

1. **Predict** Draw a line to show how the ridge of the crescent-shaped dune will likely shift over time.
2. **CCC Cause and Effect** Why do these dunes have different shapes?

....

....

....

INTERACTIVITY

Explore fast and slow changes to Earth's surface.

LESSON 2 Check

MS-ESS2-2, MS-ESS3-2

1. **Classify** Which kinds of mass movement happen quickly?

2. **CCC Stability and Change** Describe a way in which deposition by gravity slowly changes Earth's surface.

3. **CCC Patterns** Explain how the wind both builds up and wears down Earth's surface in a desert. Give examples of features that result from these processes.

4. **SEP Construct Explanations** Explain why a scientist may make a map of the location of landslides in a certain area.

5. **SEP Interpret Data** Two towns are located in the same dry region. Town X has steeper slopes than Town Y. Town Y gets heavier than normal rain for several days while Town X remains dry. Which town is more likely to experience mass movement in the near future? Explain your answer.

Quest CHECK-INS

In this lesson, you learned how gravity causes erosion and deposition. You also learned how wind causes erosion and deposition.

CCC System Models What are some ways that the effects of erosion can be mitigated in your design for the artificial island?

HANDS-ON LAB

Ingenious Island, Part I

INTERACTIVITY

Changing Landscapes

Do the hands-on lab to test your island's resistance to erosion by surface water.

Go online to explore how landscapes can be changed.

MS-ESS2-2, MS-ESS3-2

Civil Engineers SAVE THE DAY!

Who put the civil in civilization? Engineers! Civil engineers are responsible for all the works that benefit the citizens of a society. After a natural disaster, civil engineers get involved in reconstruction efforts.

Think of the networks and systems we rely on every day—roadways, train tracks, cell phone towers, the electrical grid, and gas lines. Consider the cities built on filled-in swamp or a town built over rough terrain. Think of all the bridges connecting two sides of a river—even one as wide as the Mississippi. Civil engineers and the construction workers they guided made all of this possible.

Whether planning a new road or bridge, civil engineers must take into account the forces that change Earth's surface. Water and wind erosion, for example, have serious effects on roadways and can cause costly damage. A civil engineer's job is to determine how to build the road in a way that minimizes nature's potentially damaging effects.

If you want to be a civil engineer, you'll need to study science and math. You'll also need to develop your imagination, because solutions require creativity as well as analytical thinking.

VIDEO

Watch what's involved in being a civil engineer.

MY CAREER

Type "civil engineer" into an online search engine to learn more about this career.

Civil engineers survey and measure the surface of Earth. The data they collect are used to plan construction projects such as this bridge.

LESSON

3 Water Erosion

Guiding Questions

- How does moving water change Earth's surface?
- What landforms form from water erosion and deposition?
- How does groundwater change Earth?

Connection

Literacy Cite Textual Evidence

MS-ESS2-2

HANDS-ON LAB

uInvestigate Trace the paths raindrops can follow after hitting the ground.

Vocabulary

runoff
stream
tributary
flood plain
delta
alluvial fan
groundwater

Academic Vocabulary

develop
suggest

Connect It!

Draw a line showing where Niagara Falls may have been in the past.

SEP Construct Explanations How do you think Niagara Falls formed?

....

....

....

SEP Apply Scientific Reasoning What do you think this waterfall and all other waterfalls have in common?

....

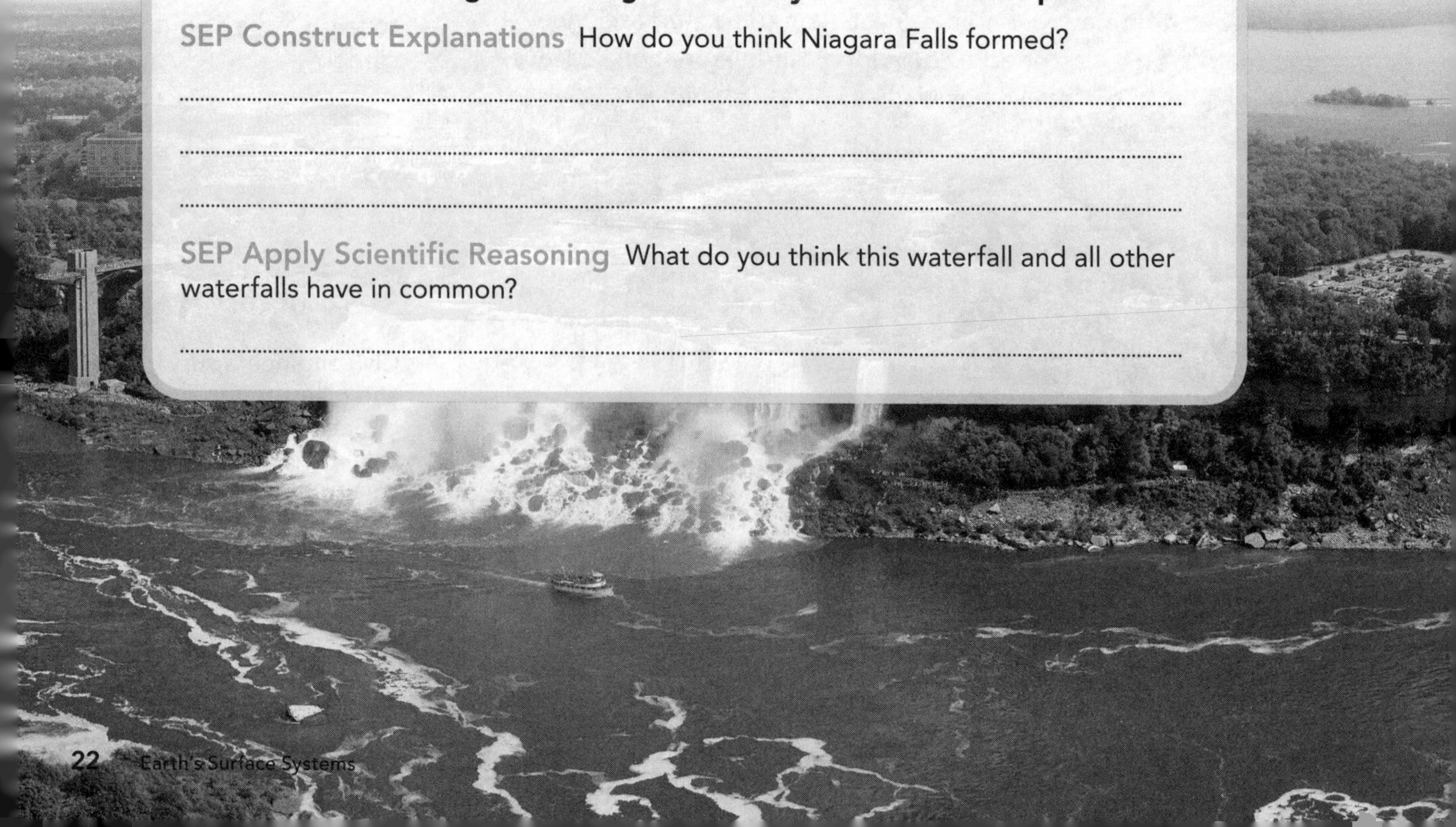

How Water Causes Erosion

Erosion by water doesn't start with a giant waterfall, such as the one in **Figure 1**. It begins with a little splash of rain. Some rainfall sinks into the ground, where it is absorbed by plant roots. Some water evaporates, while the rest of the water runs off over the land surface. Moving water of the hydrosphere is the primary agent of the erosion that shaped Earth's land surface, the geosphere, for billions of years. It continues to shape the surface today in small and large ways.

INTERACTIVITY

Locate evidence of water erosion and determine why it happened.

Runoff As water moves over the land, it picks up and carries sediment. This moving water is called **runoff**. When runoff flows over the land, it may cause a type of erosion called sheet erosion, where thin layers of soil are removed. The amount of runoff in an area depends on five main factors. The first factor is the amount of rain an area gets. A heavy or lengthy rainfall can add water to the surface more quickly than the surface can absorb it. A second factor is vegetation. Grasses, shrubs, and trees reduce runoff by absorbing water and holding soil in place. A third factor is the type of soil. Different types of soils absorb different amounts of water. A fourth factor is the shape of the land. Runoff is more likely to occur on steeply sloped land than on flatter land. Finally, a fifth factor is how people use land. For example, pavement does not absorb water. All the rain that falls on it becomes runoff. Runoff also increases when trees or crops are cut down, because this removes vegetation from the land.

Literacy Connection

Cite Textual Evidence As you read the second paragraph, number the factors that affect runoff.

Factors that reduce runoff also reduce erosion. Even though deserts have little rainfall, they often have high runoff and erosion because they have few plants and thin, sandy soil. In wet areas, such as rain forests and wetlands, runoff and erosion may be low because there are more plants to protect the soil.

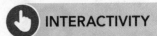

Taking the Plunge

Figure 1 The powerful Niagara River plunges more than 50 meters from the highest point of Niagara Falls. Here, the hydrosphere (river) interacts with the geosphere (land) and shapes Earth's surface.

HANDS-ON LAB

Investigate Trace the paths raindrops can follow after hitting the ground.

Stream Formation Gravity causes runoff and the sediment it carries to flow downhill. As runoff moves across the land, it flows together to form rills, gullies, and streams, as shown in **Figure 2**.

Rills and Gullies As runoff travels, it forms tiny grooves in the soil called rills. Many rills flow into one another to form a gully. A gully is a large groove, or channel, in the soil that carries runoff after a rainstorm. As water flows through gullies, it picks up and moves sediment with it, thus enlarging the gullies through erosion.

Streams and Rivers Gullies join to form a stream. A **stream** is a channel along which water is continually flowing down a slope. Unlike gullies, streams rarely dry up. Small streams are also known as creeks or brooks. As streams flow together, they form larger bodies of flowing water called rivers.

Tributaries A **tributary** is a stream or river that flows into a larger river. For example, the Missouri and Ohio rivers are tributaries of the Mississippi River. A drainage basin, or watershed, is the area from which a river and its tributaries collect their water.

READING CHECK **Integrate With Visuals** Review the information in paragraph 2 and in **Figure 2**. How does the amount of water change as it moves from rills and gullies to streams?

....

....

Stream Formation

Figure 2 In the diagram, shade only the arrows that indicate the direction of runoff flow that causes erosion.

CCC Cause and Effect How will the depth of the channel likely change with further erosion?

....

....

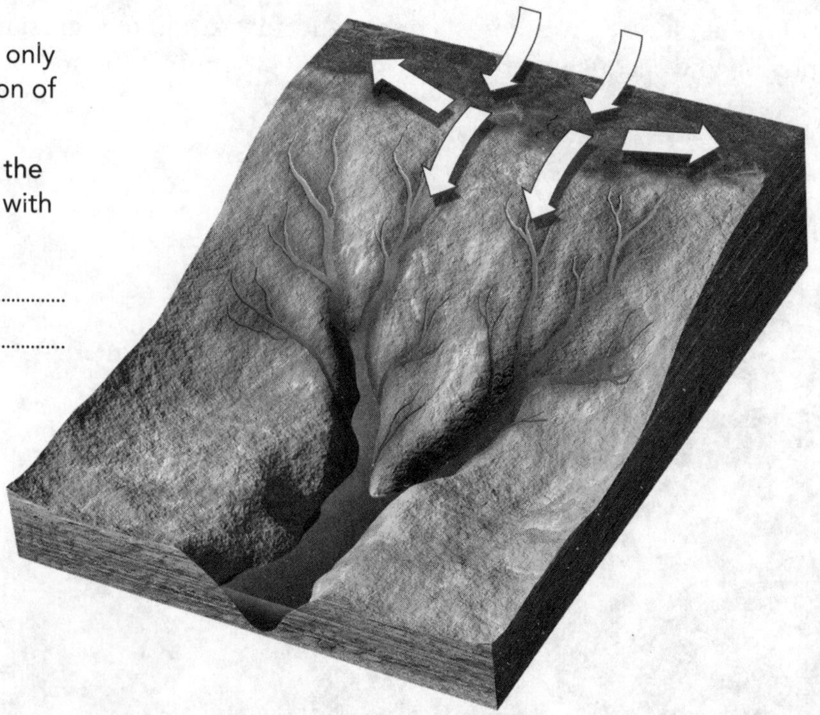

Waterfalls

Figure 3 Waterfalls form where rivers erode hard and soft rock layers at different rates.

1. **SEP Use Models** The rock at the top of the waterfall erodes at a (slower/faster) rate than the rock below it.

2. **Predict** How do you think erosion will change this waterfall in the next 100 years?

....

....

....

....

....

Water Erosion and Deposition Change Earth's Surface

Some landforms result from erosion by rivers and streams, while others result from deposition. Still other landforms are created from a combination of these processes. Erosion by water removes particles on Earth's surface, while deposition by water builds it up.

Water Erosion

Many rivers begin on steep mountain slopes as flowing rain water or melted snow. This running water starts out fast-flowing and generally follows a straight, narrow course. The steep slopes along the river erode rapidly, resulting in a deep, V-shaped valley. As a river flows to the sea, it forms other features such as waterfalls, flood plains, meanders, and oxbow lakes.

Waterfalls Waterfalls, as shown in **Figure 3,** erode soft rock, leaving a ledge made up of hard, slowly eroding rock. Eventually a waterfall develops along the ledge where the softer rock has worn away. Rushing water and sediment can cause further erosion at the base of the waterfall. Rough water rapids also occur where a river tumbles over hard rock, wearing away the supporting rock base and leaving the rock above it unsupported.

Flood Plains Lower down on its course, a river usually flows over more gently sloping land. The river spreads out and erodes the land along its side, forming a wide river valley. The flat, wide area of land along a river is a **flood plain**. During a flood or a rainy season, a river overflows its banks and flows onto the flood plain. As the flood water retreats, it deposits sediment. This gradually makes the soil of a flood plain rich in nutrients.

Academic Vocabulary

What things did you develop in science class this year? Name two examples.

....

....

....

VIDEO

Explore landforms caused by water erosion.

Meanders A river often **develops** meanders where it flows through easily eroded rock or sediment. A meander is a loop-like bend in the course of a river. A meandering river erodes sediment from the outer bank and deposits the sediment on the inner bank farther downstream. The water flows faster in the deeper, outer section of each bend, causing more erosion. Over time, a meander becomes more curved.

Flood plains also follow the meander as sediment erodes more of the land to the side of the river. Here, the river's channel is often deep and wide. For example, the southern stretch of the Mississippi River meanders on a wide, gently sloping flood plain.

Oxbow Lakes Sometimes a meandering river forms a feature called an oxbow lake. An oxbow lake occurs when a meander develops such a large loop that the bends of the river join together. Sediment deposits block the ends of the bends, cutting off the river flow. Oxbow lakes are the remains of the river's former bend, seen in **Figure 4**.

READING CHECK **Cite Textual Evidence** What evidence supports the idea that a floodplain is formed by erosion and deposition?

....

....

....

Model It!

Oxbow Lakes

Figure 4 A meander may gradually form an oxbow lake.

SEP Develop Models Draw steps 2 and 4 to show how an oxbow lake forms. Then describe step 4.

1. A small obstacle creates a slight bend in the river.

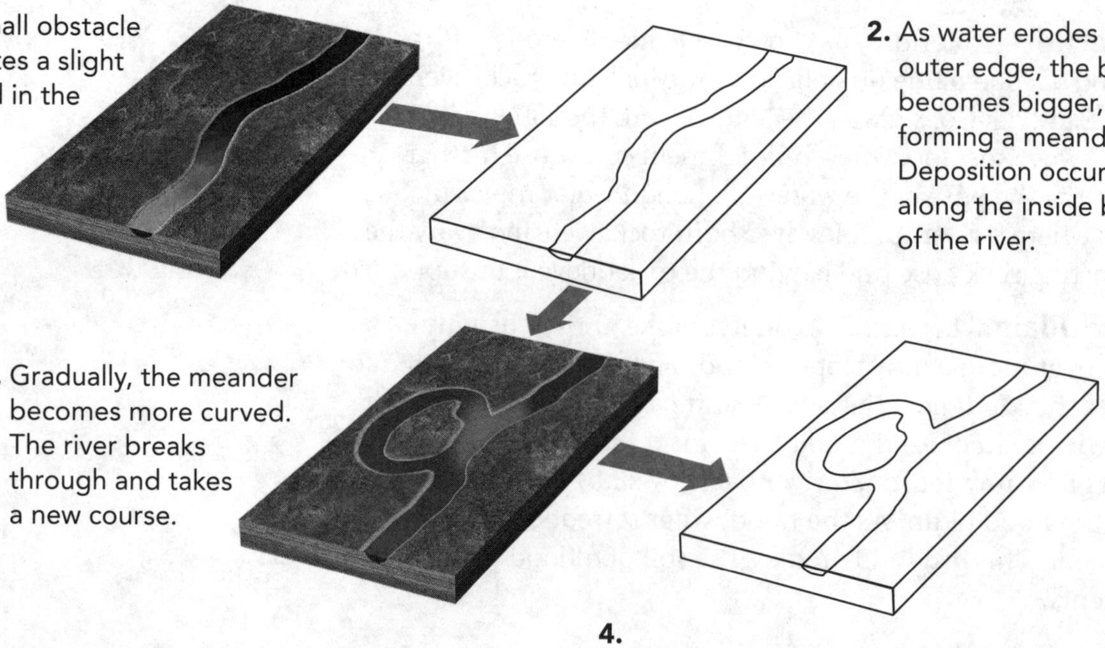

2. As water erodes the outer edge, the bend becomes bigger, forming a meander. Deposition occurs along the inside bend of the river.

3. Gradually, the meander becomes more curved. The river breaks through and takes a new course.

4. ....

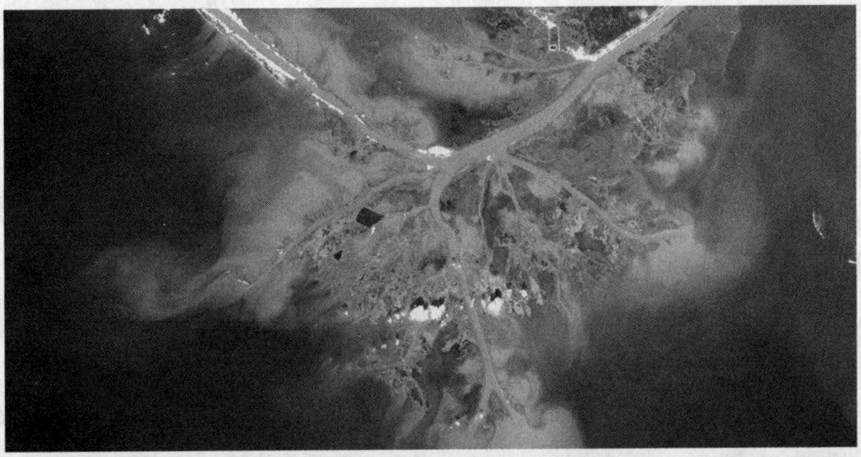

Delta and Alluvial Fan

Figure 5 ✏ Draw arrows to show the direction in which water carries sediment to each landform.

Interpret Photos Record your observations about deltas and alluvial fans.

....

....

....

....

....

....

....

Water Deposition Any time moving water slows, it deposits some of the sediment it carries. First, larger rocks stop rolling and sliding as fast-moving water starts to slow down. Then, finer and finer particles fall to the river's bed as the water flows even more slowly. In this way, water deposition builds up Earth's surface and produces landforms such as deltas and alluvial fans.

Deltas Eventually, a river flows into a body of water, such as an ocean or a lake. Because the river water no longer flows downhill, the water slows down. At this point, the sediment in the water drops to the bottom. Sediment deposited where a river flows into an ocean or lake builds up a landform called a **delta**. Some deltas are arc-shaped, while others are triangular. The delta of the Mississippi River, shown in **Figure 5**, is an example of a type of delta called a "bird's foot" delta.

Alluvial Fans When a stream flows out of a steep, narrow mountain valley, it suddenly becomes wider and shallower. The water slows down and deposits sediments in an **alluvial fan**. An alluvial fan is a wide, sloping deposit of sediment formed where a stream leaves a mountain range. As its name **suggests**, this deposit is shaped like a fan.

Academic Vocabulary

Suggest means "to mention as a possibility." Use *suggest* in a sentence.

....

....

....

....

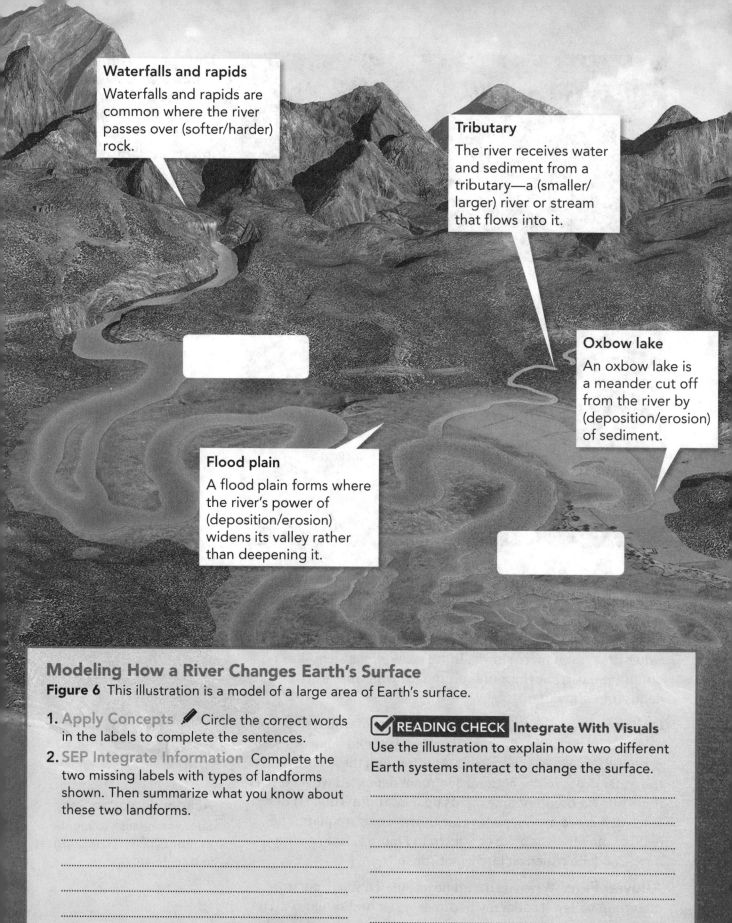

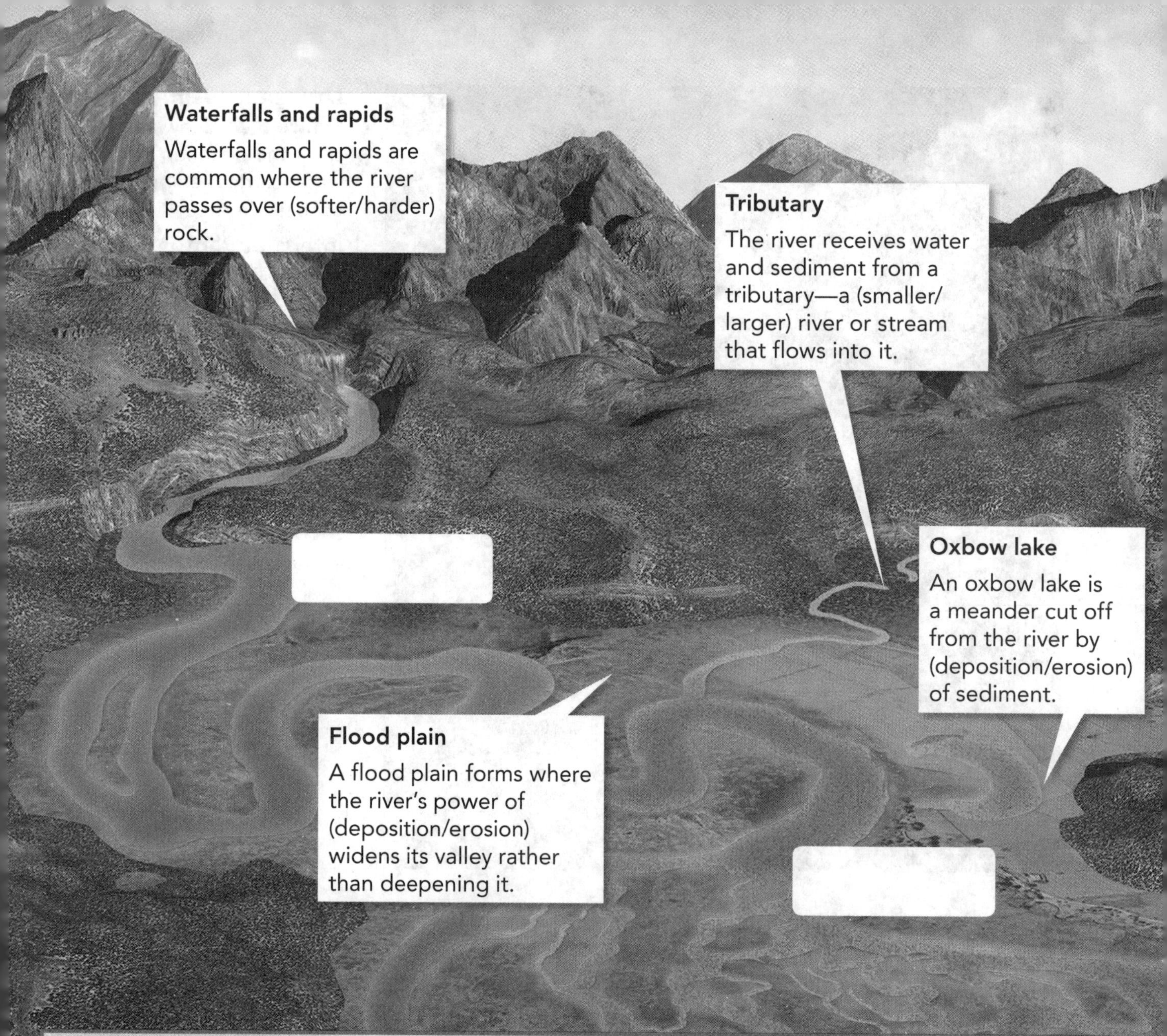

Waterfalls and rapids
Waterfalls and rapids are common where the river passes over (softer/harder) rock.
Tributary
The river receives water and sediment from a tributary—a (smaller/larger) river or stream that flows into it.
Oxbow lake
An oxbow lake is a meander cut off from the river by (deposition/erosion) of sediment.
Flood plain
A flood plain forms where the river's power of (deposition/erosion) widens its valley rather than deepening it.

Modeling How a River Changes Earth's Surface

Figure 6 This illustration is a model of a large area of Earth's surface.

1. **Apply Concepts** Circle the correct words in the labels to complete the sentences.
2. **SEP Integrate Information** Complete the two missing labels with types of landforms shown. Then summarize what you know about these two landforms.

....

....

....

....

....

....

READING CHECK **Integrate With Visuals**
Use the illustration to explain how two different Earth systems interact to change the surface.

....

....

....

....

....

....

Groundwater Changes Earth's Surface

When rain falls and snow melts, some water soaks into the ground. It trickles into cracks and spaces in layers of soil and rock. **Groundwater** is the term geologists use for this underground water. Like moving water, groundwater changes the shape of Earth's surface.

Groundwater Erosion Groundwater causes erosion by chemical weathering. In the atmosphere, rain water combines with carbon dioxide to form a weak acid called carbonic acid, which can break down limestone. Groundwater may also become more acidic as it flows through leaf debris at the surface. When groundwater flows into cracks in limestone, some of the limestone dissolves and gets carried away. This process gradually hollows out pockets in the rock. Over time, large underground holes, called caves or caverns, develop.

Groundwater Deposition The action of carbonic acid on limestone can also result in deposition. Water containing carbonic acid and calcium drips from a cave's roof. Carbon dioxide escapes from the solution, leaving behind a deposit of calcite. A deposit that hangs like an icicle from the roof of a cave is known as a stalactite (stuh LAK tyt). On the floor of the cave, a cone-shaped stalagmite (stuh LAG myt) builds up as water drops from the cave roof (**Figure 7**).

Write About It How does groundwater form caves? In your science notebook, write entries for a tourist brochure for a cave, explaining to visitors how the cave and its features formed through erosion and deposition.

INTERACTIVITY

Explore erosion caused by groundwater.

Groundwater Erosion and Deposition

Figure 7 On the photo, draw a line from each label to the formation it names.

SEP Construct Explanations How do deposition and erosion shape caves? Outline your ideas in the table.

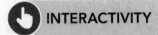

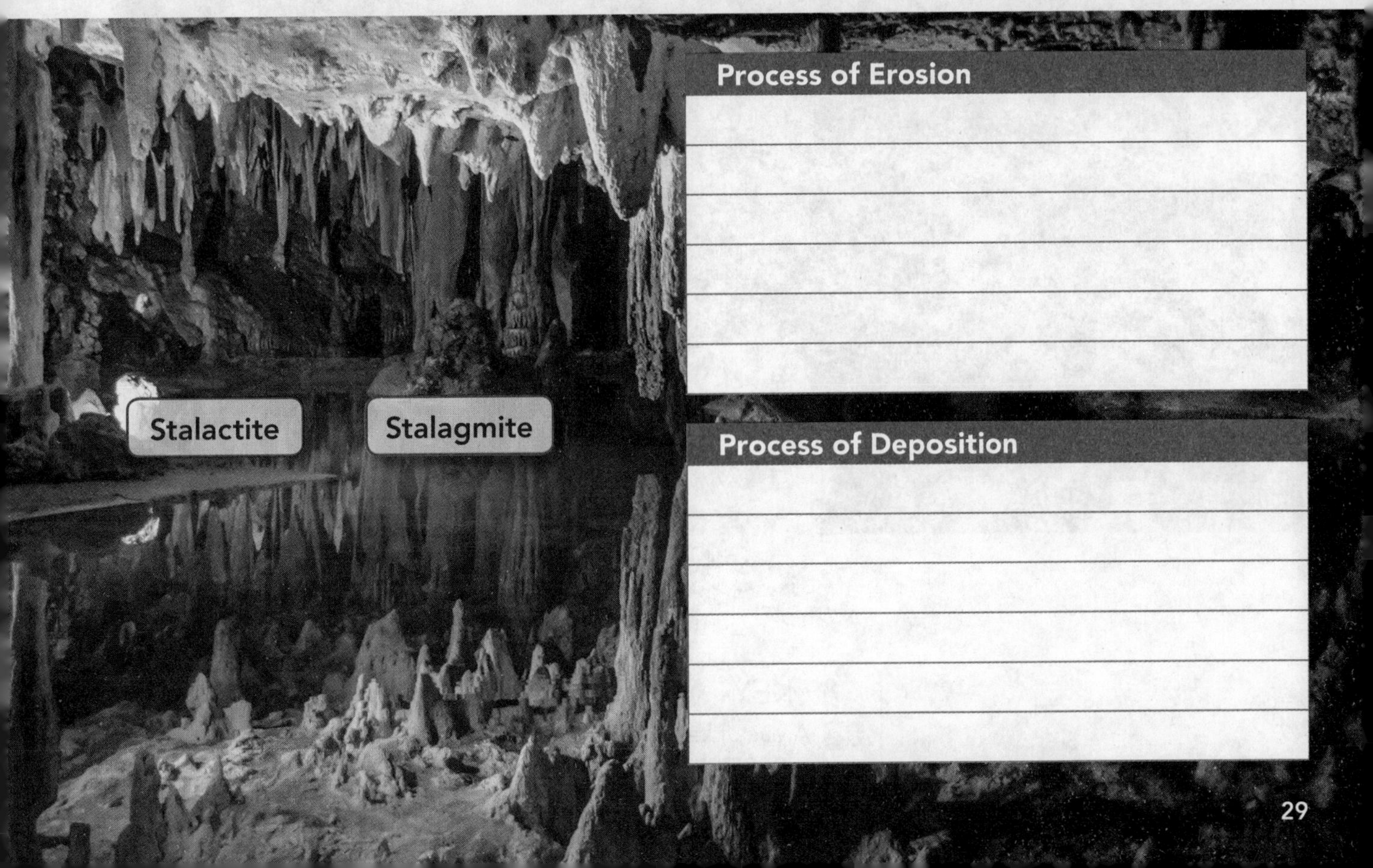

Process of Erosion

Process of Deposition

INTERACTIVITY

Explore the impact of water on Earth's surface.

Karst Topography

Figure 8 This sinkhole formed in a day in Winter Park, Florida, in 1981. What was the cause of the sinkhole?

1. **SEP Use Models** Circle the state that has the most karst topography.
2. **Identify** Identify two states that have very little karst topography.

Karst Topography In rainy regions such as Florida where there is a layer of limestone near the surface, groundwater erosion can significantly change the shape of Earth's surface. Deep valleys and caverns commonly form. If the roof of a cave collapses because of limestone erosion, the result is a depression called a sinkhole. This type of landscape is called karst topography.

The formation of karst topography happens over small to large areas and over short to very long time periods. Groundwater erosion starts with a single drop of water that dissolves a microscopic amount of limestone in seconds. After 100 years, groundwater might deposit 1 or 2 cm of calcite on the roof of a cave. Erosion might take thousands to millions of years to form a deep valley or huge cave system hundreds of kilometers long. The roof of a cave may very slowly erode over hundreds of years, but collapse within minutes to form a small or large sinkhole, as shown in **Figure 8**.

READING CHECK **Summarize** How does groundwater cause karst topography?

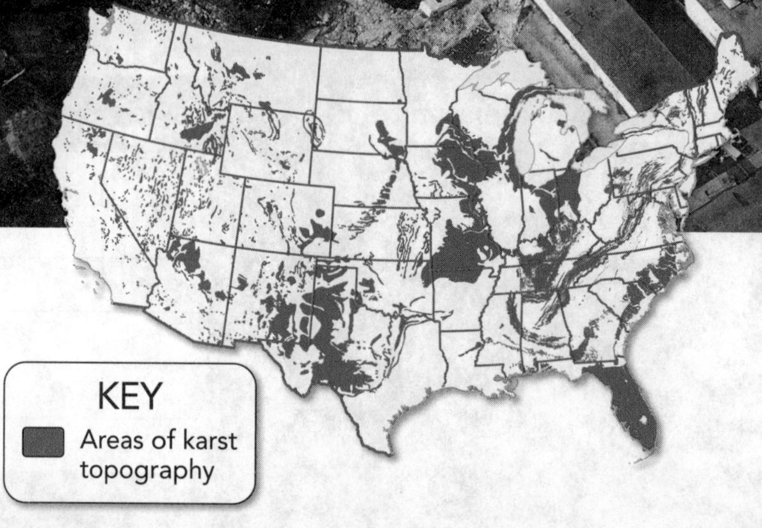

LESSON 3 Check

MS-ESS2-2

1. **Identify** What are two features that result from deposition by groundwater?

2. **CCC Cause and Effect** How does a meander form by erosion and deposition?

3. **CCC Stability and Change** Identify and describe a landform that results from water wearing down Earth's surface.

4. **CCC Patterns** How will Niagara Falls most likely change naturally in the future?

5. **SEP Evaluate Information** Suggest two things a property owner could do to reduce water erosion on soil-covered land that has a steep slope.

Quest CHECK-IN

In this lesson, you learned how water on Earth's surface causes erosion and deposition. You also found out how groundwater causes erosion and deposition.

SEP Evaluate Your Solution Why is it important to take different types of erosion and deposition into account when designing an artificial island?

HANDS-ON LAB

Ingenious Island: Part II

Investigate how you can use a model to test the effects of the agents of erosion on your artificial island.

Case Study

MS-ESS2-2

Buyer Beware!

When a cavity forms in limestone below the ground, a sinkhole can form when the ground eventually collapses into the cavity.

It may sound like something out of a science fiction movie, but the United States is home to monsters that can destroy a roadway or swallow an entire house in a single gulp. They're known as sinkholes.

Geologic Hazards

Sinkholes come in all sizes—from an area the size of a small carpet and 30 centimeters deep to an area spreading over hundreds of acres and several hundreds of meters deep. The size of a sinkhole depends on the surrounding land features. Collapse sinkholes, for example, tend to happen in regions with clay sediments on top of limestone bedrock. As their name suggests, collapse sinkholes form quickly. The ceiling of an underground cavity suddenly gives way, and everything on the surface above that cavity collapses down into it.

In addition to the natural processes, such as heavy rainfall or extreme drought, that form sinkholes, human activities can have an impact. As we turn more of the countryside into housing developments, more people are living in areas prone to sinkholes. As we develop land, we use more water. Overuse of the groundwater, digging new water wells, or creating artificial ponds of surface water can all increase the chances of sinkhole formation.

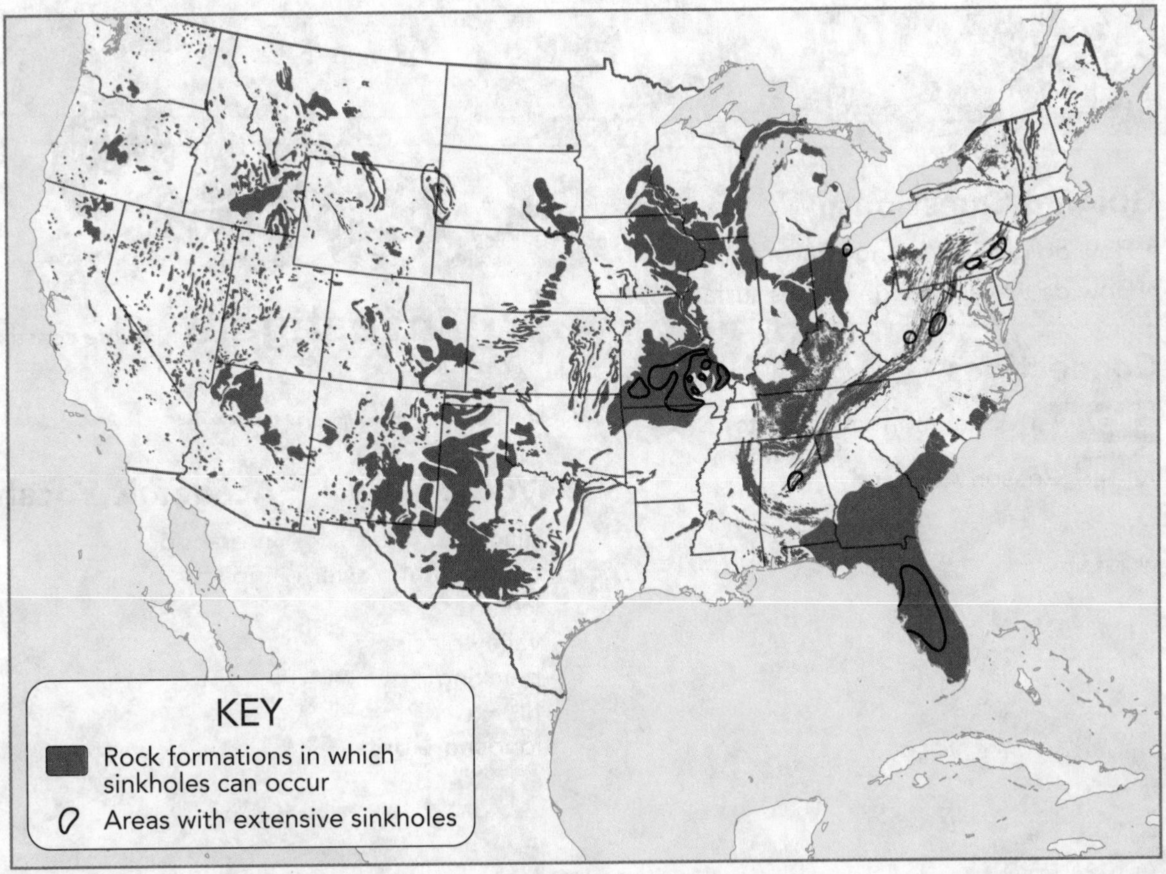

Sinkholes are more common in some parts of the U.S. than in others.

1. Patterns What patterns do you observe in the map? What might account for these patterns?

2. Interpret Diagrams Based on the map, why do you think that the overuse of groundwater can cause a sinkhole to form?

3. Form an Opinion How might communities prevent the damage and destruction caused by sinkholes?

LESSON

4 Glacial and Wave Erosion

Guiding Questions

- How do glaciers change Earth's surface?
- How do waves change Earth's surface?

Connections

Literacy Write Informative Texts

Math Reason Abstractly

MS-ESS2-2

HANDS-ON LAB

uInvestigate Explore coastline erosion.

Vocabulary

glacier
continental glacier
ice age
valley glacier
plucking
till
longshore drift

Academic Vocabulary

interaction
impact

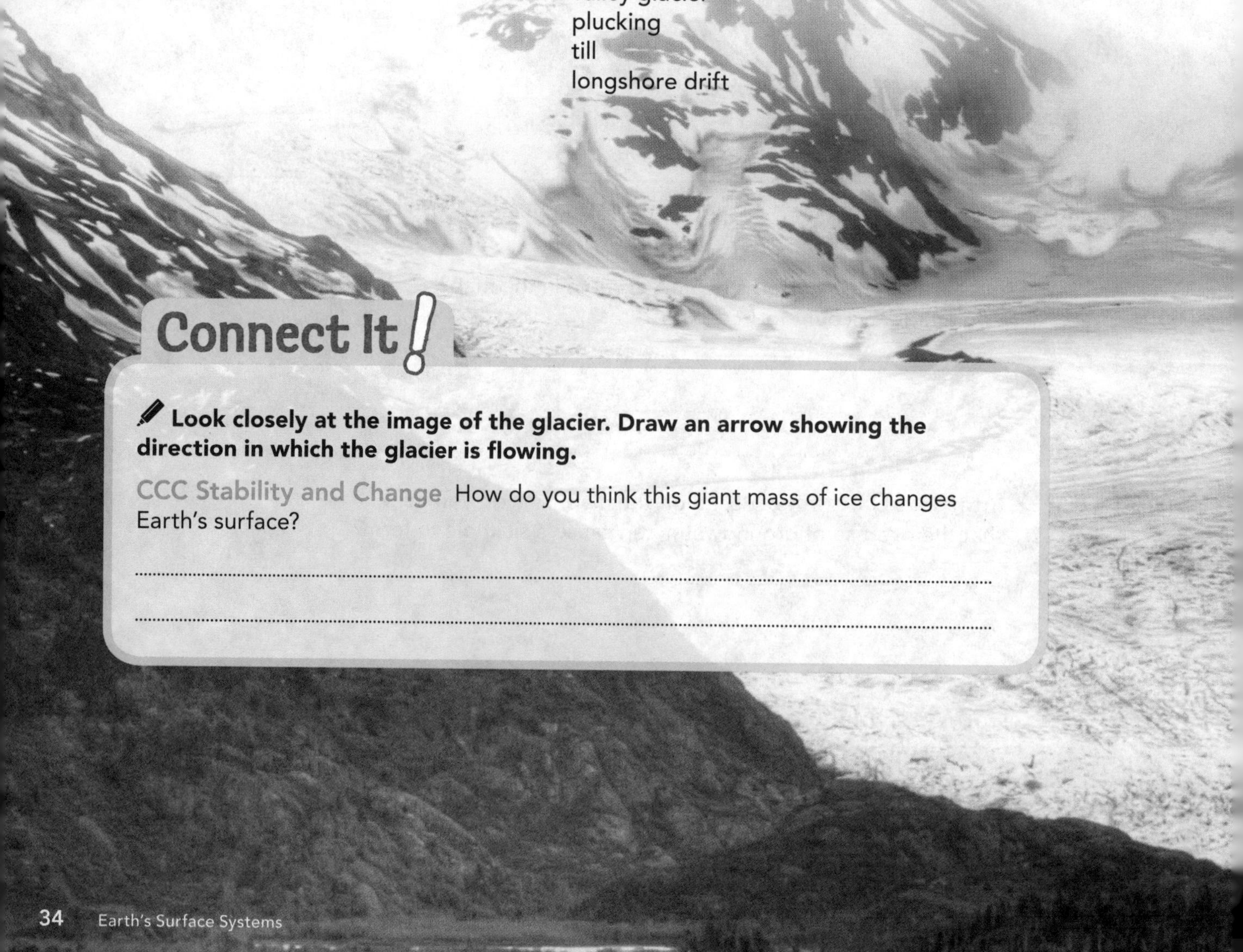

Connect It!

Look closely at the image of the glacier. Draw an arrow showing the direction in which the glacier is flowing.

CCC Stability and Change How do you think this giant mass of ice changes Earth's surface?

....

....

Glaciers Change Earth's Surface

If you were to fly over Alaska, you would see snowcapped mountains and evergreen forests. Between the mountains and the Gulf of Alaska, you would also see a thick, winding mass of ice. This river of ice in **Figure 1** is a glacier. Geologists define a **glacier** (GLAY shur) as any large mass of ice that moves slowly over land.

Glaciers occur in the coldest places on Earth. That's because they can form only in an area where more snow falls than melts. Layers of snow pile on top of more layers of snow. Over time, the weight of the layers presses the particles of snow so tightly together that they form a solid block of ice.

Glaciers are part of the cryosphere (KRI oh sfear), which includes all the frozen water on Earth. As glaciers move slowly over land, the cryosphere interacts with the rocky upper layer of the geosphere that is known as the lithosphere. This **interaction** changes Earth's surface through weathering, erosion, and deposition. When the ice of the cryosphere melts, it becomes part of the hydrosphere.

HANDS-ON LAB

Examine how glaciers move across Earth's surface.

Academic Vocabulary

Describe an interaction you observed and one you took part in. Be sure to identify the people and things involved in the interaction.

....

....

....

....

....

Giant Bulldozer of Ice

Figure 1 Like a slow-moving bulldozer, Alaska's Bering Glacier, the largest glacier in North America, plows across Earth's surface.

> **INTERACTIVITY**
>
> Learn about the effects of glaciers.

Continental Glaciers A **continental glacier** is a glacier that covers much of a continent or large island. It can spread out over millions of square kilometers and flow in all directions. Today, continental glaciers cover about 10 percent of Earth's land, including Antarctica and most of Greenland.

During **ice ages**, continental glaciers covered larger parts of Earth's surface. The glaciers gradually advanced and retreated several times, changing the shape of Earth's surface each time.

Valley Glaciers A **valley glacier** is a long, narrow glacier that forms when snow and ice build up in a mountain valley. High mountains keep these glaciers from spreading out in all directions, and gravity pulls the glacier downhill. Valley glaciers usually move slowly down valleys that have already been cut by rivers. Sometimes a valley glacier can experience a surge, or a quick slide, and move about 6 kilometers in one year. Alaska's Bering Glacier, shown in **Figure 1**, is a valley glacier.

Math Toolbox

Comparing Glacier Thickness

The graph shows the cumulative mass balance of a set of glaciers observed by scientists from 1945 to 2015. The cumulative mass balance is the total amount of ice the glaciers have gained or lost since 1945. The curve is always negative, so the glaciers have lost ice since 1945. The slope of the curve (how steep it is) shows how fast or slow the glaciers are losing ice.

1. **Reason Abstractly** What does a flat slope indicate? What does a steep slope indicate?

   ....

   ....

   ....

   ....

2. **SEP Use Models** According to the data, the reference glaciers have melted and lost ice in every decade. In which decade did the glaciers lose ice slowest? In which decade did they lose ice quickest?

   ....

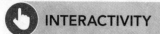

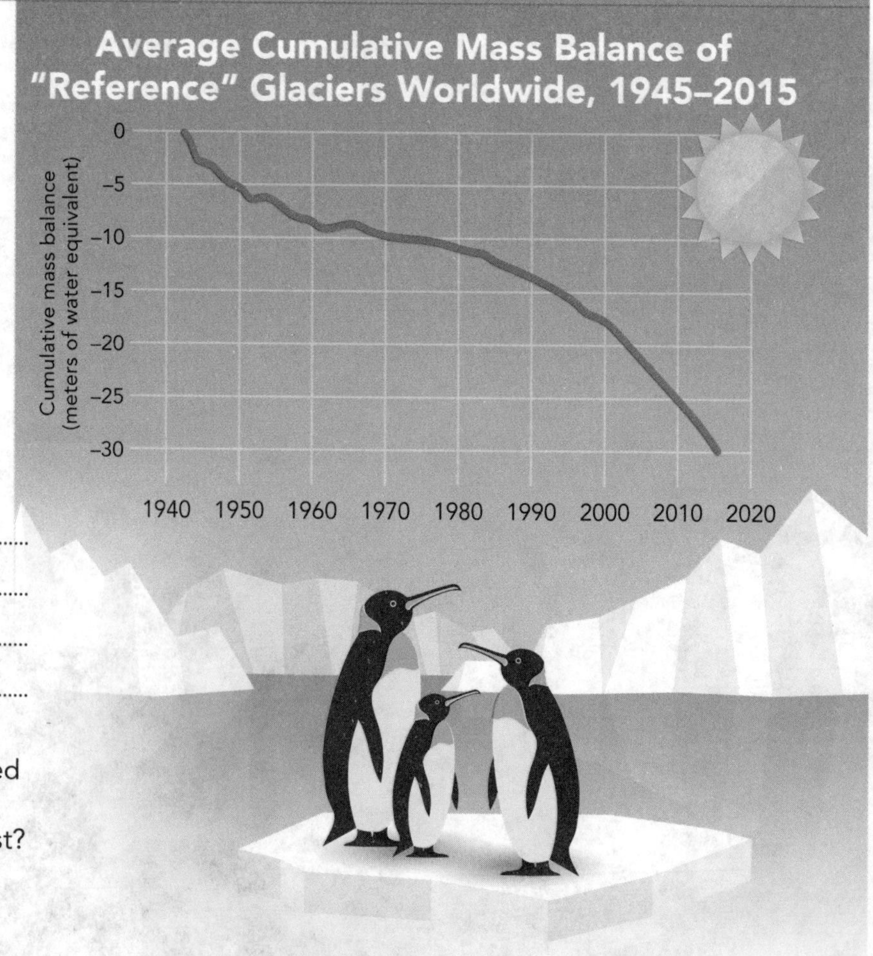

Source: World Glacier Monitoring Service, 2016

Glacial Erosion

Figure 2 Glaciers wear down Earth's surface by plucking and abrasion.

1. **Interpret Diagrams** Draw an arrow in the diagram to show the direction in which the ice is moving. Draw an *X* where you think abrasion is occurring. Draw a circle where plucking is happening.

2. **SEP Construct Explanations** In your own words, describe the glacial erosion taking place in the diagram.

....

....

....

....

....

....

....

Glacial Erosion The movement of a glacier slowly changes the land beneath it. The two processes by which glaciers erode the land are plucking and abrasion.

As a glacier flows over the land, it picks up rocks in a process called **plucking**. The weight of the ice breaks rocks into fragments that freeze to the bottom of the glacier. Then the rock fragments get carried with the glacier, as shown in **Figure 2**. Plucking leaves behind a jagged landscape.

Many rocks remain embedded on the bottom and sides of the glacier, and the glacier drags them across the land much like sandpaper in a process called abrasion. Land is worn away and deep gouges and scratches form in the bedrock.

For most glaciers, advancing, retreating, and eroding the land are very slow events. It can take years for scientists to observe any change in a glacier or its effects. Sometimes, however, glaciers move unusually fast. In 2012, scientists determined that a glacier in Greenland advanced up to 46 meters per day, faster than any other glacier recorded.

Although glaciers move and work slowly, they are a major force of erosion. They can take years to carve tiny scratches in bedrock. They can also carve out huge valleys hundreds of kilometers long over thousands of years. Through slow movement and erosion, glaciers dramatically change the shape of large areas of Earth's surface.

INTERACTIVITY

Examine water's effect on glaciers.

Glacial Deposition A glacier carries large amounts of rock and soil as it erodes the land in its path. As the glacier melts, it deposits the sediment it eroded from the land, creating various landforms, detailed in **Figure 3**. These landforms remain for thousands of years after the glacier has melted. The mixture of sediments that a glacier deposits directly on the surface is called **till**, which includes clay, silt, sand, gravel, boulders, and even rock ground so finely it is called rock flour.

Moraine The till deposited at the edges of a glacier forms a ridge called a moraine. Lateral moraines are deposits of sediment along the sides of a glacier. A terminal moraine is the ridge of till that is dropped at the farthest point reached by a glacier.

Landforms of Glacial Erosion and Deposition

Figure 3 Glacial erosion and deposition wear down and build up Earth's surface, producing landforms.

Classify In the model of a landscape shaped by glaciers, identify the features of erosion and deposition. In the circles, write *E* for erosion and *D* for deposition.

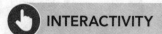

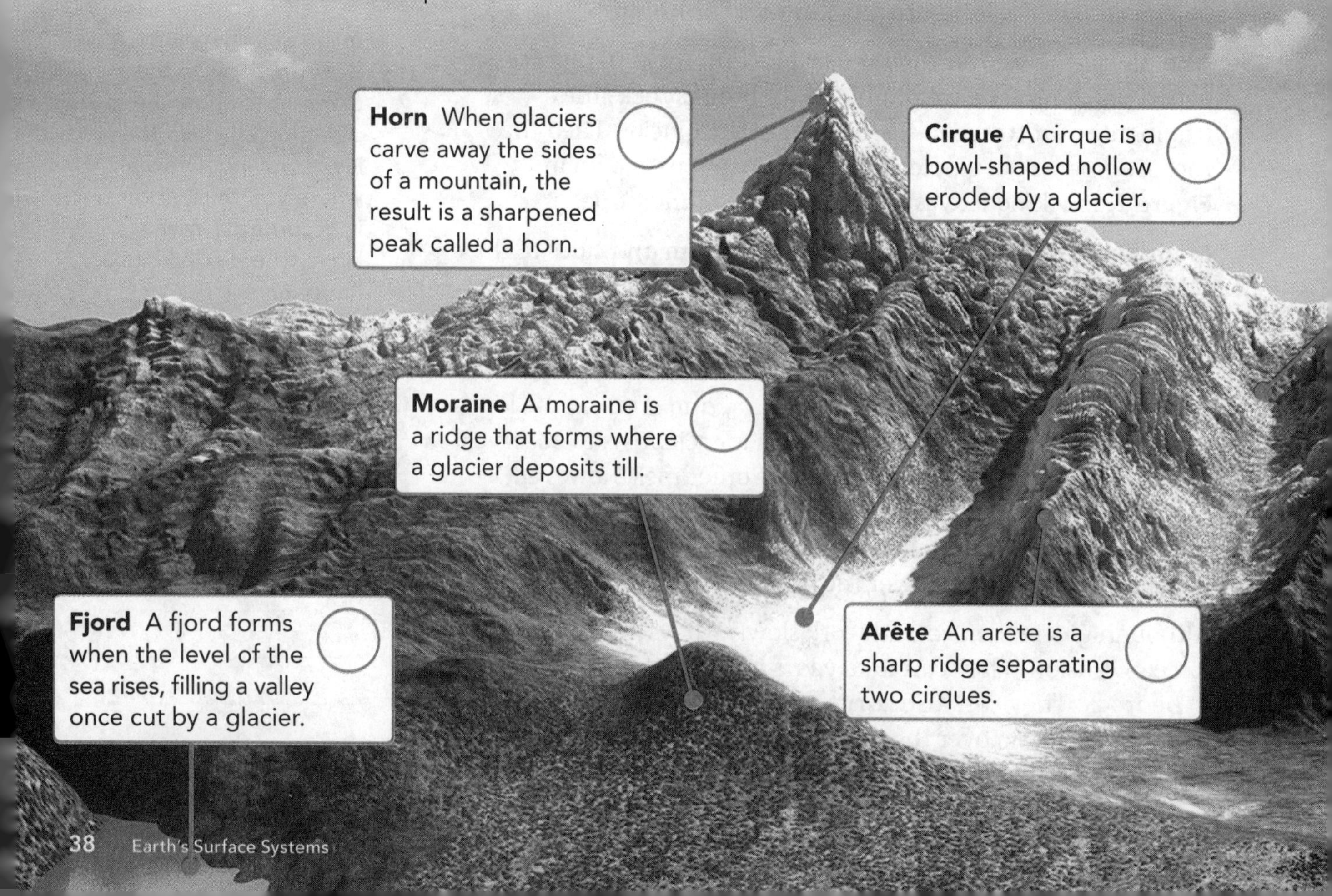

Horn When glaciers carve away the sides of a mountain, the result is a sharpened peak called a horn.
Cirque A cirque is a bowl-shaped hollow eroded by a glacier.
Moraine A moraine is a ridge that forms where a glacier deposits till.
Fjord A fjord forms when the level of the sea rises, filling a valley once cut by a glacier.
Arête An arête is a sharp ridge separating two cirques.

Kettle Retreating, or melting, glaciers also create features called kettles. A kettle is a steep-sided depression that forms when a chunk of ice is left in glacial till. When the ice melts, the kettle remains. The continental glacier of the last ice age left behind many kettles. Kettles often fill with water, forming small ponds or lakes called kettle lakes. Such lakes are common in areas such as Wisconsin that were once covered with glaciers.

READING CHECK **Write Informative Texts** What are the effects of glacial deposition?

....

....

....

....

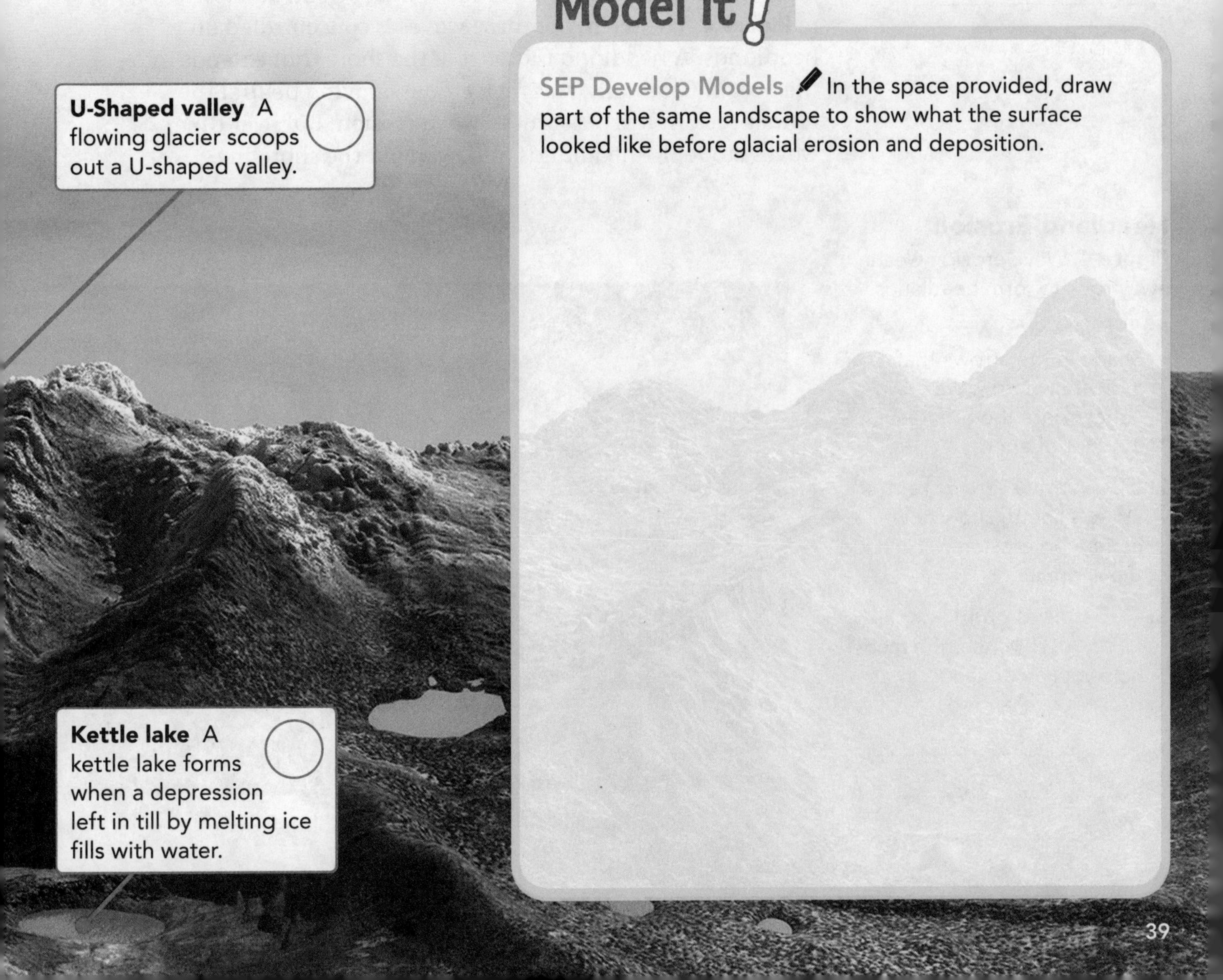

U-Shaped valley A flowing glacier scoops out a U-shaped valley.
Kettle lake A kettle lake forms when a depression left in till by melting ice fills with water.

Model It!

SEP Develop Models In the space provided, draw part of the same landscape to show what the surface looked like before glacial erosion and deposition.

Waves Change Earth's Surface

HANDS-ON LAB

Investigate Explore coastline erosion.

Like glaciers, waves change Earth's surface. The energy in most waves comes from the wind. Stronger winds cause larger waves. The friction between the wave and the ocean floor slows the wave. Then the water breaks powerfully on the shore. This forward-moving water provides the force that changes the land along the shoreline.

Wave Erosion Waves shape the coast through weathering and erosion by breaking down rock and moving sand and other sediments. Large waves can hit rocks along the shore with great force, or **impact**. Over time, waves can enlarge small cracks in rocks and cause pieces of rock to break off. Waves also break apart rocks by abrasion. As a wave approaches shallow water, it picks up and carries sediment, including sand and gravel. When the wave hits land, the sediment wears away rock like sandpaper slowly wearing away wood.

Academic Vocabulary

How might you use the word *impact* in everyday life? Write a sentence using the word.

....

....

....

....

....

Waves approaching the shore gradually change direction as different parts of the waves drag on the bottom, as shown in **Figure 4**. The energy of these waves is concentrated on headlands. A headland is a part of the shore that extends into the ocean. Gradually, soft rock erodes, leaving behind the harder rock that is resistant to wave erosion. But over time, waves erode the headlands and even out the shoreline.

Headland Erosion

Figure 4 Wave erosion wears away rock to form headlands.

1. SEP Develop Models Shade in the arrows that indicate where waves concentrate the greatest amount of energy.
2. CCC Cause and Effect Draw a line to show how continued erosion will change the shoreline.
3. CCC Stability and Change How does this model help you understand a system or process of change?

....

....

....

....

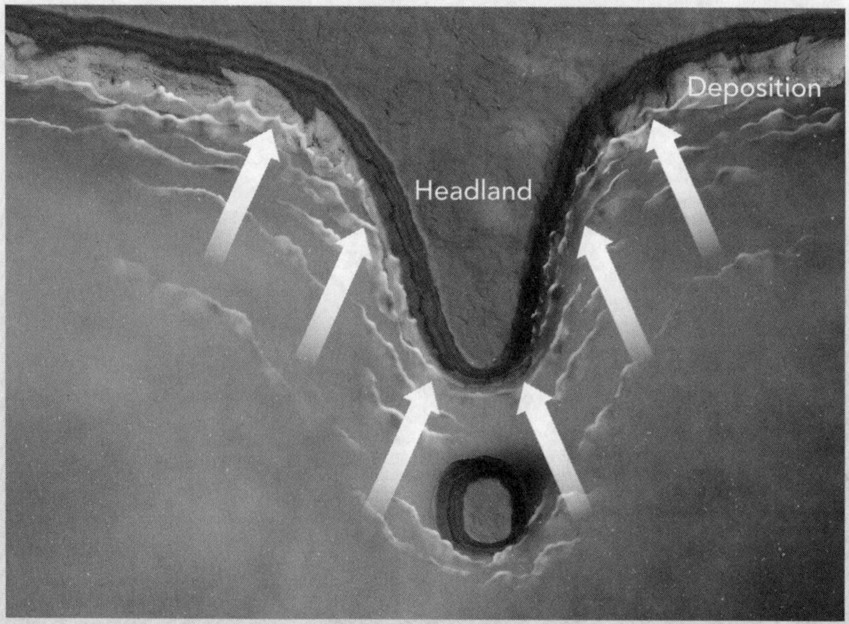

Landforms Formed by Wave Erosion

When an ax strikes the base of a tree trunk, the cut gets bigger and deeper with each strike. Similarly, when ocean waves hit a steep, rocky coast, they erode the base of the land. Waves erode the softer rock first. Over time, the waves may erode a hollow notch in the rock called a sea cave. Eventually, waves may erode the base of a cliff so much that the cliff collapses. The rubble is washed out by wave action and the result is a wave-cut platform at the cliff's base, which is all that remains of the eroded cliff. A sea arch is another feature of wave erosion that forms when waves erode a layer of softer rock that underlies a layer of harder rock. If an arch collapses, a pillar of rock called a sea stack may result.

Wave erosion changes Earth's surface at different rates. Sometimes it changes the land quickly. During a single powerful storm with strong winds that form high-energy waves, part of a cliff or sea stack may crumble. Waves may pick up and carry away large amounts of sediment along a shore. In general, waves erode rock slowly, cutting cliffs and headlands back centimeters to meters in a year. Waves may take hundreds to thousands of years to wear away headlands and even out shorelines.

READING CHECK **Write Explanatory Texts** Reread the text. Then explain how you think a sea cave might become a sea arch.

....

....

Landforms Formed by Wave Erosion

Figure 5 Identify and label the landforms in the photo.

Literacy Connection

Write Informative Texts
As you read, think about how you could help another student understand the concepts. Then, in your own words, describe how waves cause erosion.

....

....

....

....

....

....

....

INTERACTIVITY

Investigate wind and water erosion in Florida.

Wave Deposition Deposition occurs when waves lose energy and slow down, causing the water to drop the sediment it carries. Waves change the shape of a coast when they deposit sediment and form landforms.

Landforms Formed by Wave Deposition A beach is an area of wave-washed sediment along a coast. The sediment deposited on beaches is usually sand. Some beaches are made of coral or seashell fragments piled up by wave action. Florida has many such beaches.

Waves usually hit the beach at an angle, creating a current that runs parallel to the coastline. As waves repeatedly hit the beach, some of the sediment gets carried along the beach with the current, in a process called **longshore drift**.

Longshore drift also builds up sandbars and creates barrier islands. Sandbars are long ridges of sand parallel to the shore. A spit is an extended part of a beach that is connected by one end to the mainland. A barrier island forms when waves pile up large amounts of sand above sea level, forming a long, narrow island parallel to the coast. Barrier islands are found in Florida and numerous other places along the Atlantic coast of the United States. Barrier islands are constantly changing from wave erosion and deposition that occur during hurricanes and other storms.

READING CHECK **Translate Information** Use the information in the text and **Figure 6** to determine how the coastline might change if large amounts of sand built up higher than sea level as a result of storm deposition.

Landforms Formed by Wave Deposition

Figure 6 On the diagram, draw arrows and label them to show the direction of longshore drift and the flow of sediment from the river to the sea.

LESSON 4 Check

MS-ESS2-2

1. **Identify** What are three landforms formed by wave deposition?

2. **CCC Stability and Change** How are the ways in which glaciers and waves wear down Earth's surface similar?

3. **CCC Cause and Effect** A valley in the Rocky Mountains contains a glacier. How might the glacier change this valley in the future?

4. **SEP Develop Models** Draw and label diagrams to show how a sea arch might form from a headland.

Quest CHECK-IN

In this lesson, you discovered how erosion and deposition by glaciers change Earth's surface. You also learned how erosion and deposition by waves change Earth's surface.

CCC System Models Why is it important to consider the effects of wave erosion and deposition when designing an artificial island?

INTERACTIVITY

Breaking Waves

Go online to examine how wave erosion might impact the location of your island, and adjust your design as needed.

TOPIC 1 Review and Assess

1 Weathering and Soil

MS-ESS2-2

1. How does acid rain cause weathering?
   A. through abrasion
   B. through oxidation
   C. by dissolving rock
   D. by carrying rock away

2. Mechanical weathering breaks some limestone into pieces. What effect would this have on chemical weathering of the limestone?
   A. Chemical weathering would stop occurring.
   B. Chemical weathering would remain the same.
   C. Chemical weathering would occur at a slower rate.
   D. Chemical weathering would occur at a faster rate.

3. The process of .... is an example of .... weathering in which rock splits through repeated freezing and thawing.

4. **SEP Develop Models** Draw a diagram of the A, B, and C horizons of soil. Label the horizons and describe the processes that formed each layer. Include examples of weathering in your description.

....
....
....
....
....
....

2 Erosion and Deposition

MS-ESS2-2, MS-ESS3-2

5. Which change occurs as a result of wind slowing down?
   A. erosion
   B. deposition
   C. chemical weathering
   D. mechanical weathering

6. How are erosion and deposition alike?
   A. Both change Earth's surface over time.
   B. Both build up Earth's surface quickly.
   C. Both wear down Earth's surface slowly.
   D. Neither changes Earth's surface.

7. Which type of mass movement occurs rapidly when a single mass of soil and rock suddenly slip downhill?
   A. creep
   B. landslide
   C. mudslide
   D. slump

8. Deposition by .... causes sand .... to form.

9. **CCC Stability and Change** A scientist observes that over several decades, fence posts placed in soil on a slope became tilted. Have erosion, deposition, or both occurred in this area? Use evidence to explain how you know.

....
....
....
....
....
....
....

ASSESSMENT

Evaluate your understanding by taking a Topic Test.

3 Water Erosion

MS-ESS2-2

10. Which landform develops as a result of river deposition?

A. cave
B. delta
C. stalactite
D. waterfall

11. Which of the following processes causes sinkholes to form?

A. erosion of sediment by runoff
B. deposition of sediment by a river
C. deposition of calcite by groundwater
D. erosion of limestone by groundwater

12. Sediments get deposited in an alluvial fan because ....

....

13. SEP Develop Models Complete the flow chart to model a process that changes Earth's surface. Be sure to give the model a title.

Raindrops strike ground.
↓
Runoff forms.
↓

↓

↓

↓

4 Glacial and Wave Erosion

MS-ESS2-2

14. Which term describes sediment of mixed sizes deposited directly by a glacier?

A. kettle
B. loess
C. slump
D. till

15. How does longshore drift affect Earth's surface?

A. Rivers carry sediment to the ocean.
B. Rock cliffs break apart from impact.
C. Sediment moves down a beach with the current.
D. Waves concentrate their energy on headlands.

16. Which landform is created as a direct result of waves slowly eroding rocks?

A. beach
B. sandbar
C. sea stack
D. spit

17. Glaciers erode Earth's surface through the processes of .... and ....

18. CCC Cause and Effect You are in a mountain valley studying a glacier. How could you use local landforms to tell whether the glacier is advancing or retreating?

....

....

....

....

....

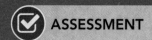

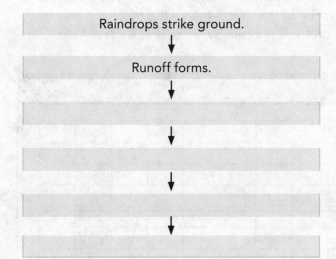

MS-ESS2-2, MS-ESS3-2

Evidence-Based Assessment

A team of researchers is studying a massive landslide that occurred on the scenic stretch of California's coast known as Big Sur on May 20, 2017. Millions of tons of rock and dirt collapsed down a seaside slope onto the highway and spilled into the sea.

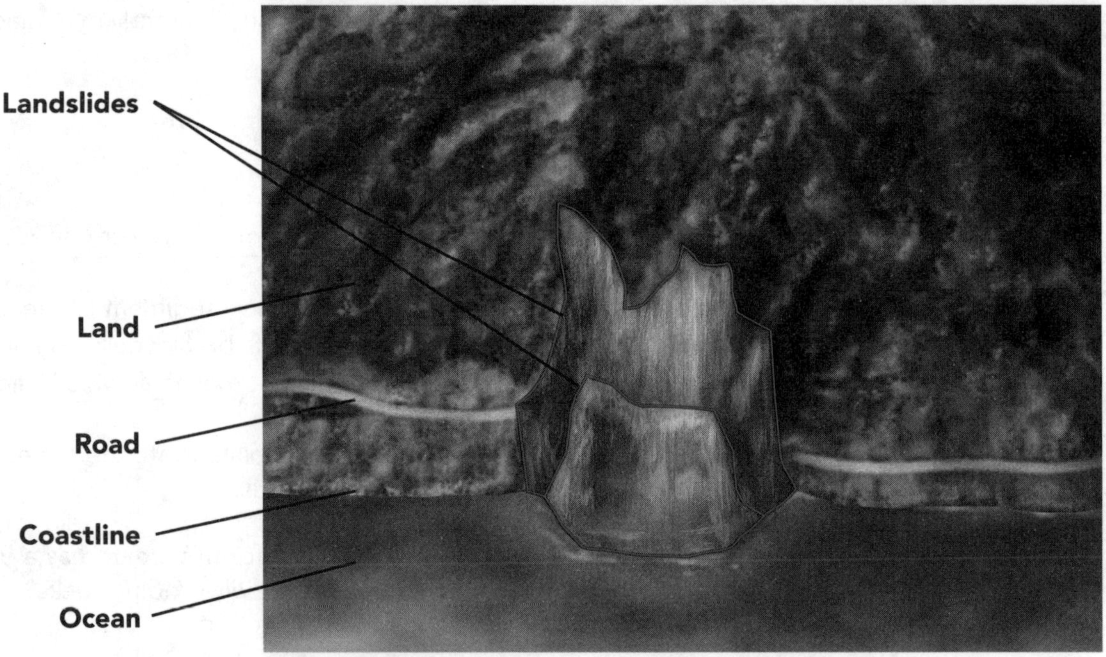

To understand what happened in Big Sur, researchers are analyzing average winter precipitation data collected over a thirty-year period. The data is displayed in the graph. The solid line across the middle of the graph marks the mean, or average, winter precipitation for California over the entire thirty-year period.

California Winter Precipitation 1987–2017

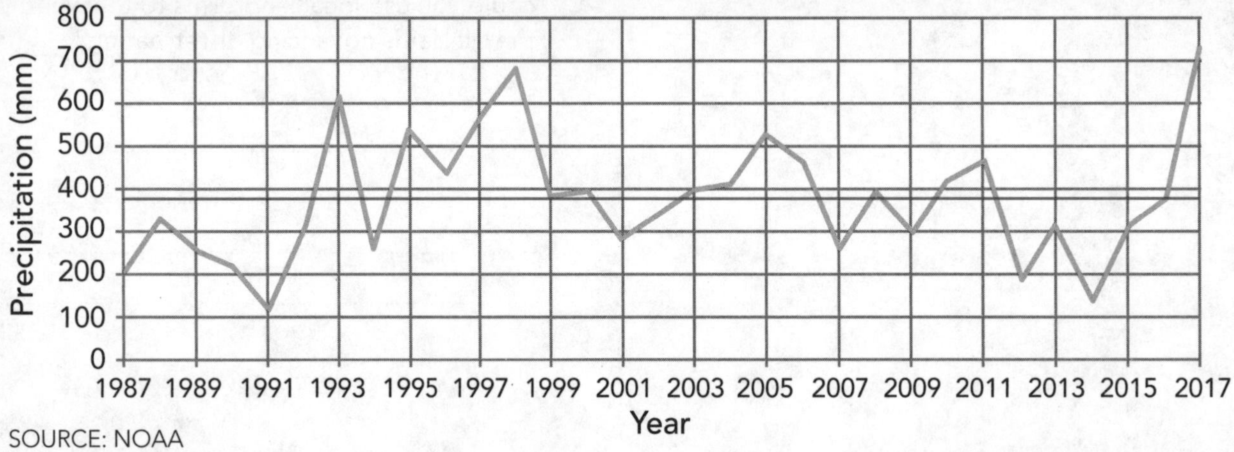

SOURCE: NOAA

1. **SEP Analyze Data** How much precipitation did California receive in the winter prior to the May 20 landslide of 2017?
A. 710 mm **B.** 390 mm
C. 520 mm **D.** 800 mm

2. **SEP Interpret Data** How would you describe California's precipitation in the five winters prior to 2017? Select all the statements that apply.
- [ ] It was above average for the five winters.
- [ ] It was below average for four winters, and average for one.
- [ ] It was below average for the five winters.
- [ ] It was mostly above average.
- [ ] It was mostly below average.
- [ ] It was above average for four winters, and below average for one.

3. **CCC Stability and Change** In the image of the coast at Big Sur, what are three visible indications that a large landslide occurred?

4. **CCC Cause and Effect** How do you think weathering and erosion will affect the base of the deposited sediment, which is in the ocean? How will this affect the coastline in the future?

5. **SEP Construct Explanations** What do you think is the connection between the precipitation in the winter of 2017 and the landslide?

Quest FINDINGS

Complete the Quest!

Phenomenon Reflect on how changes to Earth's surface will impact an artificial island. Then, prepare and deliver an oral or written presentation explaining your island design and your model.

CCC System Models What are three things you learned about the processes that shape Earth's surface that helped you to design your artificial island?

INTERACTIVITY

Reflect on Your Ingenious Island

MS-ESS2-2, MS-ESS3-2

Materials on a Slope

How can you use a **model** to determine the likelihood of **mass movement**?

Background

Phenomenon Geoscience processes such as rapid mass movement result in large amounts of sediment moving down hillsides.

In this investigation, you will work as part of a landslide monitoring team. You will develop and use a model to explore the relationship between the height and width of a hill. You will gain understanding about how these factors affect the hill's stability and the likelihood that mass movement will occur.

Safety

Be sure to follow all safety guidelines provided by your teacher. The Safety Appendix of your textbook provides more details about the safety icons.

Materials

(per group)

- tray (about 15 cm × 45 cm × 60 cm)
- several sheets of white paper
- masking tape
- cardboard tube
- spoon or paper cup
- dry sand (500 mL) in container
- wooden skewer
- metric ruler
- pencil or crayon
- graph paper

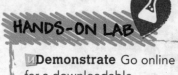

Landslides are destructive events that not only damage roadways and buildings, but also result in the loss of life.

Plan Your Investigation

HANDS-ON LAB

Demonstrate Go online for a downloadable worksheet of this lab.

☐ Use the metric ruler to mark off centimeters across the length of the paper. Take the tray provided by your teacher and use the paper to cover its interior surface. Secure the paper with tape. In the middle of the tray, stand the cardboard tube upright. Use a spoon or cup to fill the tube with sand.

☐ When the tube is nearly full, slowly and steadily pull the tube straight up so that the sand falls out of the bottom and forms a cone-shaped hill. Use different quantities of sand and observe the shapes and sizes of the sand hills created.

☐ Using the materials provided by your teacher, design an investigation to explore the relationship between the height and width of a sand hill. Determine how many sand hills you will create in your investigation.

☐ Then use the space provided to outline your procedure. Have your teacher review and approve your procedure, and then conduct your investigation. Create a data table to record your data about the heights and widths of the sand hills your group models.

Design Your Procedure

Data Table

Analyze and Interpret Data

1. **SEP Analyze Data** Study your data table. What patterns do you notice in your data?

2. **SEP Evaluate Information** What do your data suggest about the relationship between the height and width of a sand hill?

3. **SEP Identify Limitations** What are the advantages of using the sand hill model in this investigation? What are the limitations of using the model?

4. **CCC Scale, Proportion, and Quantity** How is your sand hill model similar to and different from a natural hill that undergoes mass movement?

5. **CCC Stability and Change** How could you apply the results of your investigation to help assess the likelihood of and forecast future mass movement events such as landslides? Use evidence from your investigation to support your explanation.

TOPIC

2

Distribution of Natural Resources

LESSON 1
Nonrenewable Energy Resources
uInvestigate Lab: Fossil Fuels

LESSON 2
Renewable Energy Resources
uInvestigate Lab: The Power of Wind

uEngineer It! STEM **Micro-Hydro Power**

LESSON 3
Mineral Resources
uInvestigate Lab: Cool Crystals

LESSON 4
Water Resources
uInvestigate Lab: An Artesian Well

NGSS PERFORMANCE EXPECTATIONS

MS-ESS3-1 Construct a scientific explanation based on evidence for how the uneven distributions of Earth's mineral, energy, and groundwater resources are the result of past and current geoscience processes.

MS-ESS3-3 Apply scientific principles to design a method for monitoring and minimizing a human impact on the environment.

MS-ESS3-4 Construct an argument supported by evidence for how increases in human population and per-capita consumption of natural resources impact Earth's systems.

What is responsible for these colorful rock formations?

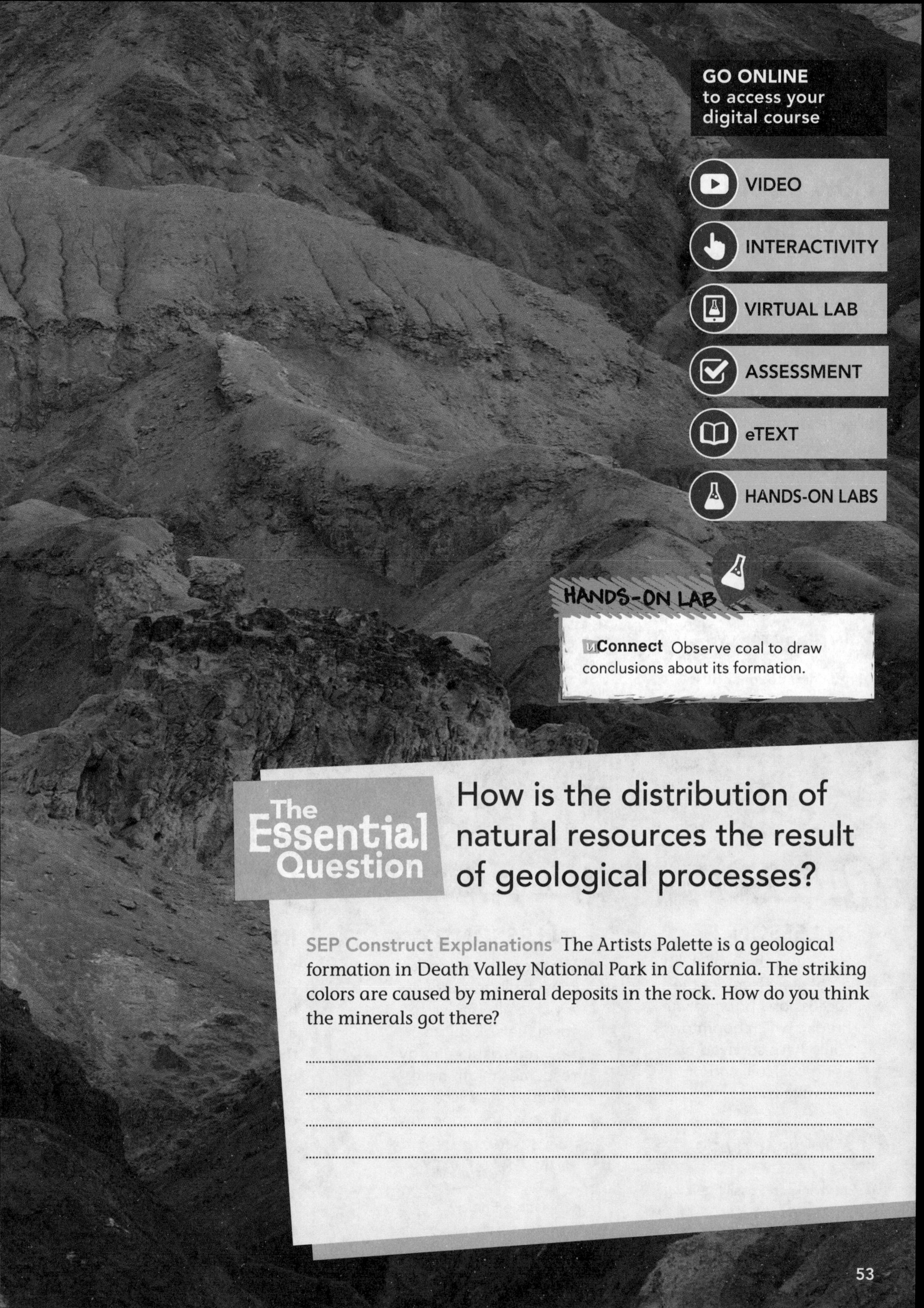

GO ONLINE to access your digital course

- VIDEO
- INTERACTIVITY
- VIRTUAL LAB
- ASSESSMENT
- eTEXT
- HANDS-ON LABS

HANDS-ON LAB

Connect Observe coal to draw conclusions about its formation.

The Essential Question

How is the distribution of natural resources the result of geological processes?

SEP Construct Explanations The Artists Palette is a geological formation in Death Valley National Park in California. The striking colors are caused by mineral deposits in the rock. How do you think the minerals got there?

....

....

....

....

Quest KICKOFF

How could natural resources have saved a ghost town?

Phenomenon In the past, the discovery of valuable or rare natural resources often led to the quick development of towns as people rushed to strike it rich. But many of these boomtowns, as they came to be known, died as quickly as they began. In this problem-based Quest activity, you will investigate how resource availability affected the longevity and success of boomtowns. By applying what you learn in each lesson, you will gather key Quest information and evidence. In the Findings activity, you will choose a boomtown to explore in more detail and explain the role that resource availability played in the fate of the town.

INTERACTIVITY

Predicting Boom or Bust

MS-ESS3-1 Construct a scientific explanation based on evidence for how the uneven distributions of Earth's mineral, energy, and groundwater resources are the result of past and current geoscience processes.

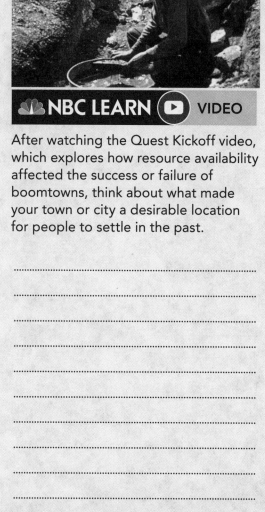

NBC LEARN VIDEO

After watching the Quest Kickoff video, which explores how resource availability affected the success or failure of boomtowns, think about what made your town or city a desirable location for people to settle in the past.

Quest CHECK-IN

IN LESSON 1

How does the availability of fossil fuels affect the success of a boomtown? Predict which boomtowns could have survived by using coal, oil, and/or natural gas.

INTERACTIVITY

Surviving on Fossil Fuels

Quest CHECK-IN

IN LESSON 2

What conditions make renewable resources a viable alternative to fossil fuels? Explore how renewable energy resources might have affected the success or failure of the boomtowns.

INTERACTIVITY

Renewable Energy

Quest CHECK-IN

IN LESSON 3

What effect does the distribution of minerals have on the success of a boomtown? Analyze the distribution of gold, copper, and salt to help you determine the fates of the boomtowns.

INTERACTIVITY

Surviving on Minerals

Many towns like the one shown here did not have the resources required to sustain growth and development.

Quest CHECK-IN

IN LESSON 4

How does access to water affect the fate of a boomtown? Predict which boomtowns might have survived based on the availability of water resources.

INTERACTIVITY

Surviving on Water

Quest FINDINGS

Complete the Quest!

Find out what happened to each boomtown and then create a travel brochure for one of the boomtowns to explain how resource availability affected the fate of that town.

INTERACTIVITY

Reflect on Boomtowns

uConnect Lab

What's in a Piece of Coal?

What evidence can you gather to **explain** what coal is made of?

Background

Phenomenon Coal is the most abundant fossil fuel in the world. About 40% the world's electricity is generated by coal, and it is also used in many industries such as steel production. Coal-fired electrical power plants use the heat given off by burning coal to make steam. Different kinds of coal release different amounts of energy when they are burned. To understand where the energy stored in coal comes from, you need to know what coal is made of and how it forms. In this activity, you will use observations of a piece of coal to try to explain its composition and formation.

Materials

(per group)

- lignite coal
- hand lens
- ruler
- paper

Safety

Be sure to follow all safety procedures provided by your teacher. The Safety Appendix of your textbook provides more details about the safety icons.

Design a Procedure

☐ **1.** Observe the piece of coal. Make a table of properties of coal that you can investigate and record your observations in the table in as much detail as possible.

☐ **2. SEP Plan an Investigation** Using the tools provided, write a procedure to test the properties you added to your table. Show your plan to your teacher before you begin. Record your observations.

....

....

....

....

....

Observations

Analyze and Interpret Data

HANDS-ON LAB

Connect Go online for a downloadable worksheet of this lab.

1. **CCC Scale, Proportion, and Quantity** Compare your initial observations to those you made using the hand lens. What did you notice?

2. **SEP Construct Explanations** Based on your observations, what do you think coal is made of?

3. **SEP Construct Explanations** Based on your observations, how do you think coal is formed?

LESSON

1 Nonrenewable Energy Resources

Guiding Questions

- What are nonrenewable resources?
- What factors affect the distribution of nonrenewable energy resources?
- How has human activity impacted the distribution of fossil fuels?

Connections

Literacy Cite Textual Evidence

Math Analyze Relationships

MS-ESS3-1, MS-ESS3-4

HANDS-ON LAB

uInvestigate Explore why fossil fuels are considered nonrenewable resources.

Vocabulary

natural resource
nonrenewable resource
fossil fuels
nuclear fission

Academic Vocabulary

renew

Connect It!

Identify and label some the materials that are being used in this construction project.

Classify Pick one of the materials you identified in the photo and explain whether you think the resource is limited or unlimited.

....

....

Natural Resources

We all rely on natural resources to survive. A **natural resource** is anything occuring naturally in the environment that humans use. We need air to breathe, water to drink, soil in which to grow plants to eat, sunlight to make those plants grow, and other natural resources. Some of these resources are essentially unlimited and renewable regardless of what we do. For example, sunlight and wind are available daily at most places on Earth. Other renewable resources can be reused or replenished, but it may require some care or planning. For example, wood from trees is a renewable resource as long as some trees are spared to reproduce and make the next generation of trees.

Other resources are **nonrenewable resources,** which cannot be replaced. This may be because there is a finite amount of the resource on Earth and we don't have a way to make more of it. The element silver, for example, cannot be made from other substances. The amount of silver on Earth is set. Other resources are considered nonrenewable because it takes very long periods of time for them to form.

HANDS-ON LAB

Classify resources that you use in a typical day.

Reflect In your science notebook, describe how a natural resource could shift from being renewable to nonrenewable.

READING CHECK **Cite Evidence** Why is wood considered to be a renewable resource?

....

....

....

Resource Use

Figure 1 This construction project relies on a number of natural resources.

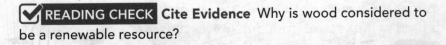

HANDS-ON LAB

Investigate Explore why fossil fuels are considered nonrenewable resources.

Lignite

Bituminous Coal

Anthracite

Types of Coal

Figure 2 Brittle, lustrous anthracite has more energy than crumbly, dull lignite.

Determine Differences Why might one type of coal contain more energy than another type of coal?

....

....

....

....

Fossil Fuels

The sources of energy commonly called fossil fuels include coal, petroleum, and natural gas. **Fossil fuels** are the energy-rich substances made from the preserved remains of organisms. The chemical energy in fossil fuels can be converted to other forms by burning them.

The energy stored in these compounds originally arrived on Earth as sunlight. Photosynthetic organisms such as algae, moss, grasses, and trees converted sunlight into carbon-based compounds. When animals ate the plants, they absorbed some of those compounds. Under certain conditions involving high temperatures and pressures, the remains of these organisms were transformed into new materials, including solid coal, liquid petroleum, and methane gas.

Coal Coal is formed from the remains of plants that died long ago in and around swampy areas. There are different grades, or types, of coal (**Figure 2**). Each grade forms under different conditions, as shown in **Figure 3**. In addition to being a source of energy, coal is used in a wide array of applications. Coal is used in water and air purification systems, as well as medical equipment such as kidney dialysis devices. Coal is used to make steel from iron ore. Coal is also an essential ingredient in carbon fiber, an extremely durable and lightweight material used to construct everything from bicycles to buildings.

Burning coal in coal-fired power plants accounts for about 30 percent of the electricity produced in the United States. Coal has long been used as a fuel because it has twice as much energy per unit of mass as wood. So, when coal can be mined at a large scale, it can be an efficient source of energy.

Unfortunately, burning coal produces pollutants and causes millions of deaths each year from health problems. Coal mining also requires large mines to be dug into the ground, or the removal of mountaintops or other surface layers to access coal beds. Removing coal causes great damage to the surrounding environment.

READING CHECK **Determine Central Ideas** What is the original source of the energy contained in coal? Explain.

....

....

....

Coal Formation and Distribution

Figure 3 Coal only forms under the right conditions. The map shows major deposits of coal around the world.

1. **SEP Use Models** Circle the three continents that have the most coal resources.

2. **SEP Construct Explanations** Why is coal not found evenly distributed around the world?

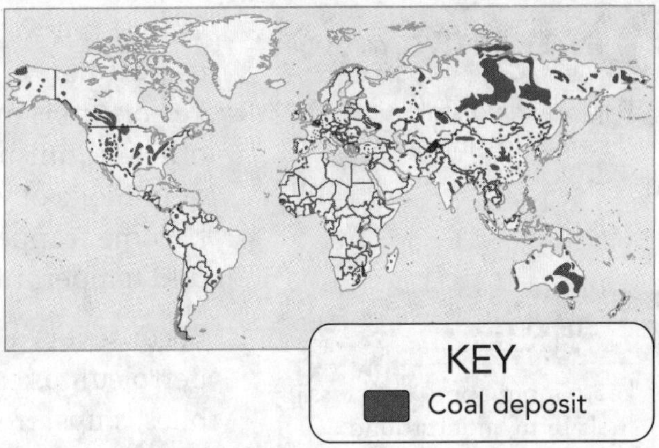

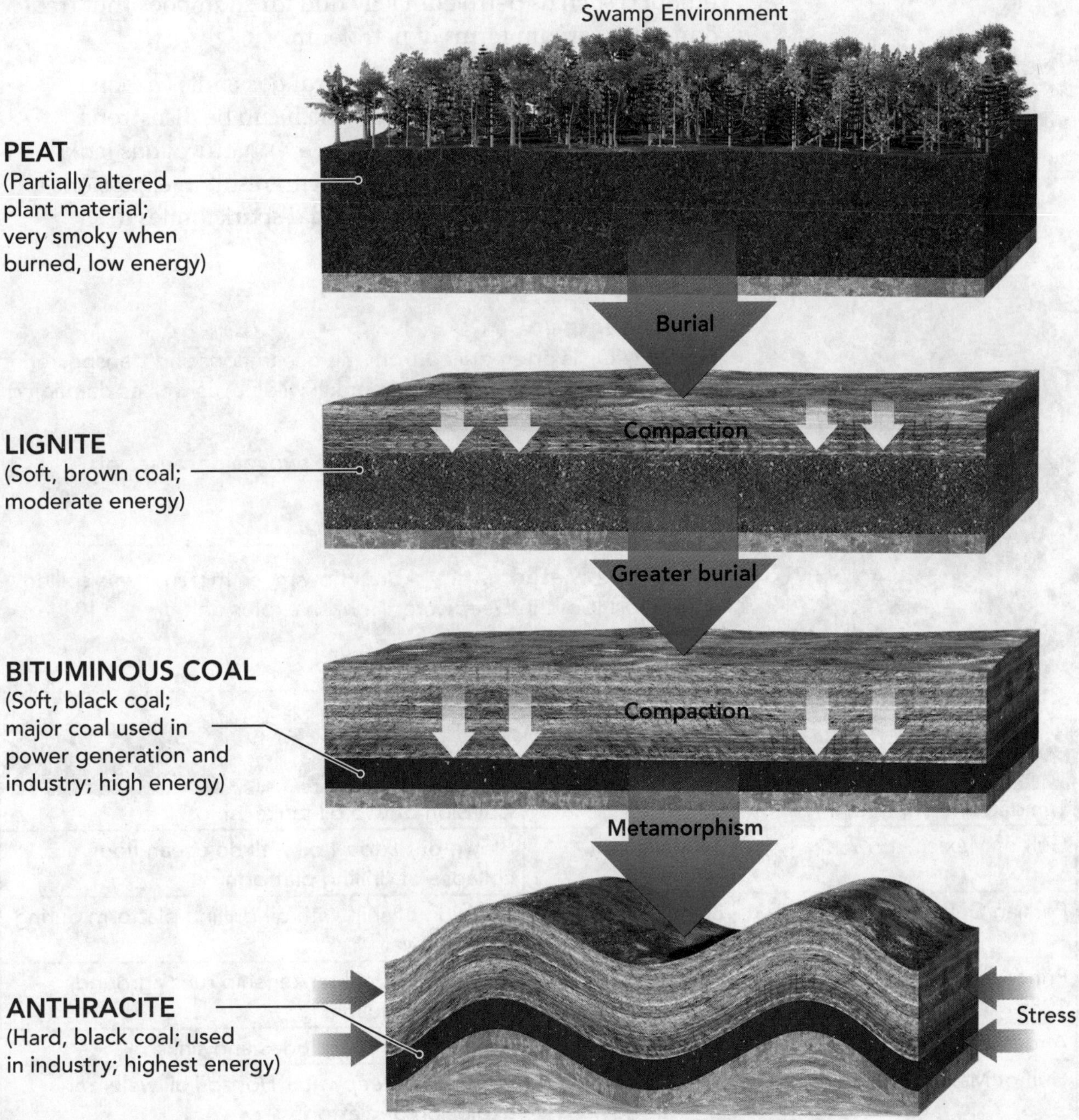

INTERACTIVITY

Explore the distribution of different fossil fuels.

VIDEO

Learn more about how fossil fuels form underground.

Oil What we commonly refer to as oil is scientifically known as **petroleum**, from the Latin terms *petra* (rock) and *oleum* (oil). Petroleum is made of the remains of small animals, algae, and other organisms that lived in marine environments hundreds of millions of years ago. Oil deposits form when these remains become trapped underground and are subject to high pressure and temperature.

Because it is a liquid and can be processed into different fuels, petroleum is especially useful for powering engines in automobiles, ships, trains, and airplanes. Petroleum also has many important industrial uses, such as making plastics, lubricants, and fertilizers. Petroleum is also the basis for synthetic fibers, such as rayon and nylon. Many cosmetic and pharmaceutical products such as petroleum jelly and tar shampoos that treat dandruff, contain forms of petroleum.

As with coal, burning oil and natural gas emits carbon dioxide. Oil can also be spilled, which can be disastrous for wildlife and water quality (**Figure 4**). Natural gas leaks contribute to global warming, and can result in explosions if the concentration of gas is high and a spark ignites it.

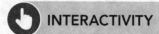

Oil Impacts

Figure 4 Oil is often drilled from the ocean floor and transported by ship. Major oil spills can harm or kill wildlife, as well as damaging habitats and water quality.

1. SEP Interpret Data What are the two major causes of accidental oil spills?

2. SEP Use Mathematics About how much more oil was spilled as a result of the *Deepwater Horizon* explosion than the *Valdez* running aground?

Location and Date	Amount Spilled (gallons)	Cause
Trinidad and Tobago, 1979	90 million	Collision of two oil tanker ships
Gulf of Mexico, 1979	140 million	Blown-out *Ixtoc 1* oil well on ocean floor, fire, collapse of drilling platform
Persian Gulf, 1983	80 million	Collision of ship with oil-drilling platform during Iraq-Iran war
Prince William Sound, Alaska, 1989	11 million	*Exxon Valdez* oil tanker ship runs aground, puncturing hull
Angola, 1991	80 million	Oil tanker ship explodes and sinks
Gulf of Mexico, 2010	181 million	Blown-out *Deepwater Horizon* oil well, explosion of platform

Petroleum Formation and Distribution

Figure 5 Petroleum has been drilled for all over the world. Wells or rigs are constructed to tap "fields" of oil hundreds or thousands of meters below Earth's surface, both on land and water.

SEP Engage in Argument ✏ A large sea once existed in the United States. Shade the area of the country where you think the sea likely existed. Then explain your choice.

....

....

....

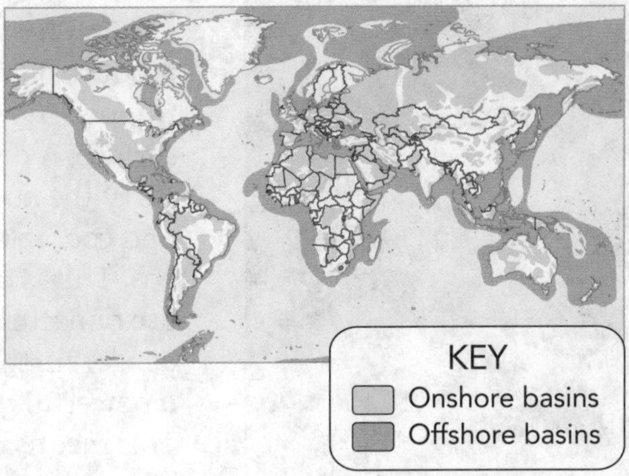

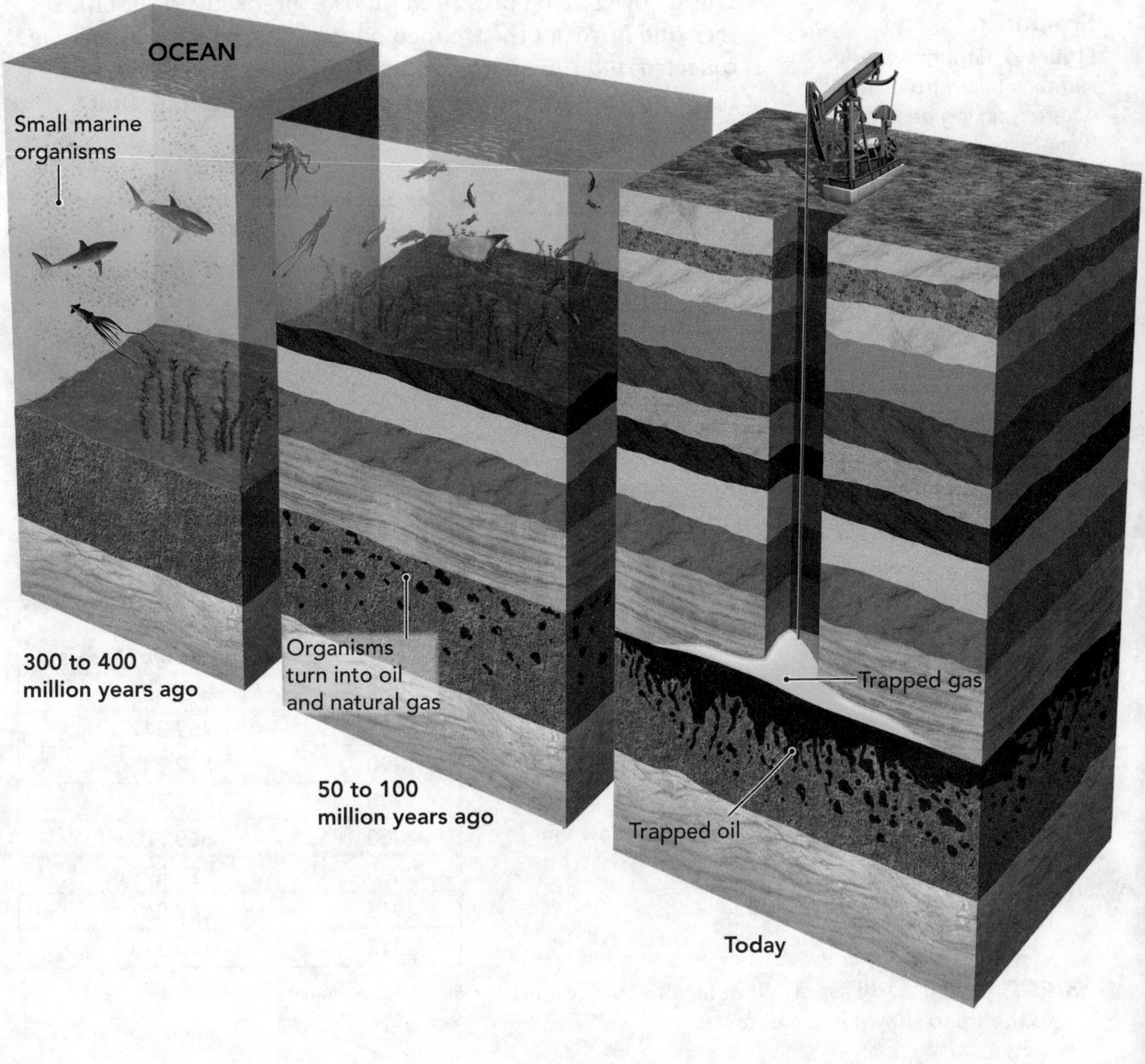

Fracking

Figure 6 Groundwater samples taken from sites where fracking has occurred have tested positive for methane and other hydrocarbons.

Natural Gas Formed from the same processes that produce oil and found in the same locations, natural gas is trapped in pockets within layers of rock deep below Earth's surface. A drill can tap the trapped gas, and then pipelines carry the gas for processing and transport. Burning petroleum and coal releases more carbon dioxide than burning natural gas. This is one reason many countries have encouraged more use of natural gas and are surveying underground basins of gas for further exploitation. On the other hand, the gas itself is a powerful greenhouse gas that contributes to global warming. This means any leaks of natural gas from wells, pipelines, and other structures pose a pollution problem.

To meet the demand for natural gas, a process called fracking has become popular. Fracking is short for hydraulic fracturing. This involves using pressured fluids to break layers of shale rock and force out the trapped natural gas, which can then be collected and transported. There are concerns that the fracking fluids are contaminating vital stores of groundwater that humans rely on (**Figure 6**).

READING CHECK **Cite Textual Evidence** Natural gas burns cleaner than coal, yet it is considered a pollutant. Why?

....

....

Math Toolbox

Natural Gas Consumption in the U.S.

In recent years, consumption patterns of natural gas have changed.

1. **SEP Use Mathematics** What was the percent increase in gas usage from 1980 to 2015? Show your work.

   ....

   ....

2. **Analyze Relationships** What trend is shown in the data?

   ....

   ....

3. **CCC Cause and Effect** What factors contributed to the trend shown in the data?

   ....

   ....

U.S. Annual Natural Gas Consumption

Year	Volume (Million Cubic Meters)
1980	562,862
1985	489,342
1990	542,935
1995	628,829
2000	660,720
2005	623,379
2010	682,062
2015	773,228

Source: U.S. Energy Information Administration

Nuclear Energy

Nuclear power is another nonrenewable energy resource used to generate much of the world's electricity. Nuclear energy provides 20 percent of the electricity in the United States. Inside a nuclear power plant, controlled nuclear fission reactions occur. **Nuclear fission** is the splitting of an atom's nucleus into two nuclei. Fission releases a great deal of energy. This energy is used to heat water, turning it into steam. The steam is then used to turn the blades of a turbine to produce electricity.

Uranium is the fuel used for nuclear fission inside nuclear reactors. It is a heavy metal that occurs in most rocks and is usually extracted through mining. The uranium found on Earth was part of the original cloud of dust and gas from which our solar system formed. Uranium is found throughout Earth's crust. But large ores of the material are formed from geological processes that only occur in certain locations on Earth (**Figure 7**).

Literacy Connection

Cite Textual Evidence As you read, underline text that supports the idea that uranium is a limited resource with finite amounts on Earth.

Source: World Nuclear Association

Distribution of Uranium

Figure 7 According to the World Nuclear Association, almost 70 percent of accessible uranium is found in only 5 countries.

1. **SEP Use Models** ✎ Circle the two countries with the greatest percentage of uranium resources.
2. **CCC Patterns** What patterns do you observe in the distribution of uranium?

....

....

....

INTERACTIVITY

Learn more about the progression of living matter to petroleum.

Using Energy Resources

Fossil fuels are among the most important nonrenewable resources for humans. As the human population has grown, these resources have become less abundant. Geologists estimate that we have already used about half the petroleum that fossilization, pressure, heat, and time have produced over hundreds of millions of years—and all in just a few centuries.

Pollution Humans are burning fossil fuels at a faster rate than the resulting carbon emissions can be absorbed by natural processes, such as photosynthesis. This is why the concentration of carbon dioxide in the atmosphere is now 45 percent higher than it was just over 200 years ago. Scientists have concluded that this is fueling global warming and climate change.

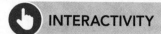

Gulf War Oil Fires

Figure 8 The oil fields that were set on fire during the first Gulf War in 1991 caused significant damage to the land and living things.

World Politics The uneven distribution of fossil fuel resources has led to political problems, including war. In 1990, Iraq invaded neighboring Kuwait in part because of disagreements over how oil fields at a shared border should be used. When the United States and other nations came to Kuwait's defense and drove out the Iraqi forces, oil fields and wells were set on fire. This resulted in hundreds of millions of gallons of oil being burned or spilled, and untreated emissions billowing into the atmosphere (**Figure 8**).

READING CHECK **Determine Conclusions** How have human activities affected the distribution of fossil fuels on Earth?

....

....

....

Plan It!

Household Energy Use

SEP Plan an Investigation Use the space to describe how you could determine how much fossil fuel is used in your home and then make recommendations about how to reduce your usage.

....

....

....

....

....

LESSON 1 Check

MS-ESS3-1, MS-ESS3-4

1. **Identify** Which fossil fuel is produced from the remains of peat?

2. **CCC Cause and Effect** A friend argues that the location of a petroleum deposit is a sign that marine organisms once lived there. Is your friend correct? Explain.

3. **Apply Scientific Reasoning** How does the abundance of a resource, and whether it is renewable or nonrenewable, affect how much it is used?

4. **SEP Engage in Argument** What advantage does coal have over wood as an energy source? What is the major disadvantage of using coal for energy?

5. **SEP Construct Explanations** Why are oil, coal, and natural gas not found evenly distributed on Earth?

Quest CHECK-IN

In this lesson, you learned about different types of nonrenewable energy resources called fossil fuels and the impacts of human activities related to extracting and using these resources.

Evaluate Why is access to energy resources such as fossil fuels important to the economic and social development of a town?

INTERACTIVITY

Surviving on Fossil Fuels

Go online to examine four different towns in the United States and determine the distribution pattern of the resources and the processes that may have resulted in the resource formation.

LESSON 2

Renewable Energy Resources

Guiding Questions

- What are renewable energy resources?
- How do renewable energy resources reduce human reliance on other natural resources?

Connections

Literacy Draw Evidence

Math Represent Quantitative Relationships

MS-ESS3-1, MS-ESS3-3

HANDS-ON LAB

uInvestigate Design, build, and test a model of wind power technology.

Vocabulary

renewable resource

Academic Vocabulary

cost

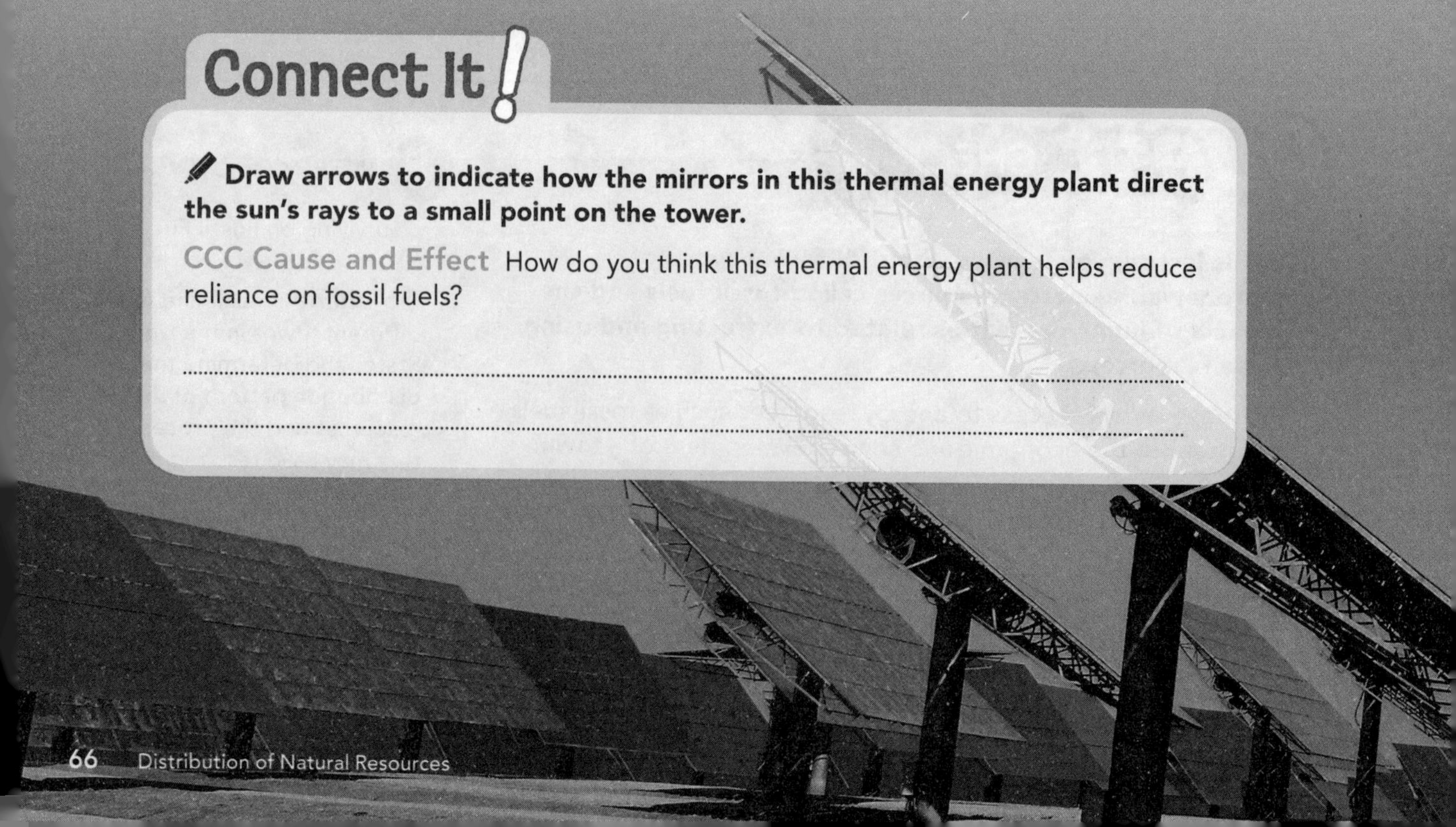

Connect It!

Draw arrows to indicate how the mirrors in this thermal energy plant direct the sun's rays to a small point on the tower.

CCC Cause and Effect How do you think this thermal energy plant helps reduce reliance on fossil fuels?

....

....

Reducing Fossil Fuel Usage

The abundance of energy-rich fossil fuels has made it easy for humankind to justify using petroleum, coal, and natural gas. However, there are both benefits and costs in terms of the short-term and long-term effects. Even though they are nonrenewable and impact Earth's systems, it was easier and less expensive in the past to mine and drill for coal, oil, and gas than to harness other sources of energy. Due to increased awareness of the consequences of mining and burning fossil fuels, as well as advances in technology, things are beginning to change in favor of alternative sources of energy.

Alternative energy resources, such as the solar power tower in **Figure 1**, are considered **renewable resources** because we cannot run out of them. They are replaced by nature, or with a little help from us.

READING CHECK **Determine Meaning** Why are some energy resources referred to as "renewable"?

INTERACTIVITY

Identify renewable resources that are most suitable for use in your community.

Thermal Power

Figure 1 This thermal energy plant uses energy from the sun to heat water and produce electricity using steam.

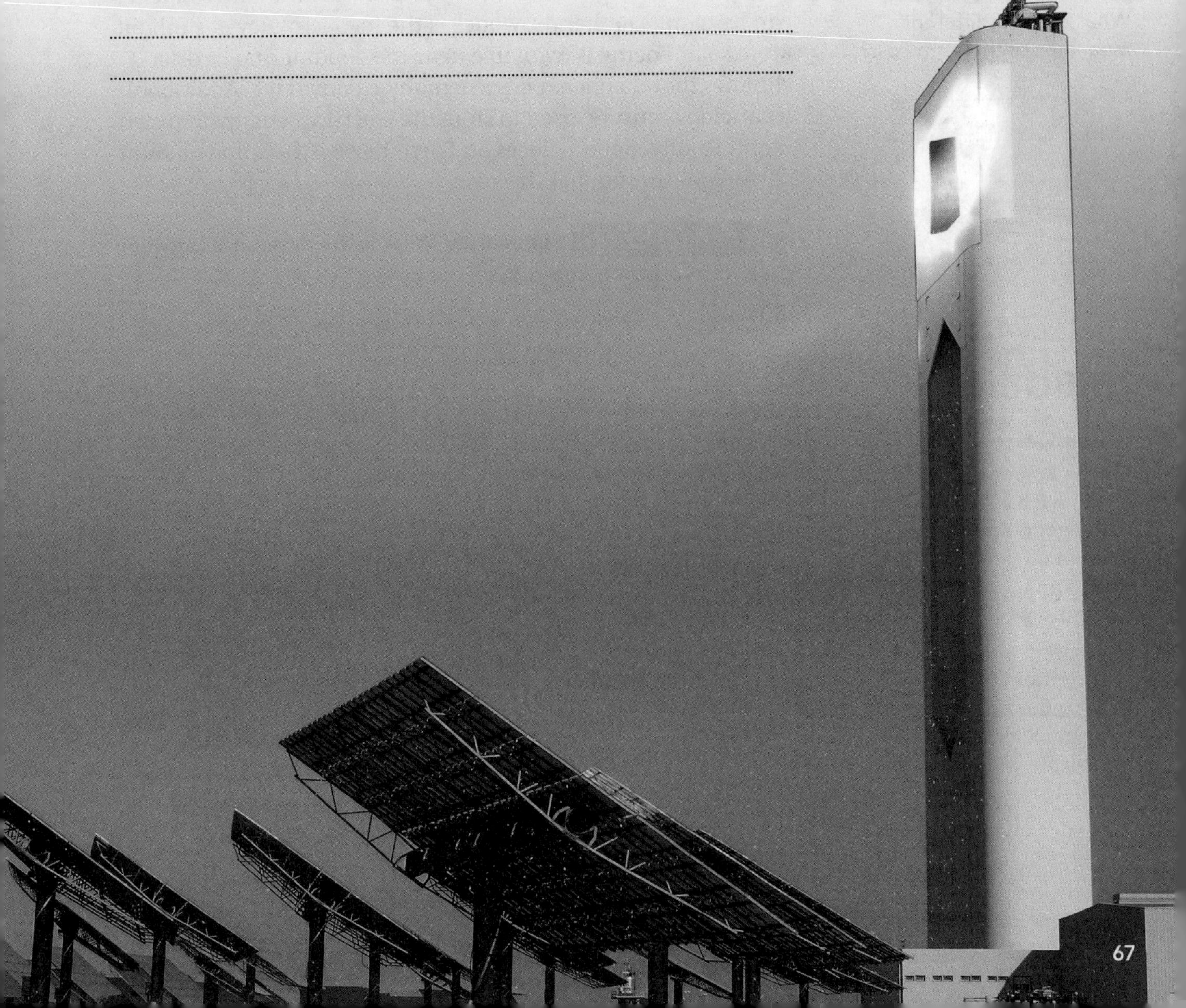

VIDEO

Learn more about the sun's role in providing energy that cycles through different processes on Earth.

Alternative Sources of Energy

Using renewable energy resources can reduce our dependence on nonrenewables and avoid some of the problems associated with them.

Solar Energy One of the most basic types of solar energy is passive solar power. It involves letting sunlight pass through glass to heat a room or building to maximize its exposure to sunlight and retain that heat. A greenhouse is a good example of passive solar power.

In an active solar power system, sunlight is captured by solar cells, which can power things as small as wristwatches or as large as entire cities. As shown in **Figure 2**, a solar (or photovoltaic) cell converts the energy from sunlight directly into electrical energy. Solar cells are not a new technology, but they are now much more efficient and less expensive than they were years ago.

Though the sunlight is free, the **costs** of the initial investment can be high. Another drawback is the inconsistency of sunlight. More solar energy is available near the equator and in drier climates that do not experience many cloudy days. Additional technology must be used to store the electrical energy for use at night. Finally, not all places on Earth receive the same amount of sunlight throughout the year.

Academic Vocabulary

What are two different meanings of the term *cost*?

....

....

....

....

....

READING CHECK **Summarize** What is the difference between passive solar power and active solar power?

....

....

Model It!

Solar Cells

Figure 2 When sunlight hits it, each solar cell in a panel generates a small amount of electricity.

SEP Develop Models Trace the path of a negative particle from the top layer to the bottom layer to indicate how electrical energy is generated.

1. Sunlight hits the solar cell, which is made up of two layers separated by a barrier.
2. Energy from the sun excites the material in each layer. One layer ends up with negative particles and the other layer with positive particles.
2. The negative particles are attracted to the positive particles, but the barrier keeps the particles apart. Instead, the negative particles are guided along a path of wiring to the other layer. This creates electrical energy that can be used to power equipment.

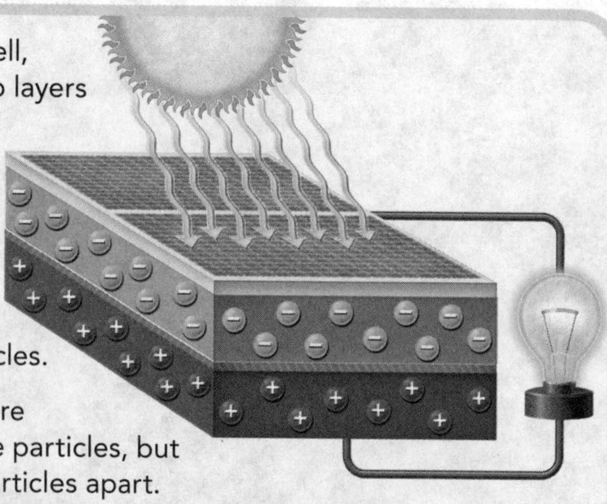

Hydroelectric Resources The sun's energy drives the water cycle, which moves large volumes of water to higher elevations from lower elevations in the form of rain and snow. Gravity pulls water downhill, giving rivers, streams, waterfalls, and tides their movement. Turbines can convert the energy of moving water into electricity.

Hydroelectric dams restrict the natural flow of a river by controlling how much water passes through turbines, as shown in **Figure 3**. Hydroelectric dams can generate a great deal of power, but they disrupt natural processes such as migrations of fish. Dams also alter habitats by creating reservoirs above the dam and reducing the width and flow of the river below. Most importantly, a dam must be close to a source of moving water.

INTERACTIVITY

Learn about renewable resources, their global distributions, and the processes necessary for them to be viable.

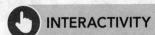

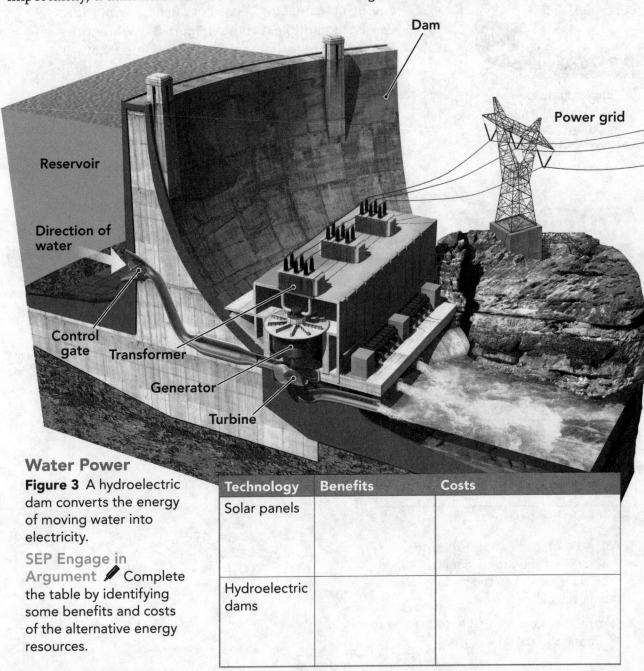

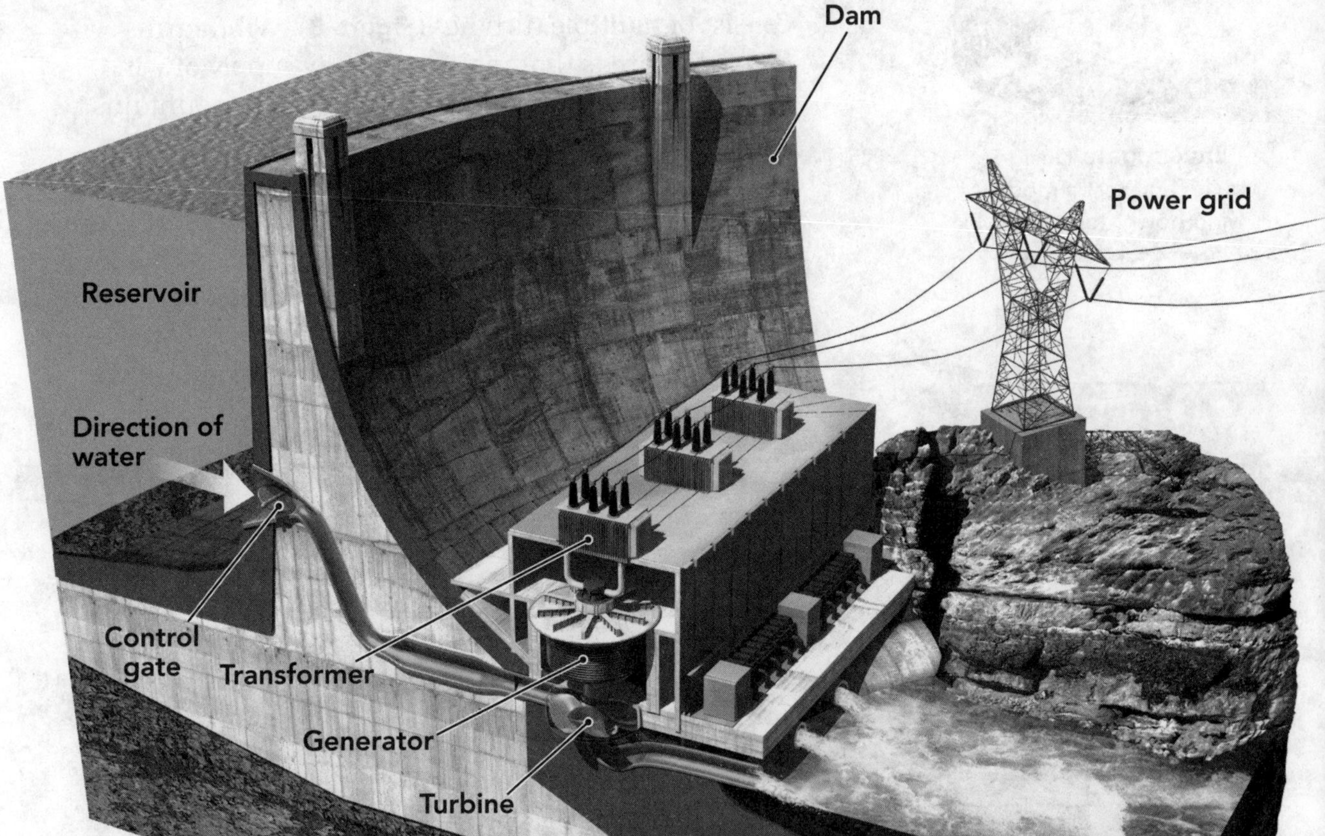

Water Power

Figure 3 A hydroelectric dam converts the energy of moving water into electricity.

SEP Engage in Argument Complete the table by identifying some benefits and costs of the alternative energy resources.

Technology	Benefits	Costs
Solar panels		
Hydroelectric dams		

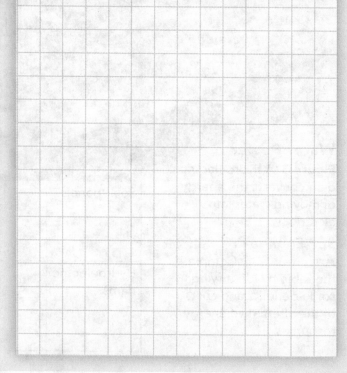

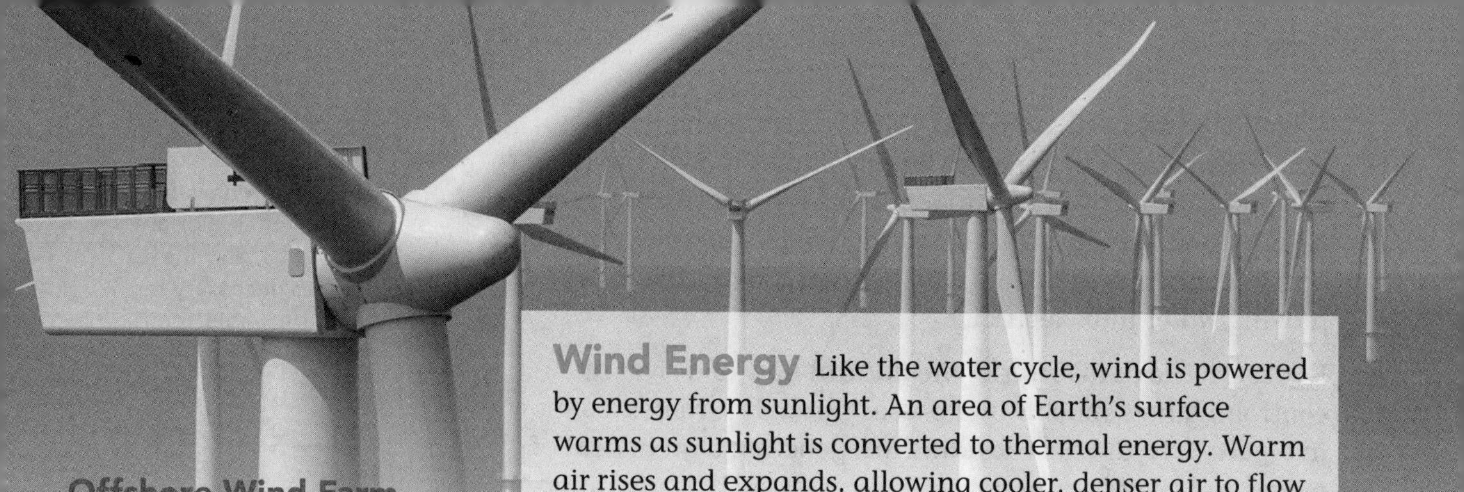

Offshore Wind Farm

Figure 3 Wind is plentiful on the water, but turbines introduce obstacles to both boats and wildlife.

Wind Energy Like the water cycle, wind is powered by energy from sunlight. An area of Earth's surface warms as sunlight is converted to thermal energy. Warm air rises and expands, allowing cooler, denser air to flow in to fill the void. We know this movement of air masses as wind. Just as turbines can be used to harness the energy in moving water, they can be used to harness the energy of wind. Land-based or offshore wind "farms" consist of multiple turbines (**Figure 3**). Wind farms do best in areas that receive a steady supply of wind. Some farms are found in valleys between mountains that channel and concentrate the wind. Others are found in the ocean, where land and sea breezes provide strong winds. The costs of constructing wind farms are considerable, and some people are concerned that large turbines threaten birds and spoil natural scenery. But wind power is already less expensive than coal power in many parts of the country, and it is the fastest-growing energy source in the world.

HANDS-ON LAB

Investigate Design, build, and test a model of wind power technology.

Math Toolbox

Wind Power

The table shows the projected production of industrial wind farms in the U.S. over the coming decades.

Year	Production (gigawatts)
2000	2.5
2010	40.2
2020	113.4
2030	224.1
2040	
2050	404.3

Source: U.S Department of Energy

1. **Analyze Quantitative Relationships** Predict what the production in 2040 should be, based on the pattern. Fill in the empty cell of the table.
2. **Represent Quantitative Relationships** Graph the data.

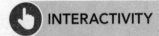

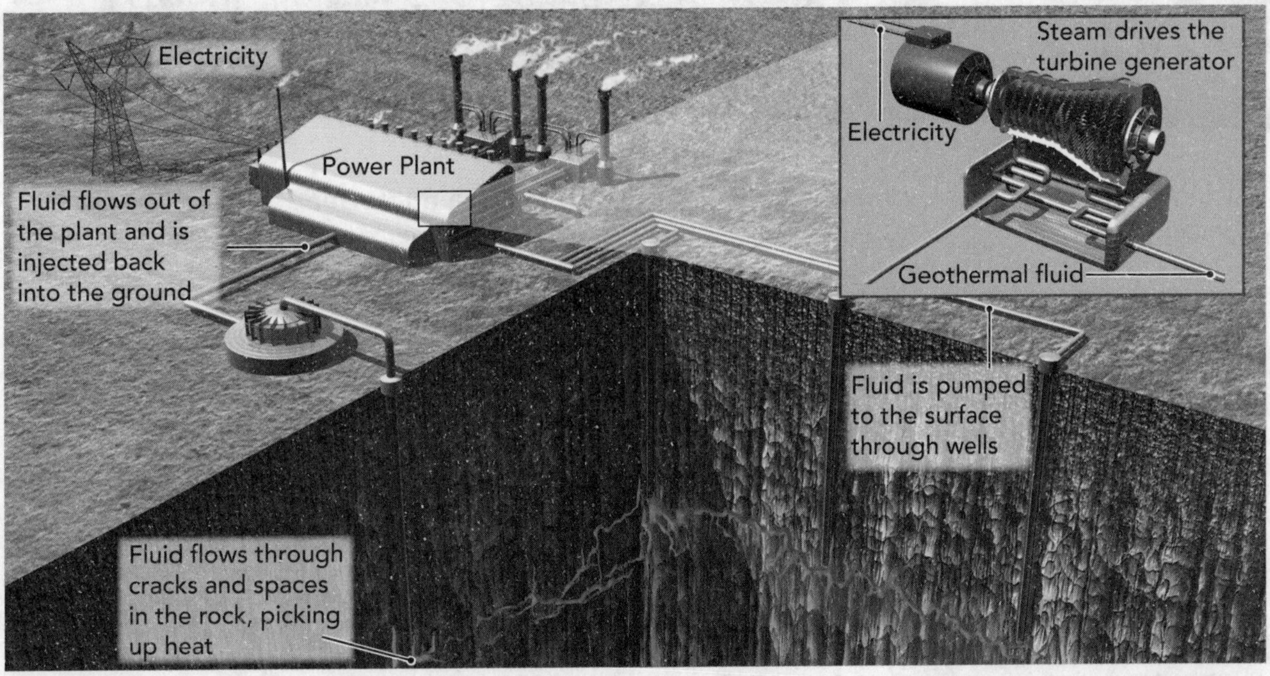
Electricity
Power Plant
Fluid flows out of the plant and is injected back into the ground
Steam drives the turbine generator
Electricity
Geothermal fluid
Fluid is pumped to the surface through wells
Fluid flows through cracks and spaces in the rock, picking up heat

Geothermal Energy One renewable energy source not originating with the sun is geothermal energy. Deep below Earth's surface, the rock of Earth's crust is hot. In some places on Earth's surface, this heat can be used on a small scale to warm homes. On a larger scale, geothermal energy plants (**Figure 4**) use this heat to generate electricity. One of the biggest drawbacks is that geothermal reservoirs are not easy to find. The site must be located over a geothermal hot spot, where the rock is hot enough to continuously reheat pumped water. The best sites are near volcanic areas. While initial costs to construct the plant and drill the pipes are expensive, the power it can provide in the long run makes up for it.

Bioenergy Resources Biomass such as wood, grasses, coconut husks, and other plant-based materials have been burned to produce light and heat for thousands of years. These resources are only limited by where they can grow. Scientists have developed ways to turn these resources into biofuels such as ethanol, which is usually made from corn or sugar cane, and biodiesel, which can be made from used cooking oil. Unfortunately, the energy that goes into producing these biofuels is often equal to or greater than the energy they yield. Also, burning biofuels is not much better for the atmosphere than burning fossil fuels.

READING CHECK **Summarize** In the long run, why might it be less expensive to construct 100 geothermal power plants than to farm the same area for corn to make ethanol?

....

....

....

Geothermal Power Plant

Figure 4 Draw arrows to indicate the flow of water through the geothermal power plant. Use the information in the text to help you.

INTERACTIVITY

Set up a dairy farm and investigate how much electricity you can generate from biogas.

Literacy Connection

Draw Evidence Underline the text that supports the idea that geothermal energy is a cost-effective solution in the long run.

LESSON 2 Check

MS-ESS3-1

1. **Identify** Name five renewable energy resources.

2. **CCC Cause and Effect** Is wind power a practical source of renewable energy everywhere on Earth? Explain.

3. **SEP Engage in Argument** Do you think the benefits of using water resources to generate electricity outweight the costs and drawbacks? Explan.

4. **SEP Obtain Information** Suppose your local government wants to encourage the use of renewable energy resources by investing in a power plant fueled by a renewable energy source. Describe how you would investigate which renewable source would be most suitable for your area.

Quest CHECK-IN

In this lesson, you learned about different renewable energy resources, or renewables, and the costs and benefits of using them.

SEP Engage in Argument What impact might the availability of renewable energy resources, such as water or wind, have on the success of a town?

INTERACTIVITY

Renewable Energy

Go online to apply what you have learned about renewable energy to supplying energy to a boomtown.

uEngineer It! Sustainable Design STEM

MS-ESS3-3

Micro-Hydro POWER

VIDEO

Examine how hydroelectric power plants and wind farms generate clean energy.

How can people without access to electricity use moving water to generate power? You engineer it!

The Challenge: To generate power from moving water.

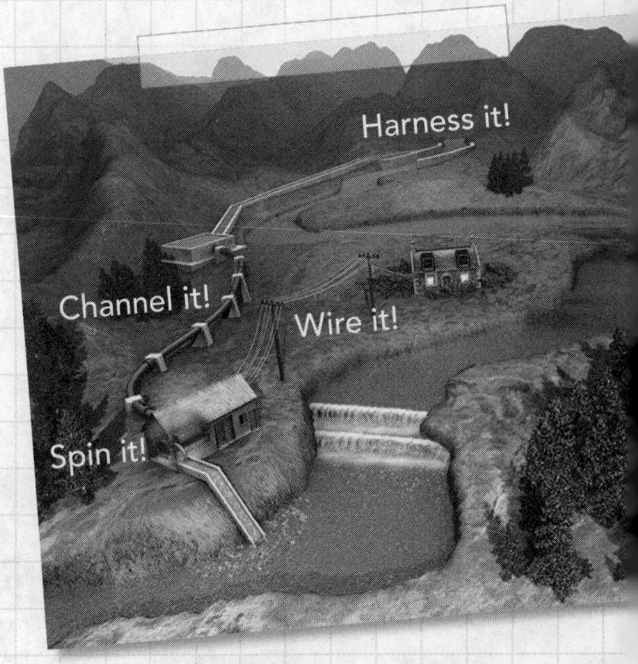

Harness it!
Channel it!
Wire it!
Spin it!

In this micro-hydro system, water from the river is channeled to the generator, which transforms the energy of the moving water into electrical energy.

Earth's water system is an excellent source of power. Centuries ago, people realized that moving water, properly channeled, can turn wheels that make machinery move. More recently, engineers designed large-scale dams to harness the energy of moving water. Water power's great advantage is that the water is always moving, so electricity can be generated 24 hours a day.

Now engineers have developed hydropower on a small scale, known as micro-hydro power. If there is a small river or stream running through your property, then you need only a few basic things: a turbine, pipes to channel the water to the turbine, and a generator that will transform the energy into electricity.

DESIGN CHALLENGE

Can you design a micro-hydro system? Go to the Engineering Design Notebook to find out!

LESSON 3

Mineral Resources

Guiding Questions

- What are mineral resources?
- What factors affect the distribution of minerals on Earth?

Connection

Literacy Determine Meaning

MS-ESS3-1, MS-ESS3-4

HANDS-ON LAB

uInvestigate Explore the geological processes that form minerals.

Vocabulary

ore

crystallize

Academic Vocabulary

distribution

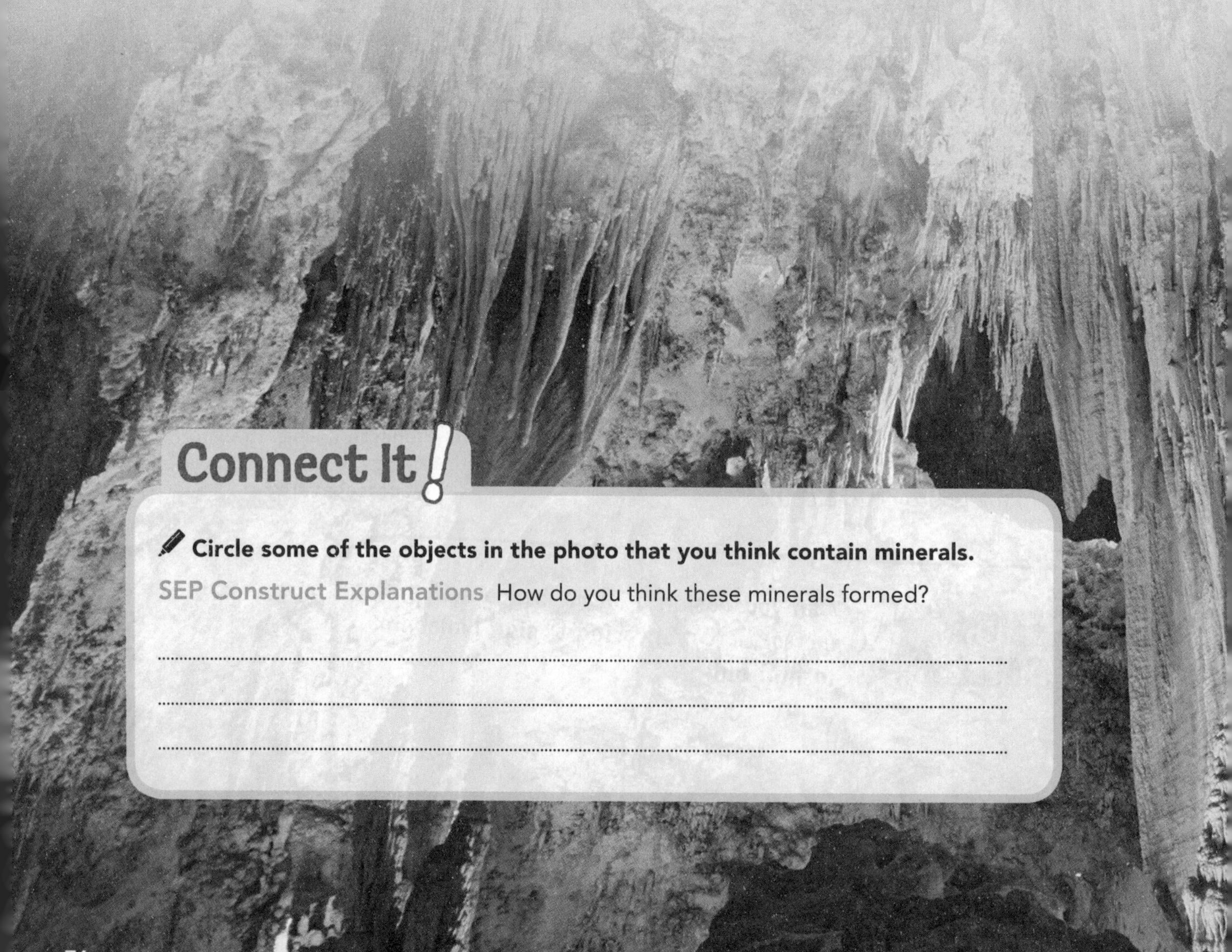

Connect It!

Circle some of the objects in the photo that you think contain minerals.

SEP Construct Explanations How do you think these minerals formed?

....

....

....

Minerals and Ores

You may think that minerals are only found in rocks. It's true that rocks are made from minerals, but if you look around, you will probably see several other things that are made from minerals. Metals are made from one or more minerals. The graphite in a pencil is a type of mineral. Computers, smartphones, and other electronic devices are made with metals and other minerals, too. Even you contain minerals, such as the calcium-bearing minerals that make up your bones and teeth.

But what is a mineral? A mineral is a solid substance that is non-living and made from a particular combination of elements. There are over 5,000 named minerals on Earth. Gold, quartz, and talc are just a few examples. When a mineral deposit is large enough and valuable enough for it to be extracted from the ground, it is known as **ore**. People remove ore from the ground so they can use it or sell it to make money.

HANDS-ON LAB

Investigate Explore the geological processes that form minerals.

Reflect Throughout the day, list some of the things you see and use that are made from minerals. Then, at the end of the day, write a paragraph explaining why minerals are important and describing some of their most important uses.

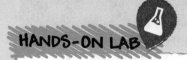

Stalactite Formation

Figure 1 These stalactites in Carlsbad Caverns National Park in New Mexico formed as minerals deposited by a dripping mineral-rich solution built up over long periods of time.

Literacy Connection

Determine Meaning
As you read, circle or underline an unknown word in the text and use context clues to help you determine the meaning. Revisit the unknown word at the end of the lesson and use a resource if you still cannot determine the meaning.

How Minerals Form Minerals form in different ways. They can form from organic materials, from mineral-rich solutions, and from cooling magma and lava.

Organic Material Corals like the ones in **Figure 2** create a hard outer skeleton that provides the coral with shape and protection. This skeleton is made from thin layers of calcium carbonate (also called calcite), a chemical compound similar to the shells of other sea animals. Once the coral is dead, the calcium carbonate skeleton is left behind. It may get buried and broken down into smaller fragments.

Minerals from Living Things

Figure 2 These corals produce a hard outer skeleton made from the mineral calcite. The skeleton will be around for a long time after the coral dies.

Apply Concepts Why wouldn't other body parts of living things, such as skin, become minerals after an organism's death?

....

....

Solutions When water contains dissolved substances it is called a solution. In some cases, the elements in these solutions will **crystallize** to form a new mineral. This can happen within bodies of water and underground. One way this happens on Earth's surface involves the process of evaporation. When the water evaporates, the elements and compounds that are left behind crystallize into new minerals such as salts. This is how the mineral formations in **Figure 3** formed.

Another way that minerals form from solutions is through a process in which a warm solution flows through a crack in existing rock. Elements and compounds leave the solution as it cools and crystallize as minerals in the crack. These form veins of ores that are different from the surrounding rock.

Magma and Lava The molten and semi-molten rock mixture found beneath Earth's surface is known as magma. In its molten, or melted state, magma is very hot. But when it cools, it hardens into solid rock. This rock is made from crystallized minerals. It may form beneath Earth's surface or above Earth's surface when magma (which is known as lava when it breaks the surface) erupts from the ground and then cools and hardens as is shown in **Figure 4.**

The types of minerals that form from magma and lava vary based on the materials and gases in the magma, as well as the rate at which it cools.

READING CHECK Analyze Text Structure Examine the way the text on these two pages has been organized. Describe how the author has organized the text so that it supports the reader's comprehension.

....

....

....

....

....

....

Minerals from Solutions

Figure 3 These mineral deposits in Mammoth Hot Springs in Yellowstone National Park formed from a solution.

SEP Analyze Data Draw an X on the solution the minerals formed from. Circle some of the mineral deposits.

Minerals from Magma

Figure 4 As this lava cools, it will harden and crystallize into minerals.

CCC Cause and Effect Where would you expect to find minerals that have formed in this way?

....

....

....

INTERACTIVITY

Find out more about mineral resources and their distributions.

VIDEO

Learn why some minerals are only found in certain places.

Academic Vocabulary

Explain what *distributed* means and give one or two examples of something that is distributed.

Distribution of Minerals

The distribution of mineral resources on Earth depends on how and when the minerals form. Common minerals, such as the ones that make up most of the rocks in Earth's crust, are found roughly evenly distributed around the planet. Other minerals are rare because they only form as a result of tremendous heat and pressure near volcanic systems. Therefore, these minerals will only be found near subduction zones or other regions associated with volcanic activity. Other minerals may form from evaporation in the ocean or on land, such as in basins called playas. The map in **Figure 5** shows how some minerals are **distributed** around the world.

Gold, for example, is a heavy metal that formed, along with all other atoms other than hydrogen and helium, from stars that went supernova preceding the formation of our solar system. Gold is rare at the surface because most of it sank into the core when the early Earth was molten. Gold gets concentrated when hot fluids pass through the crust and pick up the gold, which doesn't fit well in the crystals of most rocks.

READING CHECK **Determine Meaning** Locate the term concentrated in the second paragraph. Using context clues, what do you think this word means? Explain your thinking.

Question It!

Minerals for Dinner?

Minerals are used in many ways in our everyday lives. We even need minerals in our diets to stay healthy. Humans need minerals that contain calcium, potassium, and magnesium to grow, fight illness, and carry out everyday functions.

Apply Scientific Reasoning Write two or three questions you would like to have answered about the importance of minerals in your diet.

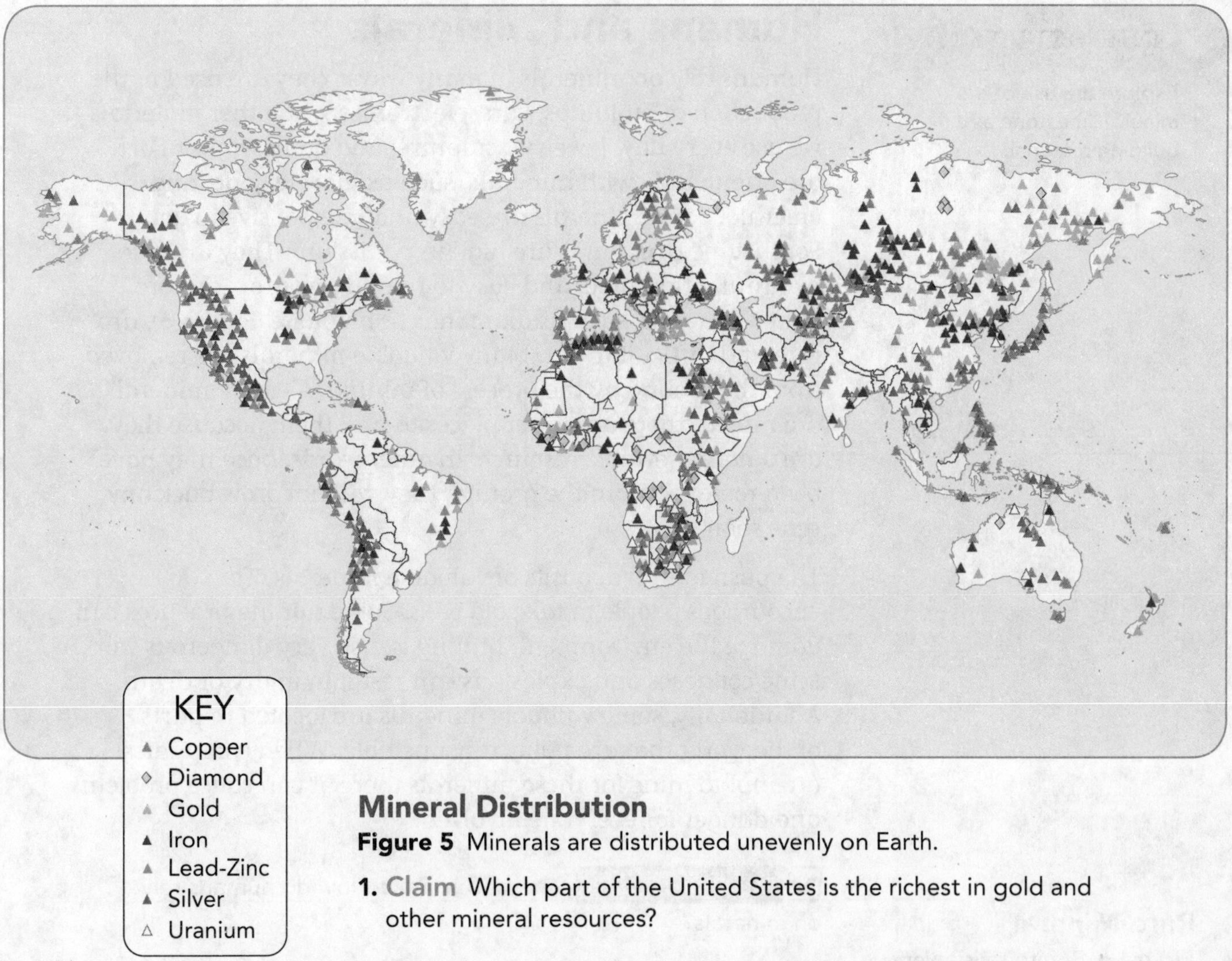

Mineral Distribution

Figure 5 Minerals are distributed unevenly on Earth.

1. Claim Which part of the United States is the richest in gold and other mineral resources?

....

....

2. Evidence Circle the area on the map that provides evidence to support your claim.

3. Reasoning Suppose you were to draw the boundaries of tectonic plates and locations of volcanic activity on the map. What patterns would you notice among plate boundaries, volcanic activity, and the distribution of different mineral resources? Explain.

....

....

....

....

....

....

....

....

INTERACTIVITY

Explore the use of the mineral limestone as a building material.

Humans and Minerals

Humans rely on minerals in many ways. They are used in the production of buildings, cars, electronics, and other materials we use every day. Jewelry, sculpture, and other works of art are often made with minerals, such as marble, jade, and emerald. Some minerals are easy and inexpensive to get. For instance, bananas are high in potassium. They are also plentiful, affordable, and easy to find in any grocery store. Other minerals, such as diamonds or benitoite (**Figure 6**), are rare and difficult to get. Many valuable minerals are removed from the ground by the process of mining. As more minerals are mined, there are fewer places to find them because they are a nonrenewable resource. In other words, once they have been removed from the ground, they will not grow back any time soon.

The push to find deposits of valuable minerals often encourages people to take big risks. Some mining practices can damage the environment. Mining is also very dangerous work. Mine collapses and explosions can result in injury or death. Additionally, some valuable minerals are located in parts of the world that are politically unstable. When companies attempt to mine for these minerals there, it can cause problems and danger for everyone involved.

READING CHECK **Summarize Text** How do humans rely on minerals?

....

....

....

Rare Mineral

Figure 6 Benitoite is a very rare blue mineral that forms as a result of hydrothermal processes in Earth's crust. It has been discovered in a few locations on Earth. But gemstone-quality benitoite can be found in only one place in California.

Connect to Society Do you think a benitoite ring would be costly or inexpensive? Explain your reasoning.

....

....

....

....

....

....

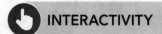

LESSON 3 Check

MS-ESS3-1

1. **Define** What are minerals? List examples.

2. **SEP Construct Explanations** Explain the relationship between minerals and ores.

3. **CCC Cause and Effect** What causes minerals to be unevenly distributed on Earth?

4. **CCC Patterns** Use drawings to show one of the ways that minerals can form.

Quest CHECK-IN

In this lesson, you learned why minerals are important resources and about how they form. You also learned that the different ways that minerals form leads to uneven distribution of different types of minerals around the world.

SEP Evaluate Information Why should you consider mineral resources when trying to determine whether a town will boom or become a ghost town?

INTERACTIVITY

Surviving on Minerals

Go online to find out more about how some mineral resources in the United States are distributed. Then, apply this information to your analysis of the town you are researching.

Case Study

MS-ESS3-1, MSS-ESS3-4

Phosphorus Fiasco

Without phosphorus, living things would not exist on Earth. All animals and plants need phosphorus to produce the energy that keeps them alive. Unfortunately, like all minerals, phosphorus is not a renewable resource. Only a certain amount exists in nature, where it moves in a natural cycle. In recent years, however, that cycle has been broken, and we run the risk of using up Earth's supply of phosphorus.

In the phosphorus cycle, animals and people eat phosphorus-rich plants. The excess phosphorus leaves the bodies of organisms as waste. The waste returns to the soil to enrich the plants, starting the cycle again.

For many centuries, farmers used manure, which is rich in phosphorus, to fertilize their crops. About 175 years ago, as the population grew, farmers looked for new sources of fertilizer to keep up with the demand for food. Engineers and geologists realized that phosphorus might be mined from underground and used to manufacture fertilizers. Most of the world's phosphorus reserves are in the United States, China, Russia, and northern Africa.

Phosphorus mining has altered the natural phosphorus cycle.

The "phosphorus fiasco" is a result of improved technology that has interrupted the natural phosphorus cycle. Because most human waste now ends up in sewer and water treatment systems, phosphorus ends up in the ocean. More manufactured fertilizer is used to fertilize plants and crops. We still get our required phosphorus, but we are using up the natural supply in the process.

World Phosphate Mine Production and Reserves			
Country	**Mine Production (tons)**		**Reserves**
	2015	**2016**	
China	120,000	138,000	3,100,000
Jordan	8,340	8,300	1,200,000
Morocco/Western Sahara	29,000	30,000	50,000,000
Russia	11,600	11,600	1,300,000
United States	27,400	27,800	1,100,000

Source: U.S. Geological Survey, 2017

Use the text and the data table to answer the following questions.

1. **CCC Scale, Proportion, and Quantity** Which country saw the greatest increase in phosphorus production between 2015 and 2016? Describe the amount of the increase as a fraction or percentage.

2. **CCC Cause and Effect** How have technological developments affected the natural phosphorus cycle? What do you think can be done to address this problem?

3. **SEP Analyze Data** Based on its current rate of production, in how many years will the United States use up its known reserves of phosphate?

4. **SEP Construct Explanations** Morocco/Western Sahara has by far the greatest reserves of phosphorus, but it is not the largest producer. Why do you think this is the case? Do you think the situation might change? Explain.

LESSON

4 Water Resources

Guiding Questions

- How do geological processes affect the distribution of groundwater on Earth?
- How is water used as a resource?

Connections

Literacy Support Author's Claim

Math Draw Comparative Inferences

MS-ESS3-1, MS-ESS3-4

HANDS-ON LAB

uInvestigate Model how an artesian well accesses groundwater.

Vocabulary

desalination

Academic Vocabulary

component
obtain

Connect It!

The drop of water on Earth represents all the water on the planet. Draw a circle inside the drop of water to represent the amount of freshwater you think exists on Earth.

CCC Systems and System Models How does water's role in Earth systems make it an important natural resource?

....

....

....

Water on Earth

Although Earth is known as the water planet, the water that living things rely on represents only a fraction of the planet's total water supply **(Figure 1)**. Most water on Earth is salt water. Freshwater is only found on the surface of our planet as surface ice or water, or within Earth's crust as groundwater.

Water is a limited resource, which means there is a finite amount of it on Earth. In addition, it is not evenly distributed around the planet as a result of meteorological and geological forces. The water cycle circulates water through Earth's ocean and other bodies of water, on and below its surface, and in the atmosphere. A tiny amount of the freshwater on Earth is in the atmosphere, and a fair amount of water is contained underground as groundwater. But most freshwater is locked up as ice at the poles and in glaciers. A very small amount of the water on the surface of the planet is immediately available for human use in lakes and rivers.

INTERACTIVITY

Predict how much water on Earth is drinkable.

Reflect How is water used in your local environment? In your science notebook, describe some ways your local environment would be affected if there were suddenly less water available.

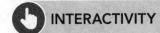

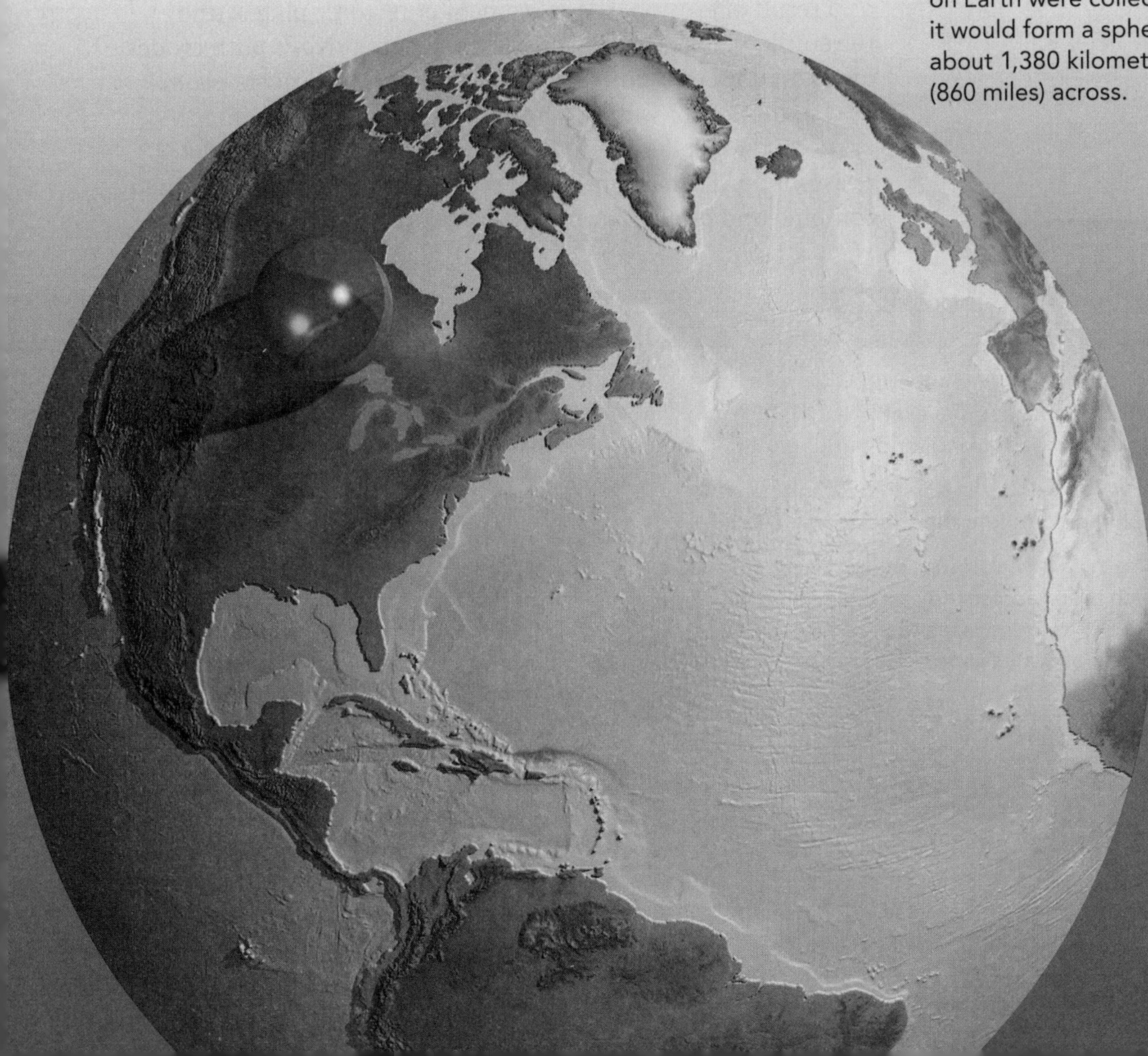

A Drop to Drink

Figure 1 If all of the water on Earth were collected, it would form a sphere about 1,380 kilometers (860 miles) across.

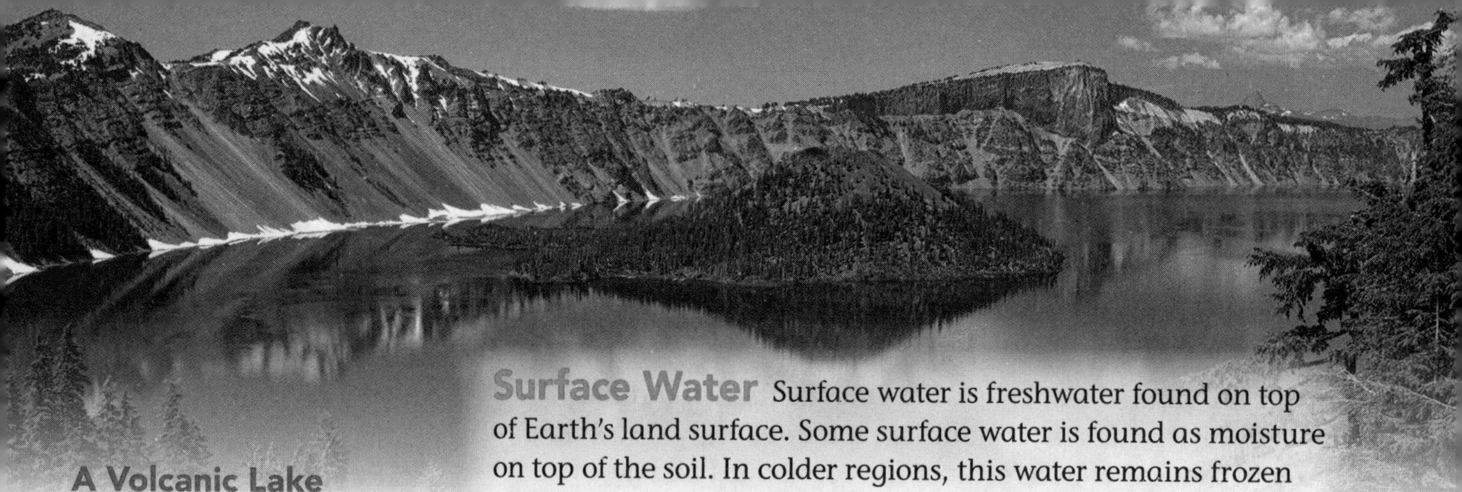

A Volcanic Lake

Figure 2 Crater Lake in Oregon sits in a bowl-shaped depression formed when a volcano erupted and collapsed into itself.

SEP Construct Explanations How do you think the water ended up in the lake?

....

....

....

....

Surface Water Surface water is freshwater found on top of Earth's land surface. Some surface water is found as moisture on top of the soil. In colder regions, this water remains frozen as permafrost. Most surface water is found in lakes, rivers, and streams, as well as swamps and marshes. Surface water, however, is not evenly distributed across Earth. Precipitation, which depends on factors such as atmospheric patterns and temperature, determines where surface water forms. Because humans require accessible water, most people live around or near sources of surface water, such as lakes and rivers.

Most of the surface water on Earth is found in lakes. Lakes form through various geological processes when water fills in depressions in Earth's surface, as in **Figure 2.** These can occur as a result of erosion, the movement of tectonic plates, and retreating glaciers. Some lakes form when a river's path erodes away an area or a dam blocks a river's flow. All rivers begin as a small flow of water caused by gravity. Runoff from rain or melting ice collects and flows downhill following the least resistant path. These small flows of water form streams, which combine and grow to form larger rivers and river systems.

Math Toolbox

Distribution of Water Resources

While most of the planet is covered in water, only a small amount of it is available to humans for cooking, drinking, and bathing.

1. **SEP Develop Models** Use the data in the graphs to complete the missing values.
2. **Draw Comparative Inferences** About how much more accessible surface freshwater is found in lakes than in the atmosphere as water vapor?

....

....

....

....

....

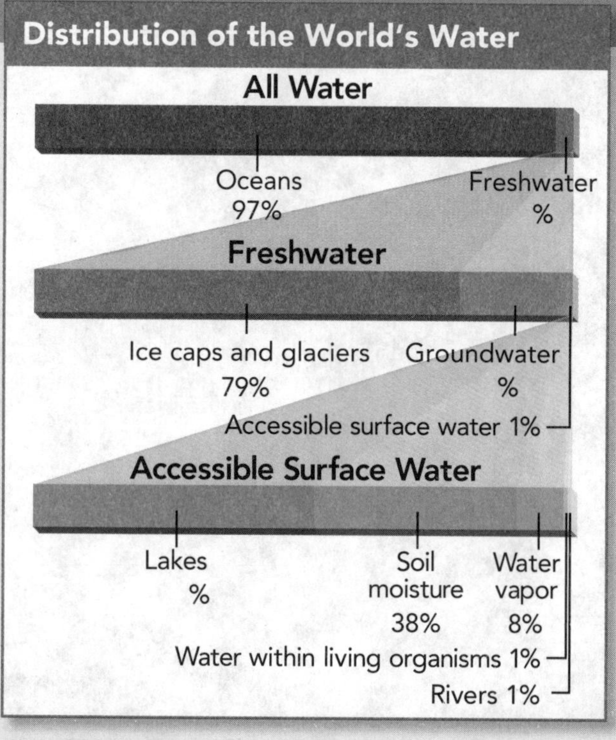

Groundwater As with surface water, groundwater is not evenly distributed across Earth **(Figure 3).** The presence of groundwater depends on the type of rock layers in Earth's crust. Groundwater forms when gravity causes water from precipitation and runoff to seep into the ground and fill the empty spaces between these rocks. Some rocks are more porous, or have more empty spaces in which water can collect. The volume of porous rock that can contain groundwater is called an aquifer. Wells are drilled into aquifers to access the water.

Deep groundwater reservoirs can take hundreds or thousands of years to accumulate, especially in arid regions where there is little rainfall or surface water to supply the aquifer. New studies of Earth's mantle reveal there may be many oceans' worth of water locked hundreds of kilometers below the surface in mineral formations. This groundwater may take millions of years to exchange with surface water through the movement of tectonic plates and mantle convection.

READING CHECK **Summarize** How does the type of rock in Earth's crust affect the distribution of groundwater?

....

....

....

INTERACTIVITY

Explore how groundwater is distributed around Earth.

HANDS-ON LAB

Investigate Model how an artesian well accesses groundwater.

Distribution of Groundwater

Figure 3 Groundwater is especially important in areas that do not have immediate access to rivers or lakes for sources of freshwater.

SEP Use Models Indicate the areas on the map with the greatest groundwater resources with a circle. Indicate the areas with the least groundwater resources with an X.

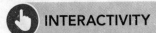

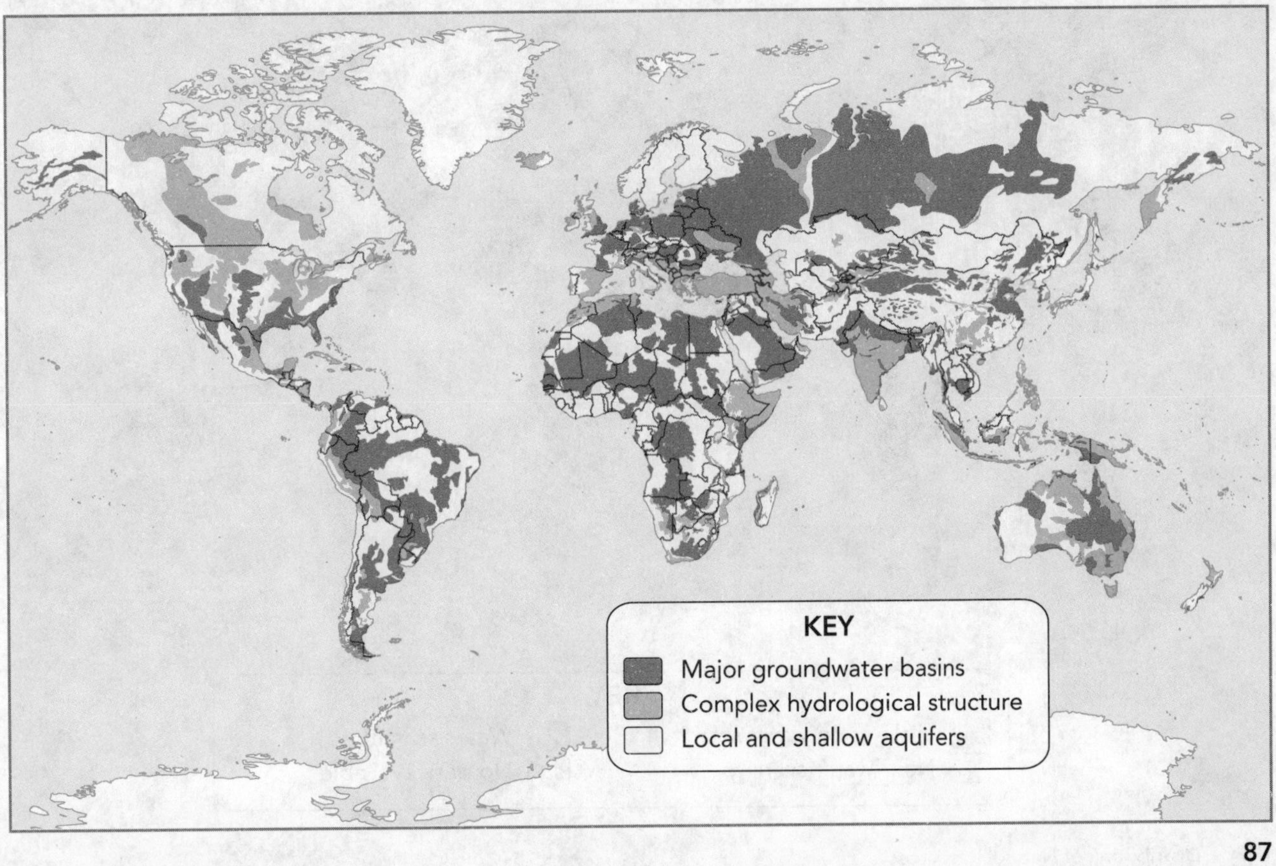

Literacy Connection

Support Author's Claim Underline the text that support the claim that human activity can cause water shortages.

Human Impacts

Humans rely on water not only to live and grow, but also for agriculture and industry. Water is needed to produce our food, manufacture products, and carry out many chemical reactions. The distribution of water resources is a result of past and current geologic processes such as the water cycle, plate tectonics, and the formation of rock. These processes take time, and in some areas humans are depleting water resources faster than they can be replenished. The human impact on water distribution is already a cause of social and economic conflict in some areas.

Using Water Humans use surface water, which often involves changing its natural path, such as with dams. This affects the amount of water that continues to flow and the ecology of the area. Humans access groundwater resources by digging wells in aquifers. But if more water is removed from an aquifer or other groundwater source than is replenished through the water cycle, water shortages can occur. As with surface water, pollution can enter groundwater supplies and impact the quality of the water. Study the effects of water scarcity in **Figure 4.**

Water Scarcity

Figure 4 Many people and regions will be affected by water scarcity in the future.

CCC Cause and Effect How might water scarcity affect economic development in an area?

....

....

....

....

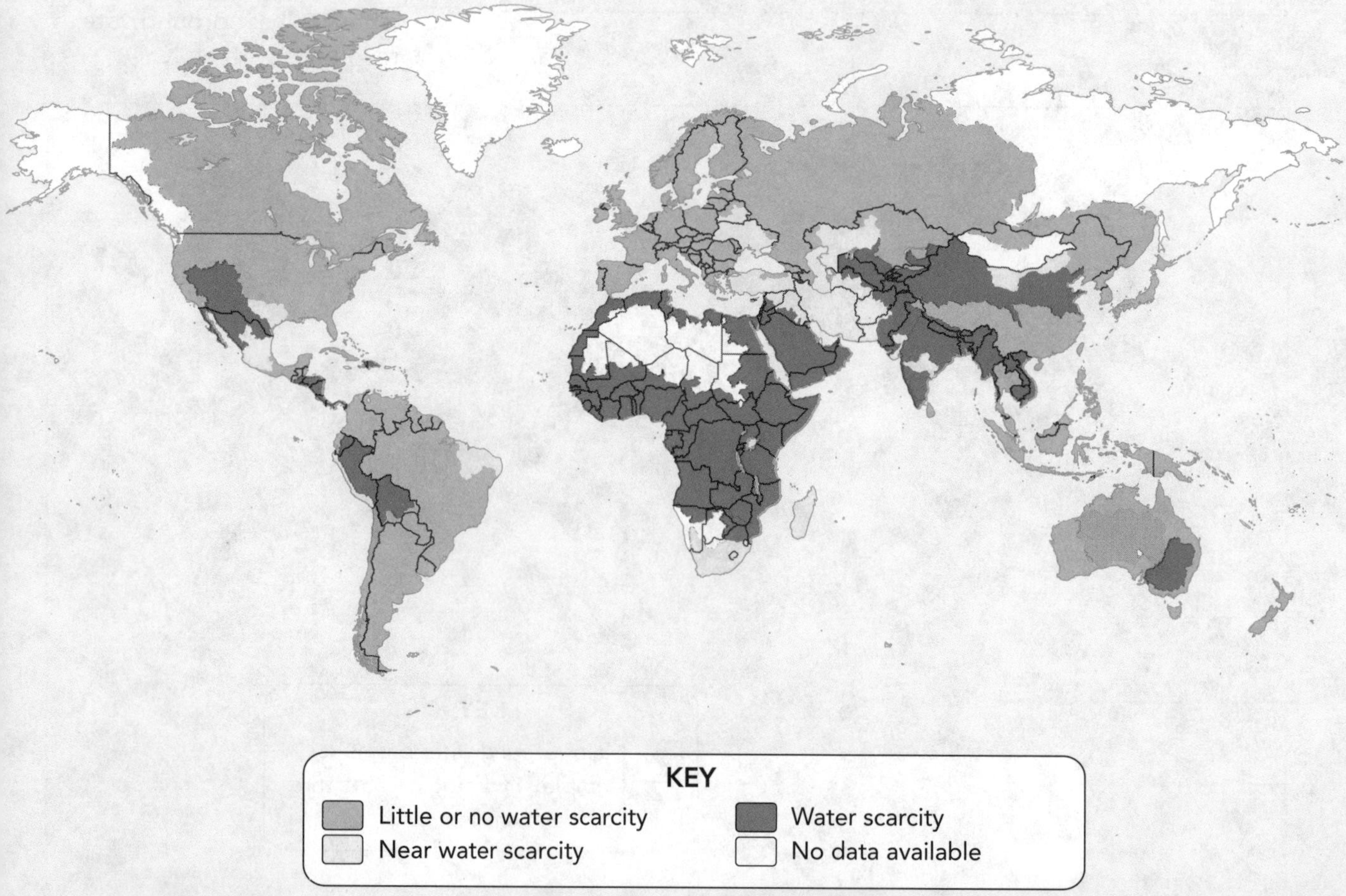

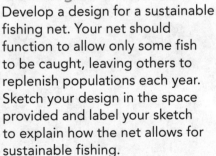

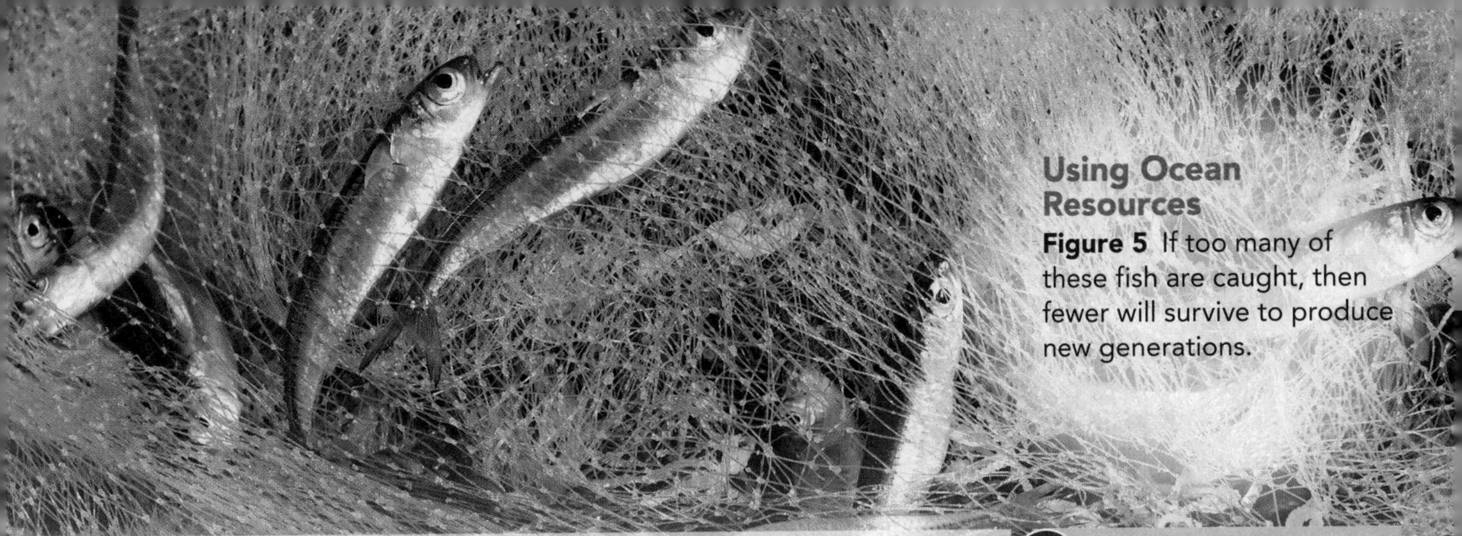

Using Ocean Resources

Figure 5 If too many of these fish are caught, then fewer will survive to produce new generations.

INTERACTIVITY

Examine the factors that affect water availability on Earth.

Desalination In the future, humans may look to technology and the ocean to meet their water needs. The process of **desalination** removes salt and minerals from saltwater to make freshwater. Today, desalination plants around the world are costly and require a lot of energy to distill saltwater. We may eventually use solar energy to convert ocean water into freshwater.

READING CHECK

Identify What are some other ocean resources humans use besides water?

Other Water Resources Humans rely on the ocean to provide a number of other important resources besides water, such as sea organisms for food and other products **(Figure 5)**. The ocean also provides salt, minerals, and fuels.

Living resources like fish are replenished through a natural cycle. However, overfishing can result in severe reductions or complete collapses of ocean ecosystems and the resources they provide. In addition, pollution and global climate change can have serious impacts on the living resources we rely on from the ocean.

Design It!

Sustainable Fishing

Fish populations are replenished only if sufficient numbers are allowed to live and reproduce in their ecosystems.

SEP Design Solutions Develop a design for a sustainable fishing net. Your net should function to allow only some fish to be caught, leaving others to replenish populations each year. Sketch your design in the space provided and label your sketch to explain how the net allows for sustainable fishing.

LESSON 4 Check

MS-ESS3-1, MS-ESS3-4

1. **Identify** What are the different sources of freshwater on Earth?

2. **SEP Construct Explanations** What factors account for the uneven distribution of groundwater on Earth?

3. **Infer** Are humans more likely to use surface water or groundwater as a freshwater source? Explain your answer.

4. **CCC Cause and Effect** Explain why some regions are more extremely affected by water scarcity than others.

5. **Connect to Society** In what way does water scarcity harm the economic development of an area?

Quest CHECK-IN

In this lesson, you learned how water is distributed on Earth and what effects geologic processes have on water resources. You also discovered how human activities are affected by water availability and limit its distribution.

SEP Define Problems Why is it important to consider how water is distributed when considering the availability of resources in a new town?

INTERACTIVITY

Surviving on Water

Go online to use what you have learned about water resources and relate it to the available resources for a ghost town.

The Pseudoscience of Water Dowsing

It's the early 1800s and you're moving westward across America. When you arrive at your land, you see that there's no nearby river or lake. As you look out, you wonder how to decide where to dig the well that will provide your freshwater. This is where someone known as a water dowser comes in.

Water dowsers claim to be able to use a simple tool to locate underground water. The two arms of a Y-shaped stick are held in the hands, with the end of the stick pointing upward. As the dowser walks around the property, he keeps an eye on the stick. When the stick pulls toward the ground, he claims that water is somewhere below.

Dowsers still work today, usually in areas where there are no easily accessible sources of groundwater. Some people believe the dowsing stick responds to the presence of water. Scientifically, though, the explanation is much simpler. In many places, groundwater is abundant enough that, in a temperate climate, you have an excellent chance of striking water no matter where you dig a well.

Geologists searching for underground water use much sounder methods. In a desert, for example, growing plants indicate there might be water present. Technology like sonar can also reveal if water lies below the ground.

CONNECT TO YOU

Do you think it's important for people to understand the difference between science and pseudoscience? Why? Discuss your ideas with a partner.

TOPIC 2 Review and Assess

1 Nonrenewable Energy Resources

MS-ESS3-1, MS-ESS3-4

1. Which of the following is considered a nonrenewable resource?
   A. sunlight
   B. wood
   C. water
   D. natural gas

2. Which of the following is *not* an effect of our growing population's use of fossil fuels?
   A. The distribution of these resources is changing.
   B. The amount of carbon dioxide in the atmosphere is increasing.
   C. The resources are now being replaced faster than they are being used.
   D. Political conflicts occur over control of these resources.

3. Which of the following is directly involved in transforming the remains of organisms into fossil fuels?
   A. pressure
   B. wind
   C. sunlight
   D. precipitation

4. Fossil fuels are .... resources that are .... distributed on Earth.

5. **SEP Construct Explanations** Why are coal and petroleum resources not commonly found across the planet?

....

....

....

....

....

....

....

....

....

2 Renewable Energy Resources

MS-ESS3-1, MS-ESS3-4

6. Which of the following renewable energy resources comes from underground?
   A. geothermal energy
   B. hydropower
   C. wind power
   D. solar power

7. Which of the following is a drawback of biofuels such as ethanol?
   A. The energy ethanol can provide is about the same as the energy required to make it.
   B. It is much more expensive than gasoline.
   C. There are few places where plants used to make ethanol can be grown.
   D. When it is burned, ethanol produces even more emissions than coal.

8. **SEP Define Problems** What areas on Earth are worst suited for using solar energy to generate electricity?

....

....

....

9. **SEP Develop Models** Draw a diagram that shows how the sun is responsible for the production of wind energy.

ASSESSMENT

Evaluate your understanding by taking a Topic Test.

3 Mineral Resources

MS-ESS3-1, MS-ESS3-4

10. Which of the following is an essential characteristic of a mineral?
  A. crystal structure
  B. artificially manufactured
  C. liquid
  D. formed from organic processes

11. Which of the following statements about minerals and ores is true?
  A. Minerals are deposits of valuable ores.
  B. Minerals are products that are made from ores.
  C. Minerals form from solutions, but ores form from volcanoes.
  D. All ores are minerals, but not all minerals are ores.

12. Many minerals are formed from .... as water ....

13. SEP Construct Explanations Gold is a valuable mineral that is found underground. It is brought closer to the surface, where it can be mined, by volcanic activity. Why do you think gold is not evenly distributed on Earth?

....
....
....
....
....
....
....
....
....
....

4 Water Resources

MS-ESS3-1, MS-ESS3-4

14. The most abundant water resource on Earth is
  A. salt water **B.** fresh water
  C. groundwater **D.** surface water

15. Most fresh water on Earth is
  A. in the atmosphere as water vapor.
  B. found on the surface in lakes and rivers.
  C. locked up in ice.
  D. located underground.

16. Factors such as precipitation, ... and surface features determine where surface water can form on Earth.

17. SEP Engage in Argument How could groundwater sources become depleted if water is constantly being cycled?

....
....
....
....
....

18. Draw Conclusions Why is the distribution of water resources a concern for the economic and social welfare of people around the world?

....
....
....
....
....
....
....

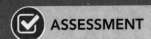

☑ TOPIC 2 Review and Assess

MS-ESS3-1

Evidence-Based Assessment

Van is researching information about the mineral copper and its distribution on Earth. Copper is used in electrical systems and even found in very small amounts in living things. Here is some of the other information Van finds, along with two maps that he finds during his research:

- copper ore can form from different geological processes
- one type of copper, called porphyry copper, is found in large deposits in certain types of rock
- most porphyry copper deposits are 340 million years old or younger
- porphyry copper forms at relatively shallow depths of about 4,500 to 9,000 meters (15,000 to 30,000 feet) in Earth's crust

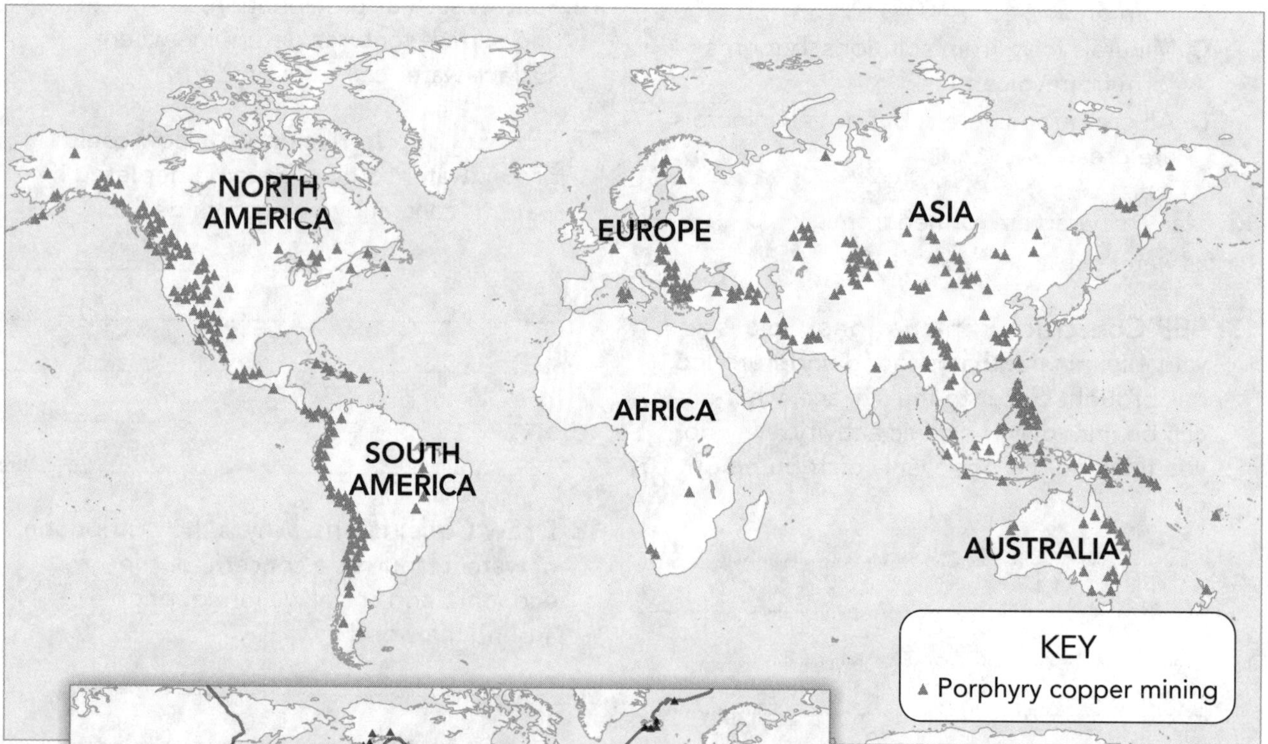

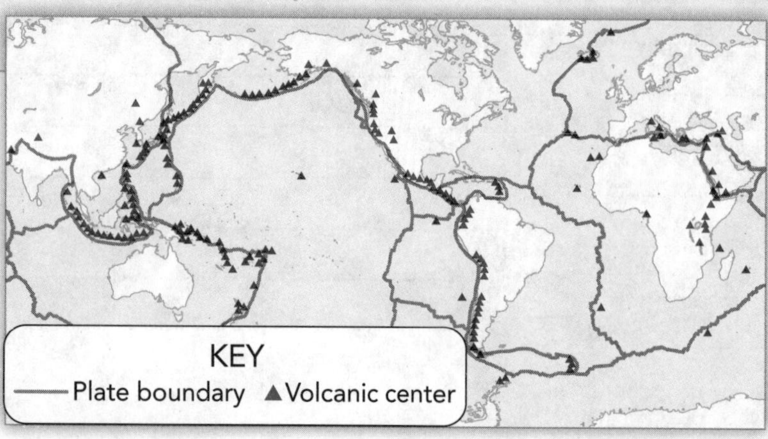

1. **SEP Analyze Data** Which of these regions seems to have the greatest concentration of porphyry copper mining?

A. Africa B. Australia
C. Europe D. South America

2. **CCC Cause and Effect** Why are there so many volcanoes around the Pacific Ocean? Support your answer with evidence from the volcanic activity map.

3. **CCC Patterns** Based on the map of porphyry copper mining, which of the following statements about the distribution of copper is correct? Select all that apply.

- ☐ Porphyry copper is distributed relatively evenly across most of the continents.
- ☐ Very little porphyry copper is found in Africa.
- ☐ A concentration of porphyry copper runs from Europe eastward through Asia and then south into Australia.
- ☐ Porphyry copper is widely distributed across South America.
- ☐ A majority of porphyry copper is found on continents that border the Pacific Ocean.
- ☐ There are fewer sources of porphyry copper in North America than in Asia.

4. **SEP Construct Explanations** Use evidence from the maps to explain why porphyry copper is not generally found near areas where volcanic activity, often associated with plate collisions, has occurred in the past.

Quest FINDINGS

Complete the Quest!

Phenomenon Choose one of the boomtowns you studied and develop a travel brochure to describe what the town was like when it was settled and what it is like now.

CCC Cause and Effect In what ways can proximity to a valuable natural resource affect the success of a town or city?

INTERACTIVITY

Reflect on Boomtowns

uDemonstrate Lab

MS-ESS3-1

To Drill or Not to Drill

How can you **use a model** to confirm the location of a **petroleum** deposit?

Materials

(per group)

- aquarium gravel
- glass baking dish
- wax crayons or candles
- plastic knife
- small weight or heavy book
- hot plate

Safety

Be sure to follow all safety guidelines provided by your teacher. The Safety Appendix of your textbook provides more details about the safety icons.

Background

Phenomenon An energy company wants to drill for oil on the outskirts of a small town. The owners of the energy company have provided evidence that the town is located near an area that was a large sea millions of years ago. Based on that evidence, they believe there is a large deposit of petroleum under the town. Town officials have hired you as an expert to look for evidence of oil under the town.

In this investigation, you will develop a model that you can use to predict whether or not the company will locate any oil below the town.

Develop Your Model

1. Using the available materials, your group must develop a model that meets the following criteria:
   - It must show how oil forms from ancient marine plants.
   - It must demonstrate the geological forces involved in the formation of oil.
   - It must indicate whether or not oil can form below the town.
2. Work with your group to develop ideas for a model that meets the criteria. Consider the following questions as you develop and design your model:
   - What materials can you use to represent the buried organic material that eventually forms oil?
   - How can your model demonstrate the geological forces that form oil?
   - What observations will you make?
3. After agreeing on a plan, write out the steps that your group will follow to develop and use the model. Include a sketch of the model that labels the materials you will be using and what they represent.
4.  After getting your teacher's approval, construct your model and use it to demonstrate how oil forms. Record your observations and data in the space provided.

Plan and Sketch

Observations

Analyze and Interpret Data

1. **SEP Use Models** Use your model to explain why oil is a nonrenewable resource.

2. **CCC Cause and Effect** What geological forces are involved in the formation of oil? How did you incorporate these forces into your model?

3. **SEP Construct Explanations** Explain whether or not oil will be found under the town. Use evidence from your model to support your explanation.

4. **Identify Limitations** In what ways is your model not reflective of the actual conditions that lead to the formation of oil? How could your group improve the model?

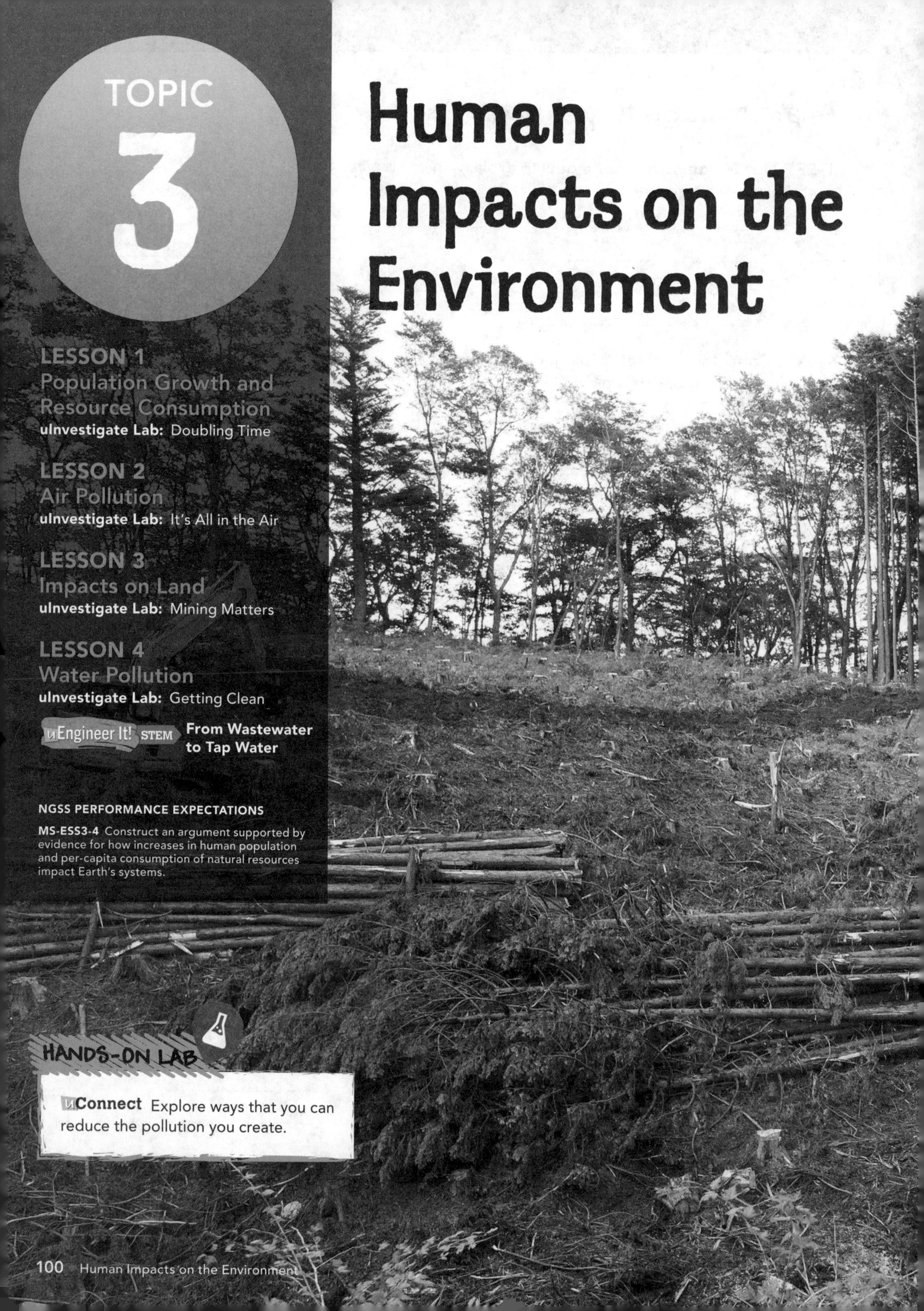

TOPIC 3

Human Impacts on the Environment

LESSON 1
Population Growth and Resource Consumption
uInvestigate Lab: Doubling Time

LESSON 2
Air Pollution
uInvestigate Lab: It's All in the Air

LESSON 3
Impacts on Land
uInvestigate Lab: Mining Matters

LESSON 4
Water Pollution
uInvestigate Lab: Getting Clean

uEngineer It! STEM **From Wastewater to Tap Water**

NGSS PERFORMANCE EXPECTATIONS

MS-ESS3-4 Construct an argument supported by evidence for how increases in human population and per-capita consumption of natural resources impact Earth's systems.

HANDS-ON LAB

uConnect Explore ways that you can reduce the pollution you create.

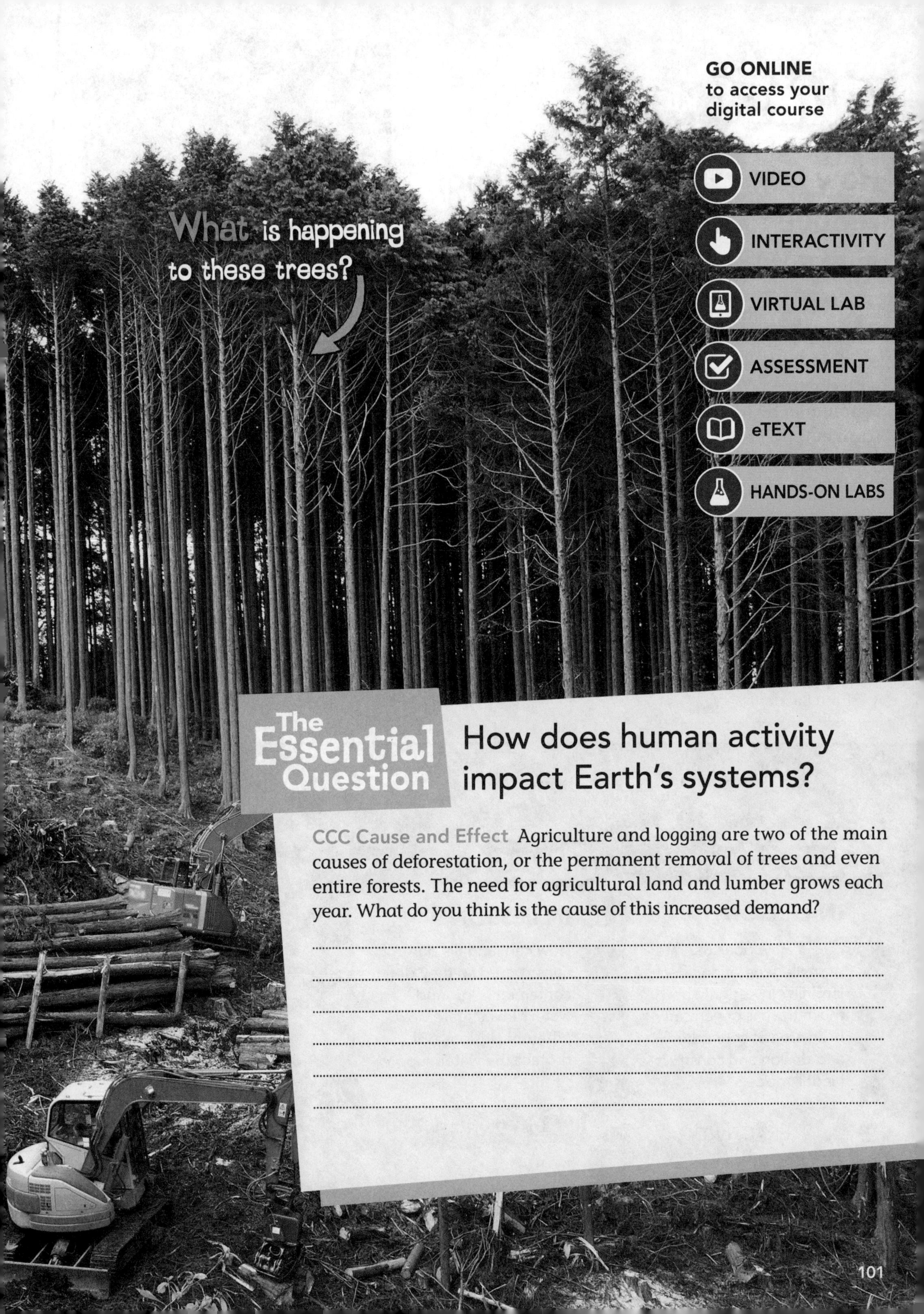
What is happening to these trees?

GO ONLINE to access your digital course

- VIDEO
- INTERACTIVITY
- VIRTUAL LAB
- ASSESSMENT
- eTEXT
- HANDS-ON LABS

The Essential Question

How does human activity impact Earth's systems?

CCC Cause and Effect Agriculture and logging are two of the main causes of deforestation, or the permanent removal of trees and even entire forests. The need for agricultural land and lumber grows each year. What do you think is the cause of this increased demand?

....

....

....

....

....

....

Quest KICKOFF

How can you help your school reduce its impact on Earth's systems?

STEM **Phenomenon** The landfill used by your community is running out of space. The community must expand it or find other ways to deal with the trash. Your principal has decided to help the community by finding ways to reduce the school's trash output. In this problem-based Quest activity, you will evaluate the trash output at your school. You will then develop a plan to decrease that output through a combination of reducing, reusing, and recycling. As you work, you should anticipate objections to your plan. Finally, you will present your plan and work to implement it at your school.

NBC LEARN VIDEO

After watching the Quest Kickoff video, which explores the plastic items that end up in the ocean, think about the trash you generate. How can you reduce, recycle, or reuse your trash?

Reduce:

....

....

Recycle:

....

....

Reuse:

....

....

INTERACTIVITY

Trash Backlash

MS-ESS3-4 Construct an argument supported by evidence for how increases in human population and per-capita consumption of natural resources impact Earth's systems.

Quest CHECK-IN

IN LESSON 1

STEM How does the rate of trash generation affect landfills? Investigate how much trash is generated in an area of your school, and design and construct landfill models.

INTERACTIVITY

More Trash, Less Space

Quest CHECK-IN

IN LESSON 2

How can landfills be constructed so they don't contaminate ground-water? Investigate how different designs will protect the water supply.

HANDS-ON LAB

Trash vs. Water

Quest CHECK-IN

IN LESSON 3

How is a landfill site chosen, and what laws regulate landfill use? Explore the stages of a landfill's life, and conduct research about laws that affect landfills.

INTERACTIVITY

Life of a Landfill

According to the U.S. Environmental Protection Agency, Americans recycled only about 35 percent of their waste in 2014. Much of the rest of the waste ended up in landfills such as this one.

Quest CHECK-IN

IN LESSON 4

How can everyone contribute to reducing waste at your school? Develop a plan to reduce trash output in at least one area of your school.

HANDS-ON LAB

Reducing Waste

Quest FINDINGS

Complete the Quest!

Refine and present your plan to reduce trash output at your school.

INTERACTIVITY

Reflect on Trash Backlash

uConnect Lab

Finding a Solution for Your Pollution

How can you **design a solution** that decreases the amount of garbage you throw away?

Background

Phenomenon Imagine it is lunchtime at school, and you have just finished eating. As you toss your trash into one of the garbage cans, you notice that the can is filled with plastic bottles and paper trays. "We would have a lot less garbage to throw away if we could recycle these bottles and trays," you say to your friend. "You're right. We should start a recycling program," your friend replies. Time to do some research, you think to yourself as you walk out of the cafeteria. In this activity, you will design a school lunch environment that generates zero waste.

Materials

(per class)

- garbage can full of cafeteria garbage
- containers
- scale

Safety

Be sure to follow all safety procedures provided by your teacher. The Safety Appendix of your textbook provides more details about the safety icons.

Design a Procedure

☐ **1. Plan an Investigation** As a class, design a procedure to gather evidence that supports the need for a zero-waste school lunch environment.

....

....

....

....

....

....

☐ **2.** Show your procedure to your teacher. Then, use your materials to carry out your investigation. Be sure to wear gloves when handling the garbage.

☐ **3.** Draw a table to record your observations and to collect evidence.

Observations

HANDS-ON LAB

Connect Go online for a downloadable worksheet of this lab.

Analyze and Conclude

1. **CCC Cause and Effect** According to the Duke Center of Sustainability and Commerce, the average person generates 4.3 pounds of waste per day. Describe the impacts all of this waste has on Earth's systems.

2. **SEP Construct an Argument** Should recycling be mandatory? Make an argument using evidence from your observations.

3. **SEP Design a Solution** Work with a partner to design a school lunch with zero waste.

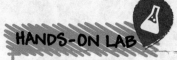

LESSON

1 Population Growth and Resource Consumption

Guiding Questions

- How has the human population changed over time?
- How is the consumption of natural resources by humans affected by changes in population size?

Connections

Literacy Determine Conclusions

Math Draw Comparative Inferences

MS-ESS3-4

HANDS-ON LAB

uInvestigate Examine how population growth affects the availability of natural resources.

Vocabulary

birth rate
death rate
exponential growth
pollution
overpopulation
conservation
sustainable use

Academic Vocabulary

estimate
constraints

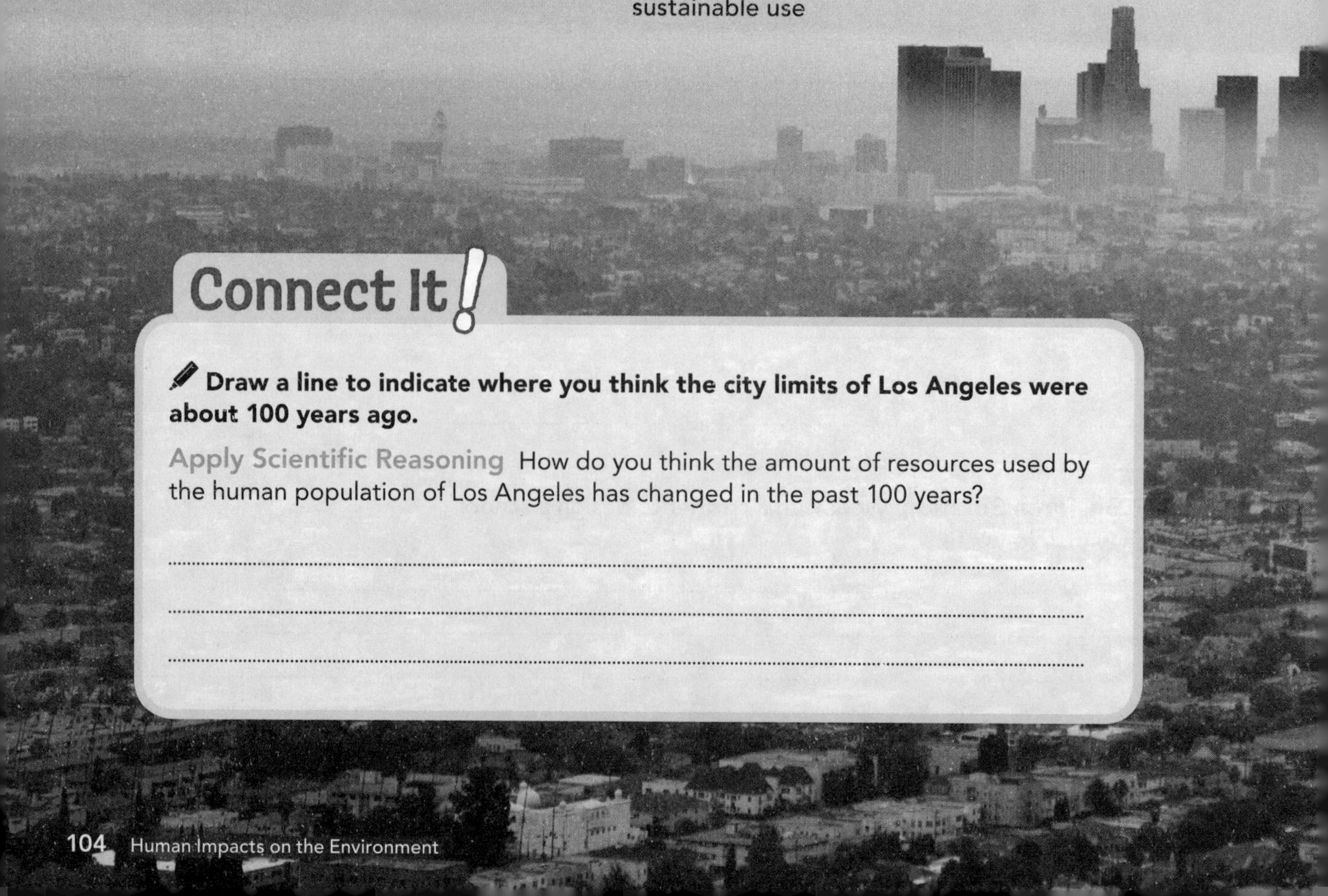

Connect It!

Draw a line to indicate where you think the city limits of Los Angeles were about 100 years ago.

Apply Scientific Reasoning How do you think the amount of resources used by the human population of Los Angeles has changed in the past 100 years?

....

....

....

The Human Population

There are more humans living on Earth today than any time in our history. Human populations have fluctuated in the past, mostly due to environmental or climate conditions. Around 60,000 years ago, the human population was generally stable at around 600,000 individuals. A warming climate and improvements in hunting and fishing techniques resulted in a rapid increase to about 6 million humans over a few thousand years.

This population remained fairly constant until about 10,000 years ago, when agriculture and livestock breeding gave rise to steady, long-term population growth. This growth dropped occasionally during war, epidemics, or invasions, but maintained a steady climb until the 1700s. Since then, unprecedented population growth has occurred, with the human population reaching 1 billion by the early 1800s. In the last 300 years, the world population has increased tenfold. As of 2017, there were 7.5 billion people on Earth.

HANDS-ON LAB

Explore how food becomes a limiting factor when population size increases.

Reflect How has the population of your community changed in your lifetime? In your science notebook, describe some ways your community would be affected if the population were to suddenly increase or decrease.

Growth of a City

Figure 1 A little over 4 million people call the city of Los Angeles home. The population has grown a great deal since the first Native American tribes settled there thousands of years ago.

INTERACTIVITY

Explore the factors that affect human population growth.

Academic Vocabulary

What other kinds of information might scientists need to estimate?

....

....

....

....

....

Population Changes

Population growth, whether in a town, a country, or the world, is determined by calculating the number of individuals who are born, die, or move into or out of an area. The number of births per 1,000 individuals for a certain time period is called the **birth rate**. On the other hand, the number of deaths per 1,000 individuals for a certain time period is called the **death rate**. When the rates of births and people moving into an area are greater than the rates of deaths and people moving out of an area, the population increases. Otherwise, the population decreases. In 2016, scientists **estimate** there were 280 births and 109 deaths every minute.

In early human history, birth rates and death rates were fairly balanced, which resulted in little change in the size of the human population. For most of human history, birth rates were only slightly higher than death rates, resulting in a slow, steady increase in population.

The graph in **Figure 2** shows human population growth beginning in 1750, around the start of the Industrial Revolution. Human population grew rapidly after the Industrial Revolution because the death rate began to decline. Advances in technology resulted in new farming and transportation methods that increased the availability of resources, such as food and clean water. Improvements in public health and general living standards also played a role in decreasing the death rate.

World Population Growth Since 1750

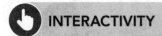

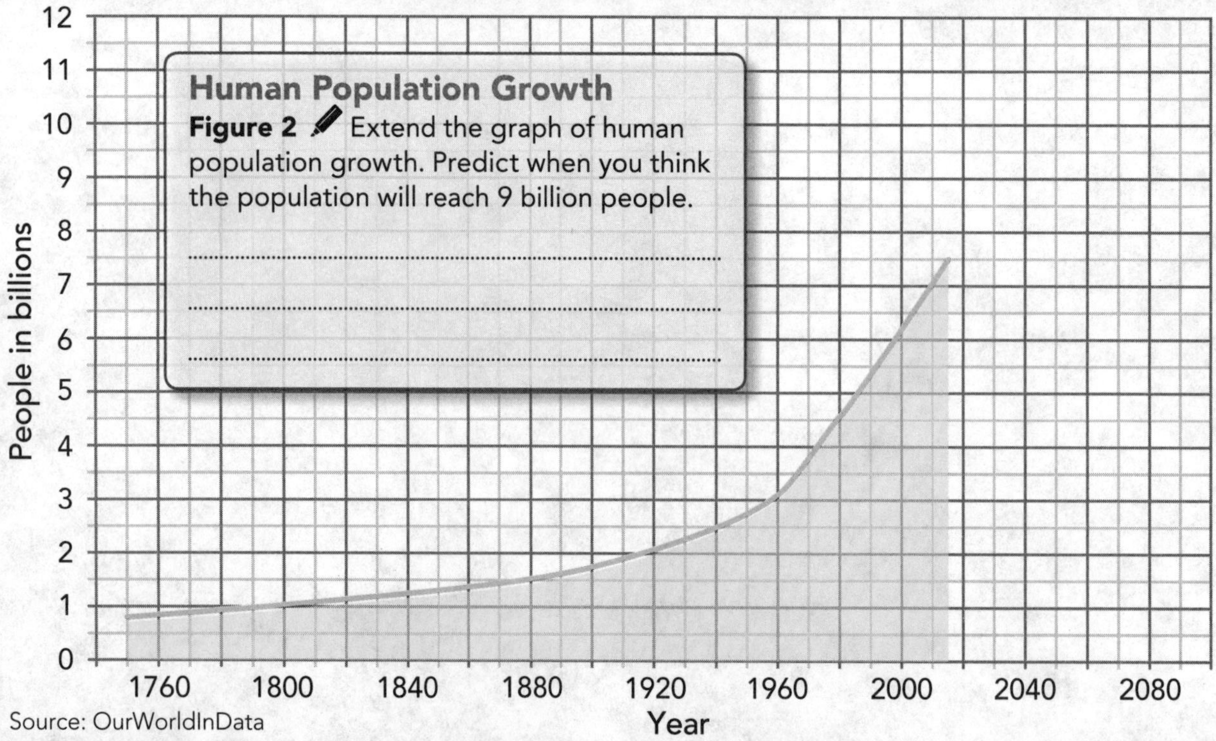

Human Population Growth

Figure 2 Extend the graph of human population growth. Predict when you think the population will reach 9 billion people.

....

....

....

Source: OurWorldInData

Population Growth Rate

Human population changes do not represent a straight line of increase on a graph. Instead the population increases more and more rapidly over time. This rate of change is called **exponential growth**—a growth pattern in which individuals in a population reproduce at a constant rate, so that the larger population gets, the faster it grows.

However, no living population can experience such extreme exponential growth for very long. Populations are limited by space and resources. Exponential growth will cease when a population reaches the upper limit of organisms its environment can support. At that point, the population will stabilize or possibly decline. Throughout history, human populations have experienced periods of growth and decline, depending on the conditions and resources available.

INTERACTIVITY

Learn about how human population growth affects Earth's systems.

READING CHECK **Determine Conclusions** What would happen if the population growth rate reached zero?

....

....

Math Toolbox

Projected Growth Rates

The rate of human population growth is not the same all around the world. Experts use existing data to predict growth rates in different countries. Some areas may experience rapid growth, while others may have no growth or a decline.

1. **SEP Interpret Data** Which country represented has the highest population growth rate? Lowest?

....

....

2. **SEP Evaluate Evidence** What conclusions can you draw from the growth rates of Angola and Germany?

....

....

....

....

Country	Population Growth Rate (%)
Angola	1.9
Australia	1.0
Canada	0.7
Germany	–0.2
Haiti	1.3
Japan	–0.2
South Korea	0.5
United States	0.8
Venezuela	1.2

Source: CIA World Factbook, 2017 estimates

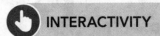

HANDS-ON LAB

Investigate Examine how population growth affects the availability of natural resources.

Academic Vocabulary
What are some other words that have the same meaning as *constraint*?

....

....

....

Using Natural Resources

Earth provides many resources that humans rely on to live, such as energy sources, minerals, water, trees, and plants. These resources are needed by all organisms on Earth. Some resources, such as water, are part of systems that affect our planet's climate and other natural cycles.

Human Activity Industries and families alike rely on energy sources such as fossil fuels to provide electricity to power our lives. We use fuel to keep us warm in the winter and cool in the summer, to travel from place to place, and to grow and transport the food we eat. We use wood from trees and minerals that are mined from the ground to build everything from the tiniest computer chips to the tallest skyscrapers. Every human being relies on fresh, clean water to survive.

As the world's population grows, so does our demand for resources. Like the human population, many resources are not evenly distributed around Earth. For example, the availability of fresh, usable water varies in different locations on Earth. It is one of the factors that may act as a **constraint** on human activities in the near future. Currently, more than 700 million people do not have access to safe, clean water. This lack of clean water forces many individuals to consume unsafe water. Experts estimate that by 2025, nearly 1.8 billion people could be suffering from water scarcity.

Question It!

Mining Salt
Salt is not only a necessary part of the human diet, it is used in numerous industrial and agricultural applications. Most of the salt used today is mined from underground deposits.

SEP Ask Questions Develop a list of questions you would ask to help determine the relationship between human population growth and salt mining.

....

....

....

....

....

....

....

....

....

....

Impact of Agriculture

Figure 3 In order to grow food for people to eat, farmers use fertilizers and other chemicals. These chemicals often run off the land and pollute lakes, rivers, and the ocean.

CCC Cause and Effect What effect does farming food for a growing population have on the environment?

....

....

....

....

....

....

....

Impact on the Earth System Using resources reduces their amounts, which is a problem for nonrenewable resources like fossil fuels. The way in which we obtain many of these resources involves drilling, mining, or clearing Earth's surface, which damages the land. As some resources such as minerals or fossil fuels become scarce, humans dig deeper and disturb more areas to keep up with our growing population. When we remove resources, it increases the potential to release harmful substances into the environment. For example, using resources creates waste. If left untreated, waste can harm the environment. Motorized vehicles, such as the one shown in **Figure 3,** burn petroleum and release gases and chemicals that can cause **pollution**, which is the contamination of Earth's land, water, or air.

Human activities also affect other life on Earth. When we mine for a mineral or divert water for our use we often destroy valuable habitats. Pollution in land and water habitats endangers the organisms that live there. Also, many organisms are over-exploited as food for growing human numbers. When the number of humans grows beyond what the available resources can support, we reach the point of **overpopulation**. Human overpopulation is a driving force of many environmental and social issues, including climate change, habitat loss, and human conflict. There may come a point at which Earth cannot adequately meet human needs at our current rate of resource use. In some parts of the world, this is already the case.

Literacy Connection

Determine Conclusions As you read, underline evidence in the text that supports your conclusions about how growing populations impact the environment.

READING CHECK **Determine Conclusions** How does a growing population impact land, air, and water resources?

....

....

INTERACTIVITY

Examine the different types of resources available on Earth.

Balancing Needs

Science can identify problems and offer possible solutions, but it is up to individuals, governments, and international organizations to decide how to manage the impacts of a growing population. There are economic, social, and environmental costs and benefits which all must be weighed against one another (**Figure 4**). For example, humans use a variety of resources to produce electricity, from burning fossil fuels to building dams. No single method works in every situation, and there are benefits and costs to each.

The practice of using less of a resource so that it can last longer is called **conservation**. To ensure that future generations have access to the same resources we enjoy now, we need to use resources in ways that maintain them at a certain quality for a certain period of time. This practice is known as **sustainable use** of living resources. It gives resources time to recover and replenish themselves.

Addressing human impacts on the environment also requires engineering new solutions to our problems. These might include using desalination to counter water shortages, or advances in solar power, wind power, and other forms of renewable energy. As human populations continue to rise, the need for new ideas and solutions will increase.

READING CHECK **Develop an Argument** Why is it important to conserve natural resources?

....

....

....

Harvesting Timber

Figure 4 We use timber, but there is an impact of our use on the environment. In the table, list the benefits and costs of logging.

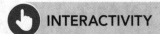

Benefits	Costs

LESSON 1 Check

MS-ESS3-4

1. **SEP Cite Evidence** What factors limited human population growth in the past?

2. **CCC Cause and Effect** How did the Industrial Revolution affect human population growth?

3. **CCC Engage in Argument** What actions should humans take to conserve natural resources?

Use the graph to answer questions 4 and 5.

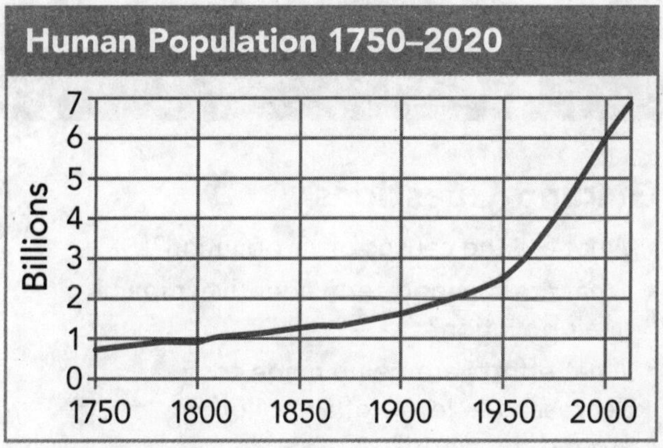

4. **CCC Evaluate Proportions** What was the approximate population growth per year from 1800 to 1925? What was the approximate growth rate from 1925 to 2000? What is the ratio between the two rates?

5. **Use Ratios** Suggest two explanations for the ratio relationship you described in question 4.

Quest CHECK-IN

In this lesson, you learned how human population has changed over time and how human population growth impacts Earth's systems.

Connect to the Environment Why is it important to consider human population growth when developing strategies for dealing with pollution?

INTERACTIVITY

More Trash, Less Space

Go online to learn about the total volume of trash generated in the United States and to determine how much trash is generated at your school.

LESSON

2 Air Pollution

Guiding Questions

- What are the causes of air pollution?
- What are the long-term negative impacts of air pollution?
- What efforts are being made to decrease the levels of air pollution around the world?

Connections

Literacy Cite Textual Evidence

Math Analyze Quantitative Relationships

MS-ESS3-4

HANDS-ON LAB

uInvestigate Evaluate how different types of pollution affect air and water clarity.

Vocabulary

point source
nonpoint source
emissions
ozone
acid rain

Academic Vocabulary

primary

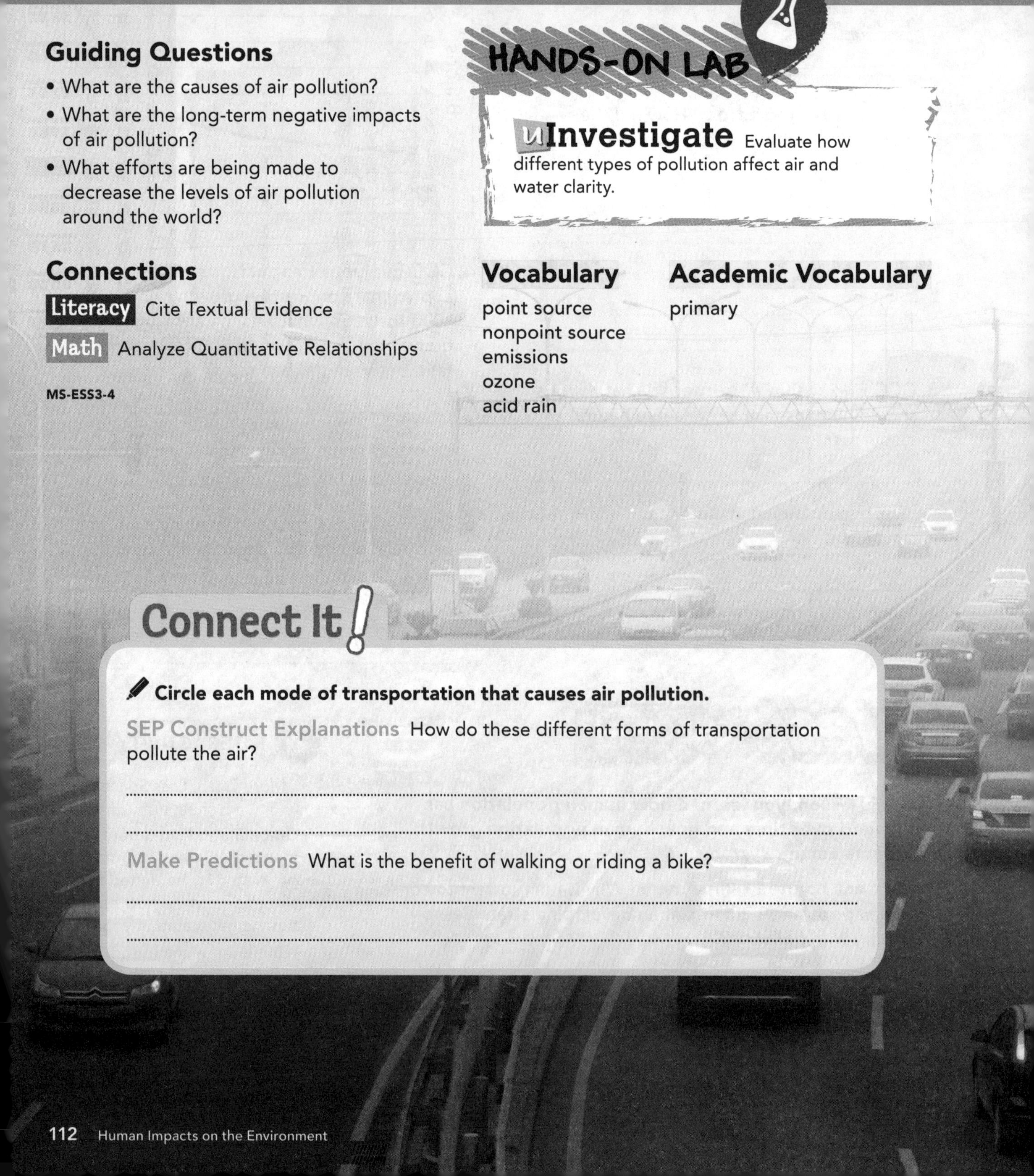

Connect It!

Circle each mode of transportation that causes air pollution.

SEP Construct Explanations How do these different forms of transportation pollute the air?

....

....

Make Predictions What is the benefit of walking or riding a bike?

....

....

Causes of Pollution

You are surrounded by air. Air is a mixture of nitrogen, oxygen, carbon dioxide, water vapor, and other gases. Almost all living things depend on these gases to survive. These gases cycle between the biosphere and the atmosphere. The cycles guarantee that the air supply will not run out, but they don't ensure that the air will be clean.

HANDS-ON LAB

Explore how particles move through the air.

Pollution

The contamination of Earth's land, water, or air is called pollution. Pollution is caused by liquids, chemicals, heat, light, and noise. Pollution can have dramatic negative effects on the environment and on living organisms.

Write About It What are the large-scale impacts of breathing polluted air?

Humans affect the levels of pollution by using natural resources and manufactured products. For example, **Figure 1** shows how the burning of gasoline pollutes the air. In addition, when coal and oil-based fuels are burned to generate electricity, carbon dioxide and sulfur dioxide are released into the air.

Types of Pollution

A specific, identifiable pollution source is called a **point source**. A sewer that drains untreated wastewater into a river is an example of a point source.

A **nonpoint source** of pollution is widely spread and cannot be tied to a specific origin. For example, the polluted air around big cities is caused by vehicles, factories, and other sources. Because it is difficult to identify the exact source of the pollution, that pollution has a nonpoint source.

READING CHECK **Determine Central Ideas** What is the difference between point and nonpoint sources of pollution?

....

....

....

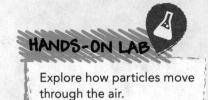

Different Sources of Pollution

Figure 1 Pollution can occur naturally or through human activities. Sometimes the level of pollution is so great that it harms people.

Sources of Air Pollution

Figure 2 ✏ Circle the natural sources of pollution. Mark an *X* on the human-made causes of pollution.

Outdoor Air Pollution

The air you are breathing is a combination of different gases. If you are in the mountains, the air might feel fresh and crisp. If you are at the shore, you might smell the salt water. In large cities, however, the air might not be as refreshing. Air pollution can be a big problem in areas where there are a lot of factories or a lot of people.

Emissions Many years ago, the main source of air pollution was the smoke being pumped out of factories. You have probably seen images of these **emissions**, or pollutants that are released into the air, as the dark smoke coming out of a factory's tall chimneys. This smoke is loaded with chemicals that mix with the gases in the air. However, today, most air pollution is released from coal-fired power plants and from motor vehicles, as shown in **Figure 2.** Emissions often contain carbon dioxide, which is also a pollutant. The increasing level of carbon dioxide is the primary contributor to the rise in average global temperatures over the past century.

Not all air pollution is caused by people. There are also some natural causes of air pollution, such as forest fires and volcanic eruptions. For example, the Hawaiian volcano Kilauea releases nearly 1,500–2,000 tons of harmful sulfur dioxide into the atmosphere each day during eruptions. However, human activities emit more than ten times as much sulfur dioxide and more than one hundred times as much carbon dioxide as all volcanoes combined.

HANDS-ON LAB

Investigate Evaluate how different types of pollution affect air and water clarity.

Smog If you live in a large city, chances are you have heard the term "smog alert." This is a warning to alert you that the amount of air pollution may make it difficult to breathe outdoors. Smog forms when certain gases and chemicals react with sunlight. This results in a thick, brownish haze that hovers over a city. Smog can cause breathing problems and diseases of the eyes and throat.

The **primary** source of smog is the emissions of cars and trucks. Among these emissions are chemicals called hydrocarbons and nitrogen oxides. These gases react in the sunlight to produce a form of oxygen called **ozone**. Ozone is toxic to humans, and it causes lung infections and harms the body's immune system.

Under normal conditions, air near the ground is heated by Earth's surface and rises up and away from the surface. Pollutants in the air are carried up into the atmosphere by the rising air. However, under certain weather conditions called temperature inversions, the normal circulation of air is blocked. As **Figure 3** shows, cool air becomes trapped below a layer of warm air during an inversion. This keeps the pollutants trapped near Earth's surface and causes them to become more concentrated and dangerous.

READING CHECK **Cite Textual Evidence** What are the main sources of air pollution and how do they cause smog?

....

....

....

Academic Vocabulary

Write a sentence using the word *primary*.

....

....

....

Temperature Inversion

Figure 3 Complete the image on the right by shading in the air pollutants to show how they are trapped during a temperature inversion.

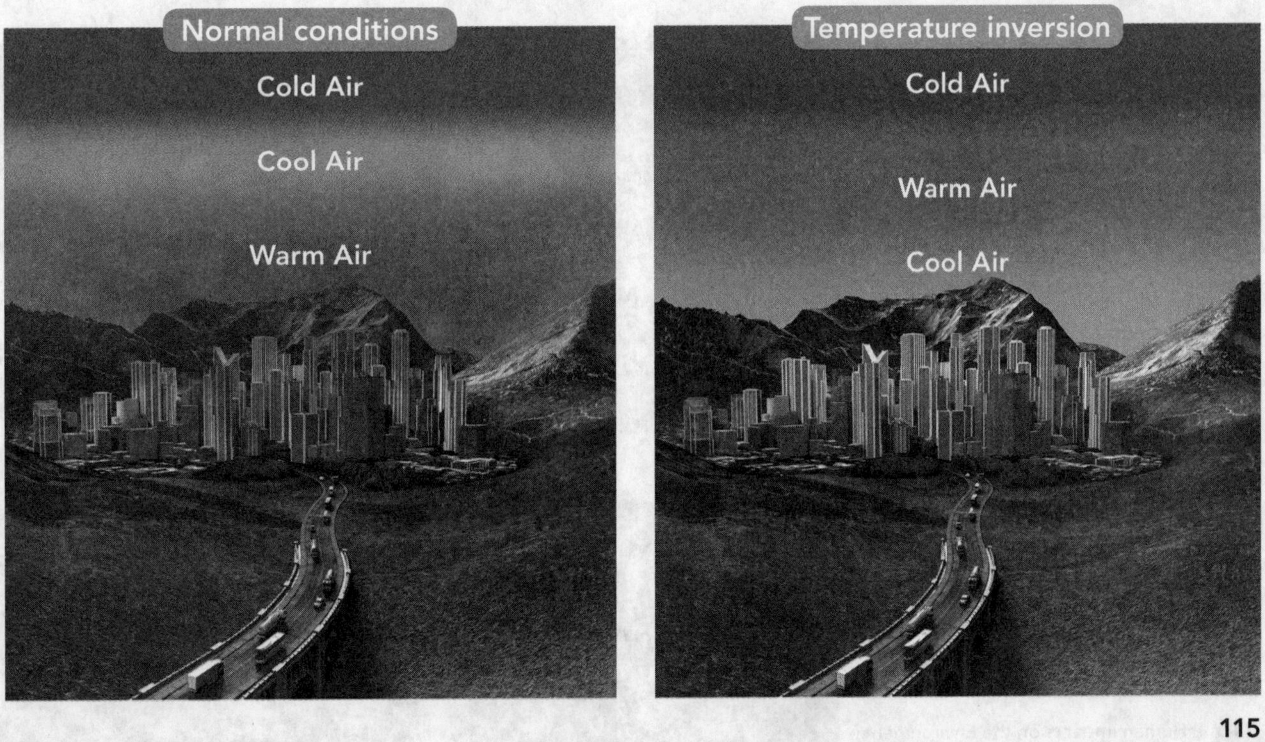

INTERACTIVITY

Examine the damaging effects of acid rain and pollution.

Acid Rain Precipitation that is more acidic than normal because of air pollution is called **acid rain**. When coal and oil are burned, they produce nitrogen oxide and sulfur dioxide gases. These gases are then released as emissions and react with the water vapor in the air to produce nitric and sulfuric acids. These acids become part of rain, snow, sleet, or fog.

When acidic precipitation falls to Earth's surface, it has damaging effects, as shown in **Figure 4**. As water and soil become more acidic, organisms will die off. Acid rain can also remove nutrients and minerals from the soil, affecting plant growth. Sometimes the effects of acid rain can be reversed by adding chemicals that neutralize the acid, but this is very expensive.

Literacy Connection

Cite Textual Evidence
As you read, underline the statements that support the idea that acid rain causes damage to living and nonliving things.

Acid rain also causes damage to nonliving things. The acid reacts with metal and stone of buildings, cars, and statues. It can cause metal to rust at a faster rate and causes the chemical weathering of stone. The effects of acid rain on these materials are irreversible.

READING CHECK **Write Arguments** Suppose your state government does not think that outdoor air pollution is a problem. What evidence could you use to convince your government that air pollution is harmful to people and the environment?

....

....

....

....

....

Effects of Acid Rain

Figure 4 Acid rain can damage nonliving things as well as living things. Explain how acid rain might affect the trees in a forest.

....

....

....

....

....

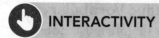

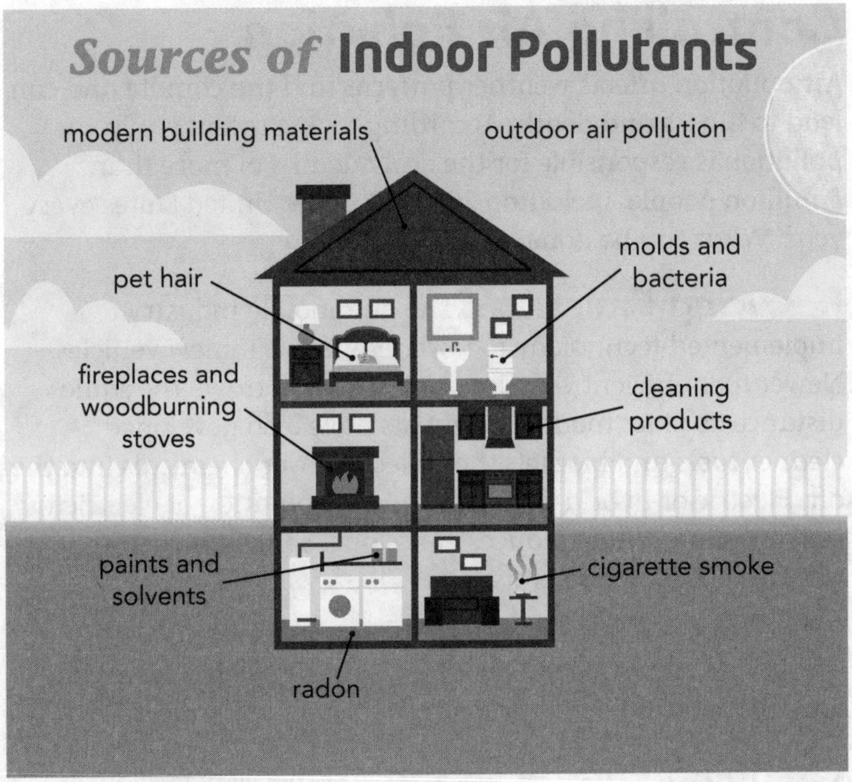

Indoor Air Pollution

Figure 5 Underline the indoor pollutants that are human-made. Circle the pollutants that occur naturally.

Indoor Air Pollution

Sometimes the quality of the air inside a building can be just as bad as the air outside. There are several things that can contribute to indoor air pollution, as shown in **Figure 5**. Some of these can be human-made, while others occur naturally.

Allergens Obvious sources of indoor air pollution include dust, mold, and pet hair. These factors, while quite common, usually affect only people who are sensitive to them. Other sources of indoor air pollution include fumes from glues, paints, and cleaning supplies and tobacco smoke from cigarettes or cigars. These can affect everyone in the home.

Indoor Gases Radon and carbon monoxide are two harmful pollutants often found in homes or other buildings. Radon is a colorless, odorless gas that is radioactive. It forms underground from the decay of certain rocks. Radon enters a home through cracks in the foundation. Breathing this gas over long periods of time can cause lung cancer and other health issues.

Carbon monoxide forms when fuels such as oil, gas, or wood are burned. Breathing carbon monoxide causes respiratory issues, nausea, headaches, and even death.

The best way to protect against carbon monoxide is to install detectors near sleeping areas. These devices alert homeowners if concentrations get too high.

VIDEO

Explore the misconception that indoor spaces do not suffer from air pollution.

READING CHECK

Integrate With Visuals
What are some ways to reduce the amount of indoor pollution in your home?

Bike Sharing

Figure 6 Bike-sharing programs provide a clean-energy alternative to driving a car or taking a bus. What actions can you take to reduce air pollution in your community?

Controlling Air Pollution

Air pollution affects weather patterns and the climate and can lead to illness and death. According to one recent study, air pollution is responsible for the early deaths of more than 5 million people, including 200,000 in the United States every year. What can be done?

Reducing Emissions The automobile industry implemented technology to lower emissions in new vehicles. Newer fuel-efficient vehicles use less fuel to travel the same distance as older models. Scientists have also developed cleaner fuels and biofuels that release fewer chemicals into the air. Electric or hybrid vehicles use a combination of electricity and gasoline, which reduces emissions. Some all-electric vehicles produce zero emissions.

Other ways to reduce emissions include carpooling, biking, or walking. You can also avoid using gas-powered lawn and garden tools and buy only energy-efficient appliances.

Changing Energy Usage Another way to reduce emissions is to transition away from fossil fuels, such as coal, oil, and natural gas. Solar, wind, hydroelectric, and geothermal energy produce only a small fraction of the harmful emissions that the burning of fossil fuels generates.

Math Toolbox

Energy Usage

The graphs show how energy consumption has changed in the United States over the past century.

1. **Use Ratios** How many times greater was energy consumption in 1908 than in 2015?

2. **Analyze Quantitative Relationships** Describe any patterns you observe in the graph showing the share of consumption for each energy source. What do you think might explain these patterns?

Energy Consumption in the United States

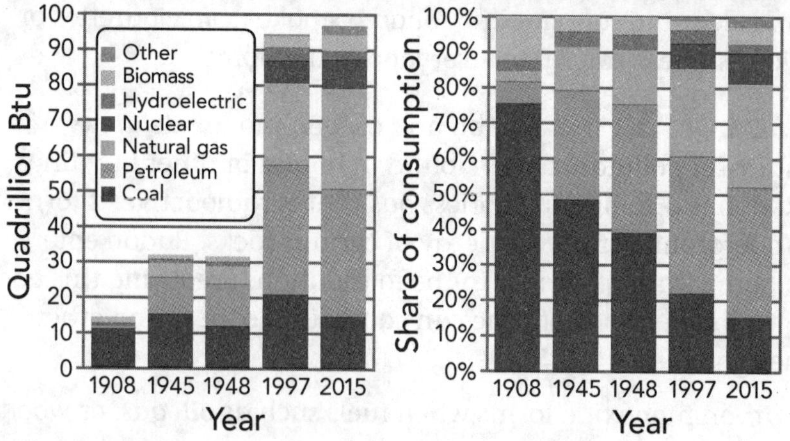

SOURCE: U.S. Energy Information Administration

Protecting the Ozone Layer If you have ever been sunburned, then you have experienced the effects of the sun's ultraviolet, or UV, radiation. The ozone layer, situated about 15 to 30 km above Earth's surface, works like a shield to protect living things from too much UV radiation.

INTERACTIVITY

Explore how to reduce your carbon footprint.

The Ozone Cycle In the ozone layer, ozone is constantly being made and destroyed in a cycle. An ozone molecule has three oxygen atoms. When sunlight hits a molecule, the ozone absorbs UV radiation. The energy causes the ozone to break apart into an oxygen gas molecule (which has two oxygen atoms) and a single oxygen atom. The oxygen atom hits an oxygen molecule and attaches itself to form a new ozone molecule.

The Ozone Hole In the late 1970s, scientists discovered an area of severe ozone depletion, or a "hole," in the ozone layer over the southern polar region, shown in **Figure 7**. The main cause of the hole was a group of gases called chlorofluorocarbons (CFCs)—human-made gases that destroy ozone molecules. As a result, more UV radiation reached Earth's surface. Nations around the world worked together to ban CFCs to help restore the amount of ozone in the atmosphere.

Ozone Hole

Figure 7 A hole in the ozone layer (in blue) allows more harmful UV radiation to reach Earth's surface in the Southern Hemisphere.

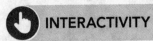

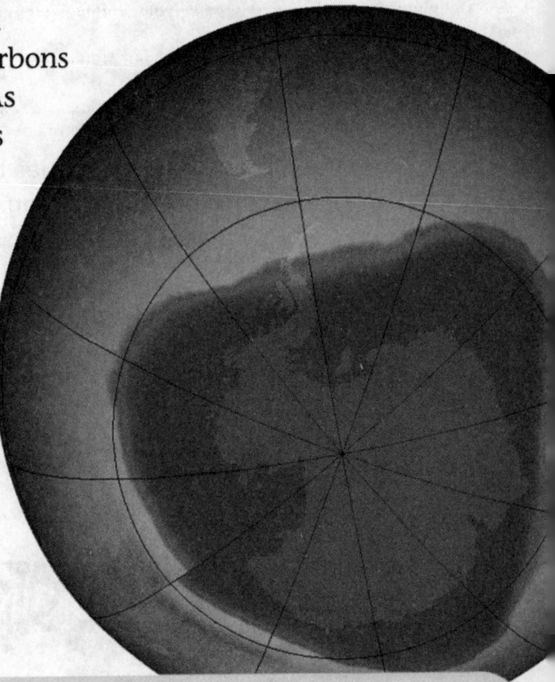

READING CHECK **Determine Conclusions** Why did countries work together to ban CFCs to help restore the ozone layer?

....

....

....

....

Model It!

Ozone Model

Re-read the paragraph about the ozone cycle.

SEP Develop Models Use the information in the text to create and label a model of an ozone molecule and how it changes during its life cycle. Explain each stage of the cycle.

....

....

....

....

....

LESSON 2 Check

MS-ESS3-4

1. **Determine Differences** What is the difference between "helpful" and "harmful" ozone?

2. **Evaluate Reasoning** Why is the use of fertilizers on lawns in residential areas an example of a nonpoint source of pollution?

3. **SEP Provide Evidence** How does burning fossil fuels affect indoor air pollution?

4. **CCC Cause and Effect** What effect does burning fossil fuels during manufacturing and energy production have on outdoor air pollution?

5. **Construct an Argument** What evidence supports the claim that walking and biking to work would have a positive effect on air pollution?

Quest CHECK-IN

In this lesson, you learned how humans affect Earth's systems by producing different forms of air pollution. You also learned how we are working to reduce the impact of air pollution.

SEP Evaluate Evidence Why is it important to work toward reducing activities that contribute to air pollution?

HANDS-ON LAB

Trash vs. Water

Download the lab to design and construct a model of a landfill.

Global to Local

MS-ESS3-4

Working Together to Reduce Air Pollution

Air pollution knows no borders. For instance, winds can carry pollution from factories in China nearly 10,000 kilometers to California. Many countries are reducing their own pollution, but they still suffer from the effects of air pollution from other countries. The only way to fight this global problem is by working together across borders.

In 2015, 196 countries came together to make a plan to reduce air pollution around the world. The Paris Agreement, as it is known, sets targets to reduce levels of carbon emissions. Carbon dioxide traps heat in the atmosphere, causing global warming. So, reducing pollution will help mitigate global warming.

It took many years to reach the Paris Agreement. Every country has different needs, industries, and laws. Some groups worry that the agreement doesn't go far enough. Others fear that environmental regulations will damage their national economies. Still, most nations believe that the Paris Agreement is necessary to reduce air pollution and protect Earth.

MY COMMUNITY

What are communities in Florida doing to reduce air pollution? Explore the Florida Climate Center website to find out.

Carbon dioxide, a by-product of burning fossil fuels, is a type of air pollution. It traps heat in Earth's atmosphere, causing global temperatures to rise. Even slight temperature increases can upset the delicate balance of life on Earth.

LESSON

3 Impacts on Land

Guiding Questions

- What natural resources are obtained from Earth's geosphere?
- Why are natural resources on land so important to Earth's systems?
- How do human activities positively and negatively affect land resources?

Connections

Literacy Cite Textual Evidence

Math Analyze Proportional Relationships

MS-ESS3-4

HANDS-ON LAB

uInvestigate Examine the impacts of mining.

Vocabulary

natural resource
renewable resource
nonrenewable resource
deforestation
erosion
desertification
sustainable

Academic Vocabulary

resource

Connect It!

Identify and label one unlimited resource and one limited resource shown in the image.

CCC Cause and Effect What impact do you think the overuse of certain resources might have on Earth's ecosystems?

....

....

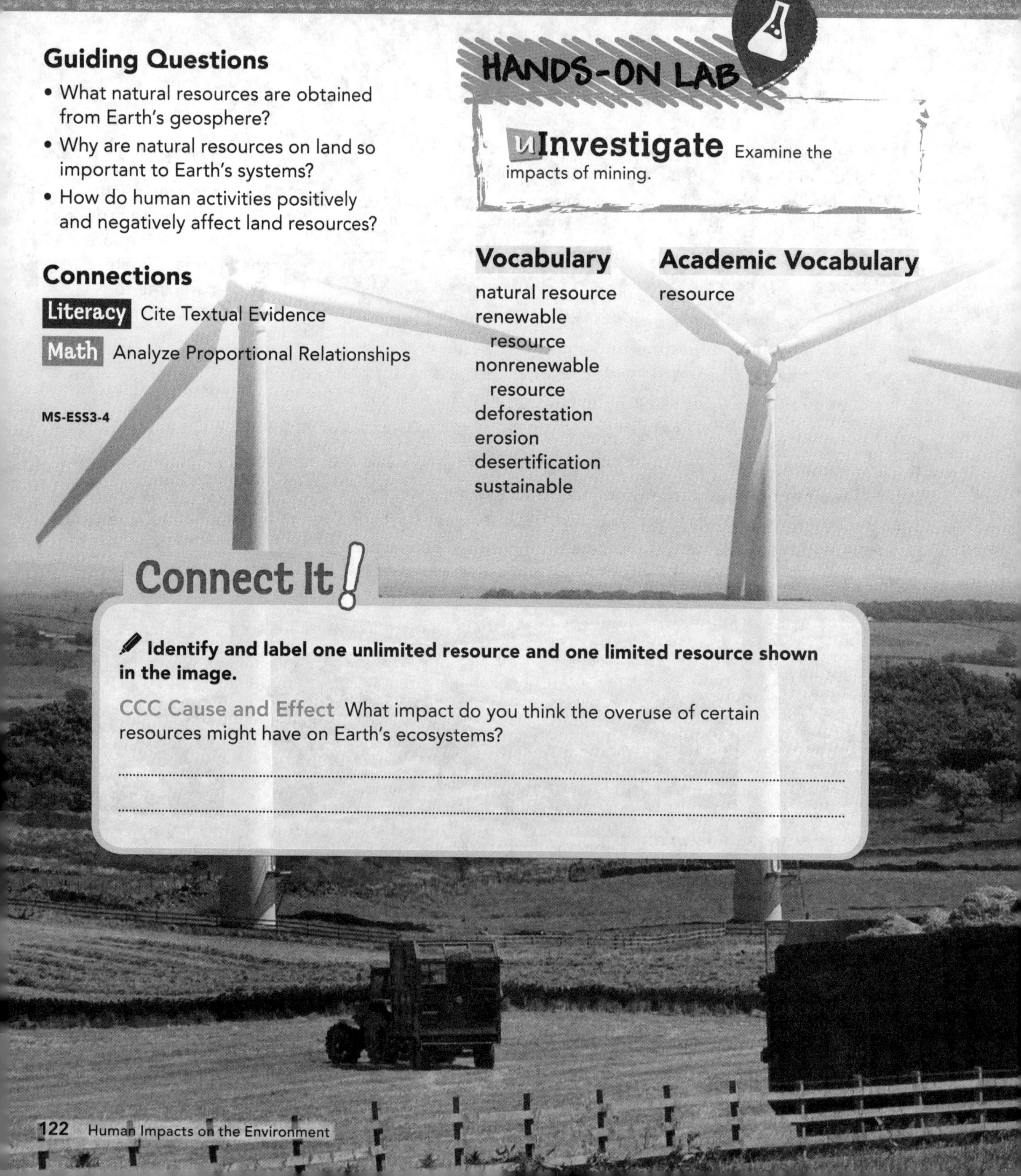

Land as a Resource

Did you drink water, turn on a light, or ride in a bus today? All of these activities, and many more, depend on Earth's **resources**. Anything we use that occurs naturally in the environment is called a **natural resource**. As **Figure 1** shows, natural resources include organisms, water, sunlight, minerals, and soil.

A **renewable resource** is either always available or is naturally replaced in a relatively short time. Some renewable resources, such as wind and sunlight, are almost always available. Other renewable resources, such as water and trees, are renewable only if they are replaced as fast as they are used.

Nonrenewable resources are resources that are not replaced within a relatively short time frame. Metals and most minerals are nonrenewable. Oil and coal are also nonrenewable resources. They were formed over millions of years from the remains of long-dead organisms. Humans use these resources faster than they can be replaced. Over time, they will be used up.

While it does not cover as much of the planet's surface as water, land is also a vital resource. Humans use its many resources to survive. As **Figure 2** will show, it is used to grow food, obtain raw materials, and provide shelter.

Academic Vocabulary

A resource is not limited to a material, such as water or trees. What other kinds of resources do you rely on in your life?

Reflect What are some renewable and nonrenewable resources that you use? In your science notebook, describe these resources.

Natural Resources

Figure 1 Humans use many different types of resources. Some of these are in limited supply, while others are essentially limitless.

HANDS-ON LAB

Investigate Examine the impacts of mining.

Agriculture

Land provides most of the food people eat. The use of land to produce food is called agriculture. Many areas of the world are not suitable for farming. New farmland is often made by draining wetlands, irrigating deserts, or deforestation. **Deforestation** is the removal of forests to use the land for other reasons. This process destroys the habitats of organisms living in these places.

Mining

The metals and plastics used to make items such as televisions, cellular phones, building materials, and cars are mined from below Earth's surface. Metals and other resources are obtained through one type of mining called strip mining. Strip mining removes the top layer of dirt, exposing the minerals or ore underneath. When heavy winds and rains come, they can wash soil and land away. With it go all the nutrients it contains. It can take thousands of years for soil to be replaced.

READING CHECK

Cite Textual Evidence Which statements from the text support the idea that land is an important resource? Underline them.

Development

Where do you live? It is a good bet that you live in a structure somewhere on the land. Whether it is a house, a camper, or an apartment building, the space your home takes up was once used as a habitat for other organisms. As the human population grows, more and more land is developed and built up with human structures, leaving no room for the living organisms of the original habitat.

Land Use

Figure 2 Humans use land is many different ways. How do these activities impact Earth's systems?

....

....

....

....

....

Importance of Soil Management

Healthy, fertile soil is essential for the success of agriculture because it contains the minerals and nutrients that plants require. Soil absorbs, stores, and filters water, which is also necessary for plant growth. Organisms living in soil, such as bacteria, fungi, and earthworms, break down the wastes and remains of living things and return them to the soil as nutrients.

Structure of Soil If you take a shovel and dig a hole in the ground, you will encounter several layers of soil, such as those shown in **Figure 3**. The first layer is called the litter. This top layer is where dead leaves and grass are found.

The next layer is called the topsoil. Topsoil is a mixture of nutrients, water, air, rock fragments, and dead and decaying organisms. Moving further down, the shovel will hit the subsoil. This layer contains the same water and air as the topsoil, but there are more rock fragments and fewer plant and animal remains here.

Underneath the subsoil is the layer of bedrock. This is the layer that makes up Earth's crust and is the basis for new soil. As time passes, water dissolves the rock, and its freezing and thawing action cracks and breaks apart the bedrock. Plant roots also help to break the bedrock by growing into cracks and then expanding. Animals such as earthworms and moles also help in the process. And as dead organisms break down, their remains contribute to the mixture of new soil.

Soil Layers

Figure 3 ✏ Fertile soil is made up of several layers. Label each layer of soil in the photo: *bedrock, litter, subsoil, topsoil.*

Plan It!

Community Considerations

CCC Cause and Effect Suppose you are part of a group that is converting an abandoned lot into a community garden. You need to plan the garden to avoid damaging the local environment further. What harmful effects should you consider and how can you minimize them?

INTERACTIVITY

Explore how agriculture has affected soil and land.

Erosion Without soil, life on land could not exist. Soil takes hundreds of years to form. Therefore, every effort must be made to protect Earth's soil. Sometimes, natural forces cause soil loss. Forces such as wind, water, and ice move particles of rocks or soil through a process called **erosion**.

Usually, plant roots growing deep into the soil help to hold it in place. Human activities such as mining, logging, construction, and farming increase erosion by taking away these plants and exposing the soil to wind and precipitation. With nothing to anchor them in place, soil particles easily move. Human activities cause erosion to happen at a much faster rate than naturally-ocurring processes do. **Figure 4** shows some examples of natural and human-caused erosion.

Erosion

Figure 4 Check the image that shows naturally-ocurring erosion. CCC Cause and Effect How did different events cause these areas to form?

Nutrient Depletion Plants make their own food through photosynthesis, but they need to take in nutrients such as nitrogen and phosphorus. Decomposers in the soil break down dead organisms, which add these and other nutrients to the soil. If a farmer plants the same crops in a field every year, the crops may use more nutrients than decomposers can supply. This leads to nutrient depletion; the soil is not adequately fertile. Nutrient depletion can directly affect humans. Crops grown in nutrient-poor soil often have less nutritional value.

Farmers add fertilizers to the soil to provide the needed nutrients. This can produce abundant, nutritious crops, but can also cause damage when rain carries the fertilizers into nearby bodies of water. Farmers often manage the soil by allowing it to sit for a season or two in between plantings. This allows the remnant crops to decompose, which replenishes the soil with nutrients.

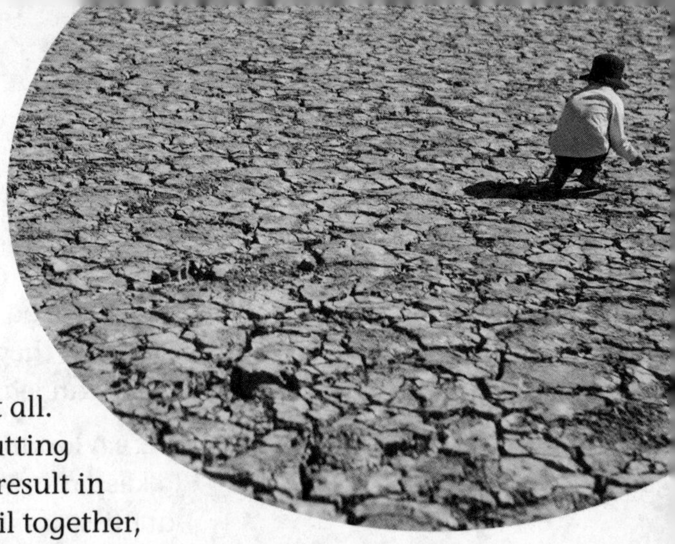

Desertification When the soil in a once-fertile area loses its moisture and nutrients, the area can become a desert. The advance of desert-like conditions into areas that were previously fertile is called **desertification**.

One cause of moisture loss is drought. During these prolonged periods of low precipitation, plants, including crops, will dry up or not grow at all. Allowing livestock to overgraze grasslands and cutting down trees without replanting the area can also result in desertification. Without plant roots to hold the soil together, erosion of fertile topsoil will occur. Plant roots also carry water deeper into the soil, so it doesn't dry out as quickly.

From 2010 to 2016, the state of California experienced a severe drought. The people of California took preventive actions to avoid desertification. The state introduced mandatory water restrictions and regulations on the use of groundwater. Farmers also reduced the growing of certain crops to lessen the need for extensive irrigation.

Desertification

Figure 5 Crops cannot grow in arid soil. As a result, many people are unable to grow their own food and must move to a town or city where food is available.

READING CHECK **Translate Information** What most likely occurred to cause the conditions in **Figure 5**?

Math Toolbox

Causes of Land Degradation

Scientists estimate that there are at least 79.5 million hectares of degraded land in North America. The graph shows the causes of land degradation by percentage.

Analyze Proportional Relationships How many more hectares were degraded by agricultural activities than by deforestation? Show your work.

Degraded Land in North America

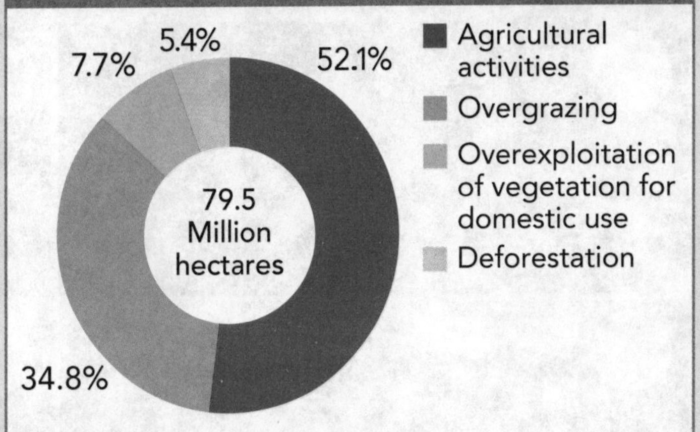

SOURCE: United Nations Environment Programme

VIDEO

Learn more about what happens when you throw something "away."

Landfills

When you are asked to take out the garbage, where does it go once it leaves your curb? Today much of the solid waste, construction debris, and agricultural and industrial waste we produce is buried in holes called landfills. These areas are designed to protect the surrounding areas from soil and water pollution. If landfills are not managed correctly, they can harm the environment. Materials from waste can leak into the groundwater, making it toxic to drink.

Once a landfill is full, it is covered with soil heavy in clay to keep rainwater from entering the waste. These "capped" landfills can be reclaimed as locations for parks and sports arenas, but they cannot be used for housing or agriculture.

Land Reclamation

It is sometimes possible to restore soil that has been lost to erosion, mining, or waste disposal. This process of restoring land to a more productive state is called land reclamation. Land reclamation could involve trucking in soil from another area. Sometimes mine operations reclaim land by storing the soil that they remove from a site, then putting it back after mining operations cease. Land reclamation can restore farming areas as well as wildlife habitats (see **Figure 6**).

Land reclamation is very expensive and difficult. It is much harder to bring back damaged land than it is to protect and conserve those resources before they become damaged.

READING CHECK **Draw Evidence** How do human actions impact land? Give one positive and one negative impact.

....

....

....

....

Land Reclamation

Figure 6 These pictures show an area that was reclaimed to include a stream. Add numbers to put these pictures in chronological order.

SEP Construct Explanations Explain what happened to the land in these pictures.

....

....

....

....

....

Wetlands

A wetland is an area in which water covers the soil for all or most of the year. They are found in all climates and on all continents except Antarctica. Other terms you may have heard for wetland include bog, marsh, and swamp.

Figure 7 shows how wetlands support both land and aquatic ecosystems. They serve as breeding and nursery grounds for many organisms, provide habitats to many species of plants, and are feeding sites for many birds, mammals, and fish.

Human activities have greatly impacted wetlands. The development of homes, businesses, and roads requires controlling the flow of water through these areas. But altering the flow of water in a wetland changes the ecosystem and destroys unique habitats. It can also lead to increases in erosion, flooding, and the pollution of water and soil. Wetland soil acts as a natural "sponge" to collect water. Without wetlands, the large amounts of rain produced by severe storms, such as hurricanes, would flow directly into rivers or populated areas. Wetlands help to protect the quality of water by trapping excess sediments and pollutants before they reach the groundwater or waterways.

READING CHECK **Integrate With Visuals** How would filling in a wetland to create a field affect the surrounding environment?

....

....

....

Literacy Connection

Cite Textual Evidence
When you write an argument, it should be based on factual evidence, not opinions. As you read, underline the evidence that supports the idea that human activities negatively affect the land.

How Wetlands Work

Figure 7 Wetland plants, soil, and bacteria protect surrounding aspects. Circle the aspects of the wetland that provide benefits to humans.

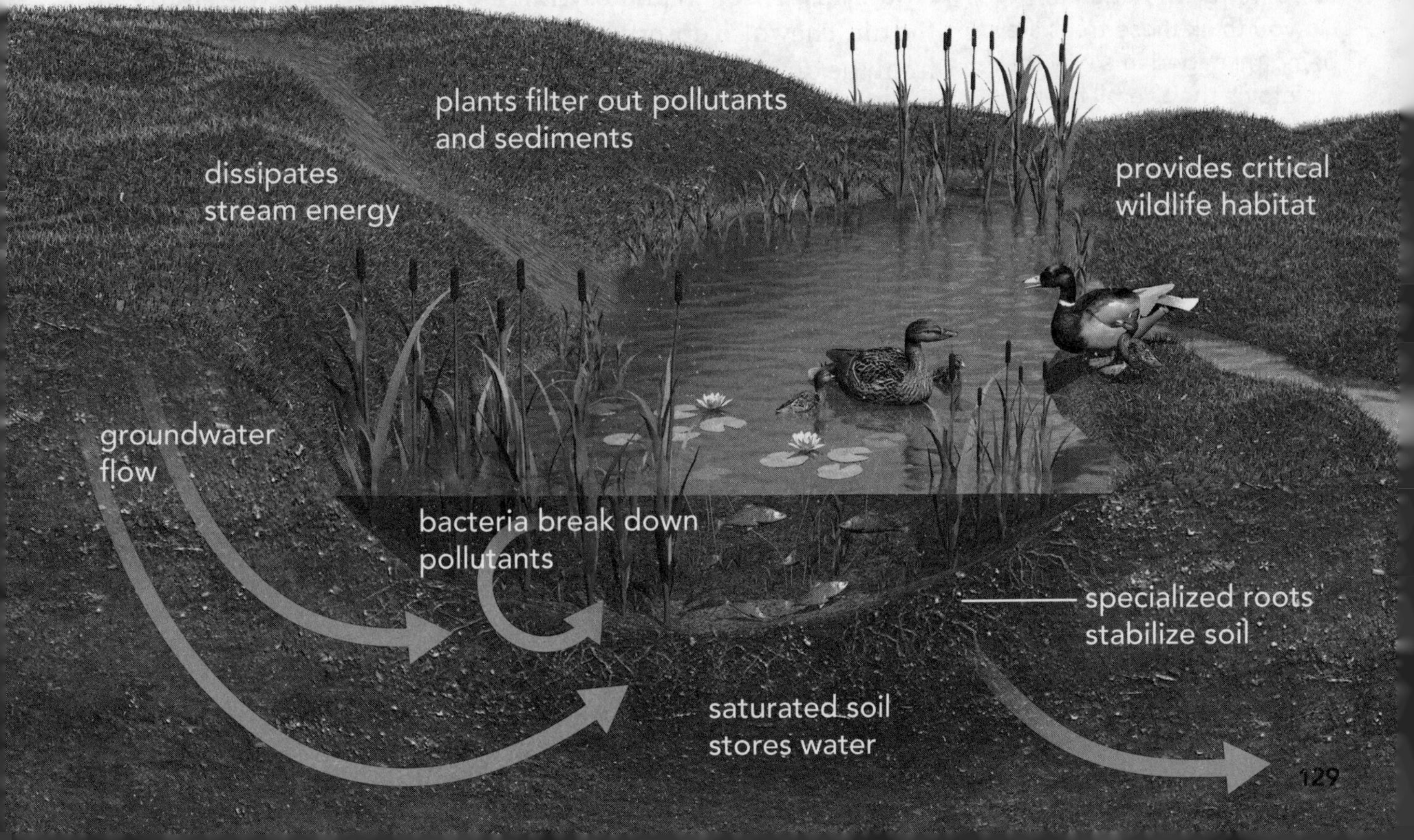

Sustainability
Figure 8 Examine the forest closely. Notice the amount of deforestation.

SEP Engage in Argument
Do you think these trees are being managed in a way that maintains the overall health of the forest? Explain.

Sustainable Forest Management

Trees and other plants, like the ones in **Figure 8**, are important land resources. They provide food and shelter for many organisms. Through photosynthesis, they release oxygen into the air. They also absorb carbon dioxide and other pollutants from the air. Their roots absorb rainwater and hold the soil together, which helps to prevent erosion and flooding.

Many products are made from the fruit, seeds, and other parts of forest plants. The wood from some trees is used for making paper, and other trees are used to build homes and furniture. Fruits and seeds from trees provide food for people and animals.

All trees, whether cultivated by farmers or growing in the wild, need to be protected and managed sustainably. Because we can plant trees to replace trees that are cut down, forests can be renewable resources. How long a resource lasts depends on how people use it. **Sustainable** use of a resource means using it in ways that maintain the resource for all future generations. Replacing and reserving trees are important ways to sustain a forest. These practices ensure that the ecosystem remains healthy and that people can still depend on forests for the resources they need.

Logging Methods There are two main methods of logging, or cutting down trees: clear-cutting and selective cutting, illustrated in **Figure 9**. Clear-cutting is the process of cutting down all the trees in an area at once. Selective cutting is the process of cutting down only some trees in a forest and leaving a mix of tree sizes and species behind.

Clear-cutting is usually faster and less expensive than selective cutting. However, selective cutting is less damaging to the forest ecosystem than clear-cutting. When a forest is cleared, all the animals' habitats are suddenly gone. Without the protection of the trees, the soil is more easily eroded by wind and rain. The soil can then be blown or washed away and into nearby streams, harming aquatic ecosystems.

Selective cutting takes much longer, as the loggers need to actively choose which trees will come down and which will remain. It is more dangerous for loggers to selectively cut trees because they have to move heavy equipment and logs around the remaining trees.

Logging Methods

Figure 9 ✎ Clear-cutting and selective cutting are two methods of tree harvesting. Label each method shown as clear-cutting or selective cutting.

INTERACTIVITY

Create a solution for a controversial use of land.

Write About It Collect information about how trees in your state are managed. In your science notebook, write an argument from the position of a conservation organization that says the yield is too high and needs to be reduced.

Sustainable Forestry

Sustainable Forestry Forests can be managed to provide a sustainable yield. A sustainable yield is the amount of a renewable resource that can be harvested regularly without reducing the future supply. Planting one tree to replace each one that is cut down ensures that the overall yield remains constant.

In sustainable forestry, after trees are harvested, young trees are planted, as shown in **Figure 10**. Trees must be planted frequently enough to maintain a constant supply. Forests containing fast-growing tree species, such as pines, can be harvested and replanted every 20 to 30 years. Forests containing slower-growing species, such as hickory, oak, and cherry, may be harvested only every 40 to 100 years. One sustainable approach is to log small patches within a forest, so different sections can be harvested every year.

READING CHECK **Draw Evidence** Why is it important to manage forests so that their yield is sustainable?

Replanting

Figure 10 Planting another generation of trees is one technique of sustainable forestry.

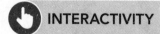

LESSON 3 Check

MS-ESS3-4

1. **Communicate** What are three different ways land is used as a resource?

2. **SEP Cite Evidence** Why are trees considered a renewable resource?

3. **Construct Arguments** How do poor farming methods impact Earth?

4. **SEP Evaluate Evidence** Give evidence to defend the claim that it is environmentally unsound to change the flow of water in a wetland.

5. **CCC Cause and Effect** How does the presence of trees maintain the stability of land resources?

Quest CHECK-IN

In this lesson, you learned about natural resources found on land and their importance to Earth's systems. You also learned how humans positively and negatively affect these resources.

SEP Evaluate Evidence Why is it important to conserve resources and not simply use them in the most convenient way?

INTERACTIVITY

Life of a Landfill

Go online to learn about where to site a landfill and how a landfill is constructed.

Case Study

MS-ESS3-4

Nothing Goes TO WASTE

One city in Texas is making sure nothing in its sewers goes to waste. The Hornsby Bend Biosolids Management Plant in Austin, Texas, recycles sewage into biosolids. Biosolids are rich in nutrients, so they make great soil and fertilizer.

Every day, Hornsby Bend receives about a million gallons of sewage solids from Austin's water treatment plants, where the sewage is separated from the wastewater. The sewage is screened, and then flows into tanks where bacteria get to work feeding on it. The bacteria break the sewage down, killing most disease organisms as they go. This process is actually not that different from how the human digestive system works. After about 60 days, the sewage is converted into biosolids.

Hornsby Bend also collects Austin's yard trimmings and mixes these with the biosolids to make nutrient-rich soil. The plant sends some soil to nearby farmers who enhance their existing soil with the mix. The rest is used to supplement the soil of Austin's public lawns, gardens, parks, and golf courses. Instead of going to an expensive landfill, the biosolids are put to good use.

Hornsby Bend is also a bird sanctuary with more than 350 types of birds.

All of the water used at the treatment plant is recycled, too. Some of it goes to irrigate the nearby farmland, and the rest goes to ponds at the treatment plant. The nutrient-rich pond water has still another benefit: the treatment plant is also a bird sanctuary. Hornsby Bend is one of the best birding sites in the state. Thanks to the Hornsby Bend Biosolids Management Plant, Austin's waste doesn't go to waste.

Use the table to answer the following questions.

Safe Levels of Pollutants in Soil on Farms Fertilized with Biosolids

Pollutant	Risk Assessment Acceptable Soil Concentration (mg/kg-soil)
Arsenic	23.5
Cadmium	19.7
Copper	769.0
Lead	161.0
Mercury	8.6
Nickel	228.0
Selenium	50.21
Zinc	1,454.0

SOURCE: Environmental Protection Agency

1. **CCC Scale, Proportion, and Quantity** One sample of biosolids contains 18.2 mg/kg mercury, 22.5 mg/kg arsenic, and 29.7 mg/kg cadmium. Are these biosolids safe to use? Why or why not?

....

....

2. **SEP Use Mathematics** A biosolids plant is picking up waste from a new factory. The level of lead in the plant's biosolids had been 121 mg/kg. With the waste from the new factory, the lead has increased 12 percent. Calculate the new lead level to determine if the biosolid is still safe to use on farmland.

....

....

....

3. **Connect to Society** Why is a chart like this important?

....

....

....

4. **SEP Engage in Argument** Are biosolids safe to use in agriculture? Make an argument to support your answer.

....

....

....

....

LESSON

4 Water Pollution

Guiding Questions

- Why is fresh water such a limited resource within Earth's systems?
- How do certain human activities cause freshwater and ocean pollution?
- What methods have humans developed to reduce freshwater and ocean pollution?

Connections

Literacy Draw Evidence

Math Analyze Proportional Relationships

MS-ESS3-4

HANDS-ON LAB

uInvestigate Practice different techniques for cleaning up oil spills.

Vocabulary

sewage
sediment
thermal pollution

Academic Vocabulary

distributed

Connect It!

Circle the areas in the photo that contain fresh water.

SEP Provide Evidence Why is water an important resource?

....

....

Water as a Resource

Water is essential for life on Earth. Most of Earth's surface is covered by some form of water, as shown in **Figure 1**. It serves as a habitat for many species. Approximately 97 percent of the water on Earth is undrinkable because it contains salt. Of the remaining 3 percent, most is frozen solid in the polar ice sheets. That leaves less than 1 percent of all the water on the planet as drinkable.

Earth's water is a renewable resource, but fresh water is a limited resource. Recall that water continually moves between the atmosphere and Earth's surface in the water cycle. However, there is not always enough water in a given place at a given time. When water usage is poorly managed, it can lead to water shortages.

The limited supply of fresh water is not evenly **distributed** around the world. Some areas have an abundant supply, while in others it is quite scarce. Water scarcity occurs when there is not enough water to meet demand. It can be caused by droughts, low levels of groundwater, unequal water distribution, or environmental factors such as water pollution. An area faces water scarcity when the water supply is less than 1,000 cubic meters per person.

READING CHECK **Draw Evidence** Why is water a limited resource even though it is renewable?

....

....

Write About It What do you think the world's freshwater supply will look like in another 100 years? In your science notebook, describe how and why our water supply might change.

Academic Vocabulary

What are some items that might get distributed? Can you think of any examples from your school?

....

....

Where is the Fresh Water?

Figure 1 Drinkable fresh water makes up less than one percent of the water on Earth.

Water Pollution

Figure 2 Most sources of freshwater pollution come from human activities.

1. Claim Mark any examples of nonpoint sources of pollution with a check mark. Mark any examples of point sources of pollution with an X.
2. Evidence What evidence did you use to identify your claims?

....

....

3. Reasoning Explain how your evidence supports your claim.

....

....

....

....

....

....

....

Sources of Freshwater Pollution

With fresh water being so limited, any form of pollution entering the water supply can have drastic results. Most water pollution is directly linked to human activities, as shown in **Figure 2**. Wastes from farming, households, industry, and mining can end up in the water supply. Water pollutants may be point or nonpoint sources, depending on how they enter the water. A point source for water pollution could be a factory output pipe or a leaking landfill. Nonpoint pollution sources could be farm pesticides, farm animal wastes, or runoff of salt and chemicals from roads.

Farming Wastes Animal wastes, fertilizers, and pesticides are sources of pollution. When it rains, animal wastes, fertilizers, and pesticides can wash away into nearby water sources and eventually the ocean. These pollutants can cause overgrowths of algae. The algae block light and deplete the water of oxygen, killing everything else in the water.

Household Pollutants The water and human wastes that are washed down sinks, showers, and toilets are called **sewage**. Sometimes, the sewage can leak into groundwater before it is treated. Because sewage contains many disease-causing bacteria, people will become ill if they drink or swim in water containing them.

Industrial Wastes The waste products of factories and mines may also pollute the water. Many manufacturing processes use or produce toxic chemicals that need to be disposed of properly. During this disposal, chemicals sometimes leak into the groundwater. Some chemicals, such as heavy metals, build up in the bodies of aquatic organisms, making them and the animals that eat them ill.

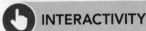

Sediment Erosion carries small particles of rocks and sand from the land into the water. These particles are called **sediment**. Sediment can cover up sources of food, nests, and eggs of aquatic organisms. Sediment also blocks sunlight, which prevents photosynthesis in plants.

Heat When heat negatively affects bodies of water, it is known as **thermal pollution**. Factories and power plants use water to cool their machinery. This heated water is often discharged back into the environment. Because it is so hot, the water can kill organisms.

Oil and Gasoline Oil and gasoline are often transported in long pipelines, either underground or above ground. Sometimes these pipelines leak into rivers, streams, or groundwater. When oil and gasoline pollute the water, it can take many years for the ecosystem to recover. Oil is difficult to collect and penetrates much of the soil in the area. It also affects the plants that grow along the water's edge. Spilled oil also has both direct and indirect effects on wildlife. It coats their fur or feathers and causes skin irritation, at the least. It kills their food sources as well.

Oil and gasoline leaks from underground storage tanks are also sources of water pollution. These leaks can seep into the groundwater, making it unfit to drink.

READING CHECK **Draw Evidence** Does most water pollution happen as a result of human activities? Explain.

....

....

....

INTERACTIVITY

Examine how pollution affects the water cycle.

Literacy Connection

Draw Evidence Sometimes you need to draw evidence to support your analysis of a certain topic. Reread the previous page and the current page. As you read, underline any pieces of evidence that support the idea that most water pollution is directly linked to human activities.

Sources of Ocean Pollution

INTERACTIVITY

Investigate whether or not human activity is responsible for odd mutations found in frogs.

It was once thought that "the solution to pollution is dilution." This meant that whatever was dumped into the ocean would just spread out and eventually go away. Today, we know that isn't true. Dumping large amounts of wastes into the ocean threatens marine organisms and the overall functioning of Earth's systems.

Natural Occurrences There are some pollutants that occur naturally. These include freshwater runoff from land after heavy rains. When this freshwater enters the ocean, the salinity drops. Some organisms cannot tolerate this, so they either move to saltier waters or die.

Human Activities Most ocean pollution is related to human activities. The chemicals, sewage, and other wastes that are dumped into the ocean come from human sources. Fertilizers and pesticides from farms run off and eventually make it to the ocean. When enough of these build up, they can create an ocean dead zone—an area where nothing can live because there is not enough oxygen in the water.

Trash Trash and plastic, as shown in **Figure 3**, are hazardous to marine animals. For example, sea turtles often mistake plastic bags floating in the water for jellyfish. Once consumed, the bags clog up the intestines of the turtles. Fishing line and nets can catch swimming animals and entangle them. One area in the Pacific Ocean contains about 2 million bits of plastic per square mile. When sea creatures consume these tiny pieces, they can become ill and die. The plastic bits can also cause health problems for animals higher up in the food chain that eat small animals with plastic inside of them.

Effects of Pollution

Figure 3 This plastic and trash was recovered from the ocean, where it can harm organisms.

SEP Design Solutions What are some ways humans can reduce the amount of plastic that ends up in the ocean?

....

....

....

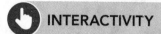

Math Toolbox

Sources of Oil Pollution

There are different ways for oil to pollute the ocean.

1. **Construct Graphs** Create a bar graph of the data.
2. **Analyze Proportional Relationships** How many times greater is the amount of pollution caused by runoff than that caused by oil spills?

....

....

....

Source of Oil Pollution	Oil Pollution (millions of liters)
Offshore drilling	80
Land runoff	1,375
Natural seeps	240
Ship repair	510
Oil spills	125

Oil Spills Oil that is accidentally spilled into the ocean is also a large source of pollution. Oil rigs that drill for oil sometimes leak into the ocean. This oil coats the feathers of birds, reducing their ability to stay warm. Oil also harms animals if they swallow it. Pollutants can build up in organisms' bodies and poison people or other marine life that feed on them.

VIDEO

Explore the misconception that the ocean cannot be harmed because it is so vast.

Aquaculture The practice of raising fish and other water-dwelling organisms for food is called aquaculture. Fish are often raised in artificial ponds and bays that replace and destroy natural habitats, such as salt marshes. The farms can cause pollution and spread diseases into wild fish populations.

READING CHECK **Determine Conclusions** How can you help to reduce the amount of pollution that ends up in the ocean?

....

....

....

....

HANDS-ON LAB

Investigate Practice different techniques for cleaning up oil spills.

INTERACTIVITY

Take a closer look at water pollution and solutions.

Reducing Water Pollution

Everyone needs clean water. But how can the pollution that currently enters the water be reduced, and what efforts can be made to prevent future pollution?

The United States and other countries have laws that regulate water-polluting substances. These laws mandate the types and amounts of substances that can be dumped into the water. While these laws help, the keys to keeping water clean are the prevention of oil and gasoline spills, effective cleanup of spills, proper sewage treatment, and reduction of pollutants.

Protecting the Ocean The ocean is a continuous body of water. Because no one country owns the ocean, it is every nation's responsibility to do whatever it can to ensure the water stays clean. To help protect the ocean, the United Nations set up regulations that say the first 22 kilometers from the coast are controlled by the nation that owns that coast. That nation also controls any resources, such as oil, natural gas, and fish, that are found out to 370 km.

Many nations are helping to protect the ocean by limiting how much can be taken from it and by establishing marine protected areas (MPAs). They also are working to reduce the amount of pollution in their coastal waters.

Cleaning Oil Spills Oil spills, such as the one in **Figure 4**, are one of the worst environmental hazards that can occur. While nature can clean small amounts of oil from the water, large spills such as the Deepwater Horizon oil spill are too much to handle. The bacteria that are able to digest oil cannot keep up with the volume of oil that is released in such a spill. Boats deploy skimming devices to collect floating oil, and barriers are set up to absorb or block oil before it reaches the shore. Chemical dispersants are also sprayed into the water to break up the oil. Cleanup of a major oil spill in the ocean can take many years.

Deepwater Horizon Disaster

Figure 4 In 2010, an oil rig in the Gulf of Mexico exploded, leaving an oil well wide open on the ocean floor. In the following days, 210 million gallons of crude oil spilled into the Gulf.

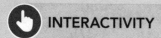

Improved Farming Methods Modern farming practices reduce water pollution. Formerly, farmers would leave fields bare in winter, allowing soil and fertilizers to wash into streams. It was also common to use large amounts of pesticides, herbicides, and fungicides. These chemicals would run off into streams, polluting the water and killing organisms. Today, farmers can reduce erosion and pollution by leaving stalks in the field or planting winter grasses that hold the soil and nutrients in place. Farmers also treat their land with a smaller amount of chemicals, and find natural predators to combat pests.

Reducing Pollutants Another way to protect Earth's waters is to reduce the amount of pollution that is created. Instead of dumping waste products directly into the environment, manufacturers can recycle them. By turning waste products into new things, the companies may even save money. Another method to reduce waste is to change the way materials are produced. Factories can eliminate the use of non-recyclable materials. By figuring out more environmentally-friendly manufacturing methods, they may make less total waste or less hazardous waste.

You can help to prevent water pollution in your home. Common household water pollutants include paints, paint thinner, motor oil, and garden chemicals. Instead of dumping these into the environment, save these materials for your community's hazardous waste collection day (**Figure 5**), or take them to a specialized facility for such wastes.

Hazardous Waste

Figure 5 Many towns and cities have special recycling centers that provide safe and proper disposal of household chemicals, such as paint and cleaning supplies.

READING CHECK **Write Explanatory Texts** What can your community do to reduce water pollution?

....

....

....

Plan It

Reducing Waste in Factories

Many factories are "going green" and changing the way they manufacture products to create less waste. Suppose there is a manufacturing company in your community that is not reducing its waste.

Construct Arguments Come up with a solution to your community's problem. Plan a presentation to convince the factory owners to "go green." How might changing their policy benefit both the community and the factory? How will making these changes impact the environment?

LESSON 4 Check

MS-ESS3-4

1. **SEP Construct Explanations** Why is it so important for sources of fresh water to be protected?

2. **CCC Cause and Effect** How do farming methods cause water pollution?

3. **SEP Provide Evidence** What evidence suggests that factories sometimes cause water pollution?

4. **CCC Analyze Systems** How does water pollution in one area affect water and organisms elsewhere?

5. **Construct Arguments** Write an argument to defend the idea that oil spills are the worst environmental hazard.

Quest CHECK-IN

In this lesson, you learned why fresh water is a limited resource within Earth's systems. You also discovered how human activities lead to water pollution and how humans can reduce freshwater and ocean pollution.

CCC Analyze Systems Why is it important to consider the effects of waste disposal on water sources?

INTERACTIVITY

Reducing Waste

Go online to determine how everyone at your school can work together to reduce wastes and help the environment. Then make a plan to reduce the trash output at your school.

MS-ESS3-4

FROM WASTEWATER TO Tap Water

VIDEO
Walk through the water treatment process.

Fresh water is a precious resource on Earth, so we reuse every drop we can. Wastewater from homes and businesses ends up being recycled for irrigation, manufacturing, and replenishing aquatic ecosystems. But how do you recycle wastewater into drinking water? You engineer it!

The Challenge: To treat wastewater so it can return to the water supply.

Phenomenon In San Diego, California, the Point Loma Wastewater Treatment plant treats wastewater and makes it safe to drink, but it takes several steps. First, water from the sewer system passes through screens that filter out large particles. Next, the water flows into tanks where gravity separates solid waste from the water. Heavy solids sink to the bottom.

The water then flows to a second set of tanks where bacteria digest waste that's still in the water. Then the water is left to settle one more time and the last sediments are removed.

Following that, the water goes through a series of filters to get rid of any small solids or harmful microorganisms. The last step is disinfection using chlorine and UV light. Finally, this water will spend about six months in storage before it arrives at a tap.

DESIGN CHALLENGE

Can you design a model for recycling wastewater or rainwater from your home or school? Go to the Engineering Design Notebook to find out!

A typical wastewater plant has many, many tanks.

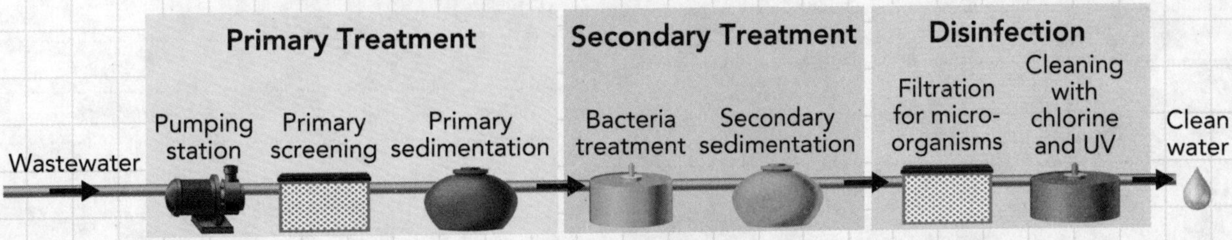

TOPIC 3 Review and Assess

1 Population Growth and Resource Consumption

MS-ESS3-4

1. Rather than increasing at a constant rate, human population growth in recent decades has increased more and more rapidly over time. This rate of change is called
   A. excessive growth.
   B. exponential growth.
   C. reverse growth.
   D. zero growth.

2. For the global population growth rate to reach zero, the number of births would have to be

   ....

   ....

3. **Connect to Society** Beginning around 1750, the global human population began to grow at a much faster rate than it had in the years before this time. What caused this change in the population growth rate?

   ....

   ....

   ....

   ....

   ....

4. **CCC Cause and Effect** How does a growing human population affect Earth's resources?

   ....

   ....

   ....

   ....

   ....

   ....

   ....

2 Air Pollution

MS-ESS3-4

5. **Evaluate Reasoning** A classmate tells you that the good thing about renewable resources like trees is that you can use them and use them and they will never run out. What is your classmate misunderstanding about renewable resources?

   ....

   ....

   ....

   ....

   ....

   ....

6. Which is a natural source of air pollution?
   A. volcanoes
   B. carbon monoxide
   C. smog
   D. ozone layer

7. Automobiles contribute to air pollution by
   A. increasing methane.
   B. decreasing oxygen.
   C. decreasing carbon dioxide.
   D. increasing carbon dioxide.

8. As human populations continue to increase, the demand for natural resources

   ....

9. **SEP Construct Explanations** Why did it take international efforts to reduce the impact of air pollution on the ozone layer?

   ....

   ....

   ....

   ....

   ....

   ....

ASSESSMENT

Evaluate your understanding by taking a Topic Test.

3 Impacts on Land

MS-ESS3-4

10. What is the difference between point and nonpoint sources of water pollution?

A. Point sources can be directly identified, and nonpoint cannot.

B. Point sources involve solid wastes, and nonpoint sources are liquids.

C. Point sources contain animal wastes, while nonpoint sources are human-made chemicals.

D. Point sources break down easily, while non-point sources break down over a long time.

11. Which of these changes can lead to desertification?

A. reduced air quality

B. increased plant life

C. reduced moisture

D. increased nutrient levels

12. What impact does logging have on the land?

A. increased nutrients

B. increased erosion

C. accelerated recycling of organic matter

D. accelerated soil deposition

13. Changing the flow of water, such as filling in a wetland for development, impacts the environment by

A. increasing desertification.

B. increasing flooding and pollution.

C. decreasing erosion.

D. decreasing nutrient depletion.

14. As human populations increase, there is a higher demand for ...., the use of land to produce food.

15. When natural forces such as wind, water, and ice move particles of rocks or soil, the process is called ....

4 Water Pollution

MS-ESS3-4

16. Construct Arguments What evidence could be used in an argument against planting the same crop in the same field year after year?

....

....

....

....

....

....

....

....

17. Which of these is a source of human-made ocean pollution?

A. fresh water

B. ozone

C. plastics

D. sediment

18. Construct an Argument What evidence supports the idea that construction companies should implement protocols that reduce the amount of sediment that runs off from land into the water?

....

....

....

....

....

....

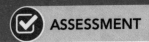

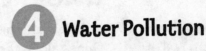

TOPIC 3 Review and Assess

MS-ESS3-4

Evidence-Based Assessment

Lange's metalmark butterfly

In 1976, ecologists made a disturbing discovery in the Antioch Dunes along the banks of the San Joaquin River in San Francisco. A butterfly, formally observed first in 1939 and only found in the dunes, was going extinct. Known as Lange's metalmark butterfly, it became one of the first insects protected as an endangered species by federal law.

Here are some important facts about the butterfly and its habitat.

- Lange's metalmark butterfly produces one crop of offspring each year, and females only lay their eggs on one species of plant, the naked-stem buckwheat plant.
- The dunes where the butterfly lives formed thousands of years ago, when sand deposited by ancient glaciers was moved and shaped by water and wind.
- When the first American settlers arrived in the early 1800s, the dunes ran along the river for about 3 kilometers (2 miles) and reached over 30 meters (100 feet) high in some places.
- As the population of San Francisco grew, parts of the dunes were leveled and developed for industry. Sand from the dunes was mined to produce bricks and other building materials. The data table shows changes in the population of San Francisco from 1850 to 2000.

San Francisco County Population, 1850–2000

Year	Population	Year	Population
1850	21,000	1930	634,394
1860	56,802	1940	634,536
1870	149,473	1950	775,357
1880	233,959	1960	740,316
1890	298,997	1970	715,674
1900	342,782	1980	678,974
1910	416,912	1990	723,959
1920	506,676	2000	776,733

1. **SEP Analyze Data** Which statement about the trends in San Francisco's population growth is valid?
   - **A.** It dropped for a few decades after 1890, but has grown almost every year since then.
   - **B.** It grew slowly each year until 1930, when the population quickly increased.
   - **C.** It increased steadily each year since 1850.
   - **D.** It grew rapidly in the mid to late 1800s and then again in the 1940s.

2. **CCC Cause and Effect** How would mining and extracting sand affect plants that live in the dunes, like the naked-stem buckwheat? Based on the population data, when you do think the most sand was removed from the dunes? Explain.

3. **Apply Scientific Reasoning** The remaining sand dunes became a national wildlife refuge in 1980. A few years later, researchers began an annual count of the butterflies. Between 1999 and 2008, the number of butterflies fell steadily. What might account for this continued drop?

4. **SEP Engage in Argument** How could an increase in the human population of San Francisco have impacted the Lange's metalmark butterflies that lived there? Use evidence from the text to support your answer.

Quest FINDINGS

Complete the Quest!

Phenomenon Refine your plan to reduce trash at your school and present the plan.

CCC Cause and Effect We produce a lot of trash that is disposed of in landfills. How would decreasing the trash we generate affect Earth's systems?

INTERACTIVITY

Reflect on Trash Backlash

MS-ESS3-4

Washing Away

How can you demonstrate the impact of **human activity** on **soil erosion?**

Background

Phenomenon A nearby town is considering a developer's plan to turn riverfront property into shops, restaurants, and apartments. The area is now an undisturbed habitat consisting of trees, bushes, and grasses. Almost all of the natural vegetation will be removed during construction. You will be part of a team tasked with providing an environmental impact report to the town board.

In this lab, you will design and conduct an investigation into the impact of vegetation and ground cover on soil erosion. You will test how quickly water runs off soil in different conditions and how much soil is carried away by the water.

Materials

(per group)

- two 2-liter beverage bottles, cut lengthwise to form troughs
- about 4 cups of potting soil, divided in half
- grass or radish seedlings
- 2 large plastic cups
- 1 liter of water
- watering can with rain spout
- stopwatch

RIVERFRONT DEVELOPMENT PLANS

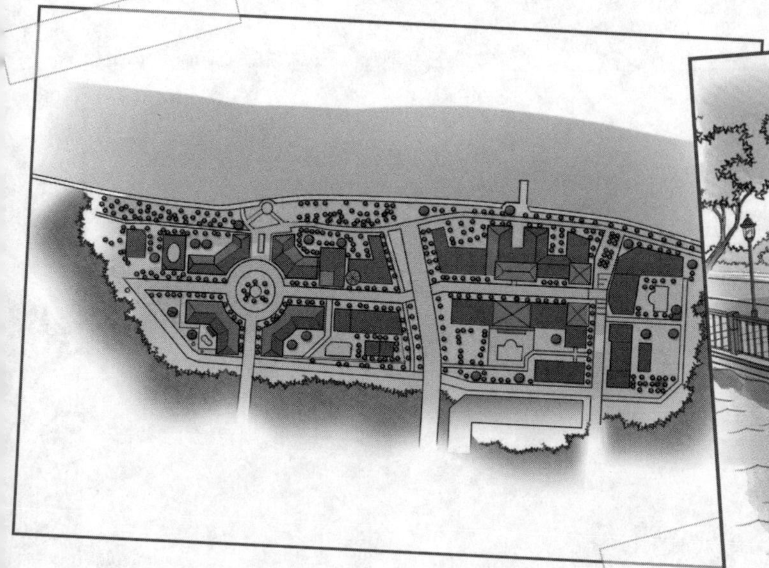

Plan Your Investigation

HANDS-ON LAB

uDemonstrate Go online for a downloadable worksheet of this lab.

- [ ] 1. Work with your partner to design an experimental setup using the materials provided by your teacher. Your experiment must test how fast water runs off the soil and how much soil is carried away in the runoff. As you design your setup, consider the following questions:
    - How would you describe the condition of the riverbank before the proposed construction?
    - How would you describe the condition of the riverbank during the construction?
    - How can you use the materials to model the condition of the riverbank before and during construction?
    - How can you design your setup so that you will be able to measure how fast the water runs off the soil and how much soil is contained in the runoff?
    - What are your dependent variable and independent variable, and the factors you hold constant?
    - How many tests will you run?
    - What observations will you make and what data will you collect?
- [ ] 2. Write a detailed procedure describing how you will investigate the effects of removing vegetation and ground cover on soil erosion. Include any sketches of your setup.
- [ ] 3. After getting teacher approval for your procedure, conduct your investigation.
- [ ] 4. Record your observations and data in the table provided.

Procedure and Sketches

Data Table

Bottle	Water Poured (mL)	Water Captured (mL)	Time (sec)	Observations of Water Collected
Grass and soil				
Soil only				

Analyze and Interpret Data

1. **Compare Data** Review the data you collected and the observations you recorded. How do the results of your tests compare?

2. **Write an Expression** Suppose you were going to graph the results of your investigation. How would you express the independent variable *Water Poured* as a variable? How would you express the results of your dependent variable *Water Captured* as a variable?.

3. **Apply Scientific Reasoning** Based on the results of your investigation, describe how soil erosion might affect the ecology of rivers, lakes, and other bodies of water.

4. **Refine Your Plan** Examine and evaluate the procedures of other teams. Based on what you learned, how might you modify your own procedure to improve the results of your investigation?

5. **SEP Engage in Argument** What would you recommend to the town board? Use the data from your investigation as evidence to justify your claim.

SEP.1, SEP.8

The Meaning of Science

Science Skills

Reflect Think about a time you misplaced something and could not find it. Write a sentence defining the problem. What science skills could you use to solve the problem? Explain how you would use at least three of the skills in the table.

Science is a way of learning about the natural world. It involves asking questions, making predictions, and collecting information to see if the answer is right or wrong.

The table lists some of the skills that scientists use. You use some of these skills every day. For example, you may observe and evaluate your lunch options before choosing what to eat.

Skill	Definition
classifying 	grouping together items that are alike or that have shared characteristics
evaluating	comparing observations and data to reach a conclusion
inferring 	explaining or interpreting observations
investigating	studying or researching a subject to discover facts or to reveal new information
making models 	creating representations of complex objects or processes
observing	using one or more of your senses to gather information
predicting 	making a statement or claim about what will happen based on past experience or evidence

Scientific Attitudes

Curiosity often drives scientists to learn about the world around them. Creativity is useful for coming up with inventive ways to solve problems. Such qualities and attitudes, and the ability to keep an open mind, are essential for scientists.

When sharing results or findings, honesty and ethics are also essential. Ethics refers to rules for knowing right from wrong.

Being skeptical is also important. This means having doubts about things based on past experiences and evidence. Skepticism helps to prevent accepting data and results that may not be true.

Scientists must also avoid bias—likes or dislikes of people, ideas, or things. They must avoid experimental bias, which is a mistake that may make an experiment's preferred outcome more likely.

Make Meaning

Think about a bias the marine biologist in the photo could show that results in paying more or less attention to one kind of organism over others. Make a prediction about how that bias could affect the biologist's survey of the coral reef.

Scientific Reasoning

Scientific reasoning depends on being logical and objective. When you are objective, you use evidence and apply logic to draw conclusions. Being subjective means basing conclusions on personal feelings, biases, or opinions. Subjective reasoning can interfere with science and skew results. Objective reasoning helps scientists use observations to reach conclusions about the natural world.

Scientists use two types of objective reasoning: deductive and inductive. Deductive reasoning involves starting with a general idea or theory and applying it to a situation. For example, the theory of plate tectonics indicates that earthquakes happen mostly where tectonic plates meet. You could then draw the conclusion, or deduce, that California has many earthquakes because tectonic plates meet there.

In inductive reasoning, you make a generalization from a specific observation. When scientists collect data in an experiment and draw a conclusion based on that data, they use inductive reasoning. For example, if fertilizer causes one set of plants to grow faster than another, you might infer that the fertilizer promotes plant growth.

Write About It

Suppose it is raining when you go to sleep one night. When you wake up the next morning, you observe frozen puddles on the ground and icicles on tree branches. Use scientific reasoning to draw a conclusion about the air temperature outside. Support your conclusion using deductive or inductive reasoning.

SEP.1, SEP.2, SEP.3, SEP.4, CCC.4

Science Processes

Scientific Inquiry

Write About It Describe a question that you posed, formally or informally, about an event in your life that you needed to investigate or resolve. Write the hypothesis you developed to answer your question, and describe how you tested the hypothesis.

Scientists contribute to scientific knowledge by conducting investigations and drawing conclusions. The process often begins with an observation that leads to a question, which is then followed by the development of a hypothesis. This is known as scientific inquiry.

One of the first steps in scientific inquiry is asking questions. However, it's important to make a question specific with a narrow focus so the investigation will not be too broad. A biologist may want to know all there is to know about wolves, for example. But a good, focused question for a specific inquiry might be "How many offspring does the average female wolf produce in her lifetime?"

A hypothesis is a possible answer to a scientific question. A hypothesis must be testable. For something to be testable, researchers must be able to carry out an investigation and gather evidence that will either support or disprove the hypothesis.

Scientific Models

Models are tools that scientists use to study phenomena indirectly. A model is any representation of an object or process. Illustrations, dioramas, globes, diagrams, computer programs, and mathematical equations are all examples of scientific models. For example, a diagram of Earth's crust and mantle can help you to picture layers deep below the surface and understand events such as volcanic eruptions.

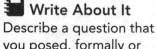

Reflect Identify the benefits and limitations of using a plastic model of DNA, as shown here.

Models also allow scientists to represent objects that are either very large, such as our solar system, or very small, such as a molecule of DNA. Models can also represent processes that occur over a long period of time, such as the changes that have occurred throughout Earth's history.

Models are helpful, but they have limitations. Physical models are not made of the same materials as the objects they represent. Most models of complex objects or processes show only major parts, stages, or relationships. Many details are left out. Therefore, you may not be able to learn as much from models as you would through direct observation.

Science Experiments

An experiment or investigation must be well planned to produce valid results. In planning an experiment, you must identify the independent and dependent variables. You must also do as much as possible to remove the effects of other variables. A controlled experiment is one in which you test only one variable at a time.

For example, suppose you plan a controlled experiment to learn how the type of material affects the speed at which sound waves travel through it. The only variable that should change is the type of material. This way, if the speed of sound changes, you know that it is a result of a change in the material, not another variable such as the thickness of the material or the type of sound used.

You should also remove bias from any investigation. You may inadvertently introduce bias by selecting subjects you like and avoiding those you don't like. Scientists often conduct investigations by taking random samples to avoid ending up with biased results.

Once you plan your investigation and begin to collect data, it's important to record and organize the data. You may wish to use a graph to display and help you to interpret the data.

Communicating is the sharing of ideas and results with others through writing and speaking. Communicating data and conclusions is a central part of science.

Scientists share knowledge, including new findings, theories, and techniques for collecting data. Conferences, journals, and websites help scientists to communicate with each other. Popular media, including newspapers, magazines, and social media sites, help scientists to share their knowledge with nonscientists. However, before the results of investigations are shared and published, other scientists should review the experiment for possible sources of error, such as bias and unsupported conclusions.

Write About It
List four ways you could communicate the results of a scientific study about the health of sea turtles in the Pacific Ocean.

SEP.1, SEP.6, SEP.7, SEP.8

Scientific Knowledge

Scientific Explanations

Suppose you learn that adult flamingos are pink because of the food they eat. This statement is a scientific explanation—it describes how something in nature works or explains why it happens. Scientists from different fields use methods such as researching information, designing experiments, and making models to form scientific explanations. Scientific explanations often result from many years of work and multiple investigations conducted by many scientists.

Write About It
Choose two fields of science that interest you. Describe a method used to develop scientific explanations in each field.

Scientific Theories and Laws

A scientific law is a statement that describes what you can expect to occur every time under a particular set of conditions. A scientific law describes an observed pattern in nature, but it does not attempt to explain it. For example, the law of superposition describes what you can expect to find in terms of the ages of layers of rock. Geologists use this observed pattern to determine the relative ages of sedimentary rock layers. But the law does not explain why the pattern occurs.

By contrast, a scientific theory is a well-tested explanation for a wide range of observations or experimental results. It provides details and describes causes of observed patterns. Something is elevated to a theory only when there is a large body of evidence that supports it. However, a scientific theory can be changed or overturned when new evidence is found.

SEP Construct Explanations Complete the table to compare and contrast a scientific theory and a scientific law.

	Scientific Theory	Scientific Law
Definition		
Does it attempt to explain a pattern observed in nature?		

Analyzing Scientific Explanations

To analyze scientific explanations that you hear on the news or read in a book such as this one, you need scientific literacy. Scientific literacy means understanding scientific terms and principles well enough to ask questions, evaluate information, and make decisions. Scientific reasoning gives you a process to apply. This includes looking for bias and errors in the research, evaluating data, and identifying faulty reasoning. For example, by evaluating how a survey was conducted, you may find a serious flaw in the researchers' methods.

Write About It
Suppose the conservation committee of a town wants to gauge residents' opinions about a proposal to stock the local ponds with fish every spring. The committee pays for a survey to appear on a web site that is popular with people who like to fish. The results of the survey show 78 people in favor of the proposal and two against it. Do you think the survey's results are valid? Explain.

Evidence and Opinions

The basis for scientific explanations is empirical evidence. Empirical evidence includes the data and observations that have been collected through scientific processes. Satellite images, photos, and maps of mountains and volcanoes are all examples of empirical evidence that support a scientific explanation about Earth's tectonic plates. Scientists look for patterns when they analyze this evidence. For example, they might see a pattern that mountains and volcanoes often occur near tectonic plate boundaries.

To evaluate scientific information, you must first distinguish between evidence and opinion. In science, evidence includes objective observations and conclusions that have been repeated. Evidence may or may not support a scientific claim. An opinion is a subjective idea that is formed from evidence, but it cannot be confirmed by evidence.

Make Meaning
Explain what empirical evidence the photograph reveals.

SEP.3, SEP.4

Tools of Science

Measurement

Making measurements using standard units is important in all fields of science. This allows scientists to repeat and reproduce other experiments, as well as to understand the precise meaning of the results of others. Scientists use a measurement system called the International System of Units, or SI.

For each type of measurement, there is a series of units that are greater or less than each other. The unit a scientist uses depends on what is being measured. For example, a geophysicist tracking the movements of tectonic plates may use centimeters, as plates tend to move small amounts each year. Meanwhile, a marine biologist might measure the movement of migrating bluefin tuna on the scale of kilometers.

Units for length, mass, volume, and density are based on powers of ten—a meter is equal to 100 centimeters or 1000 millimeters. Units of time do not follow that pattern. There are 60 seconds in a minute, 60 minutes in an hour, and 24 hours in a day. These units are based on patterns that humans perceived in nature. Units of temperature are based on scales that are set according to observations of nature. For example, 0°C is the temperature at which pure water freezes, and 100°C is the temperature at which it boils.

Write About It
Suppose you are planning an investigation in which you must measure the dimensions of several small mineral samples that fit in your hand. Which metric unit or units will you most likely use? Explain your answer.

Measurement	Metric units
Length or distance	meter (m), kilometer (km), centimeter (cm), millimeter (mm) 1 km = 1,000 m 1 cm = 10 mm 1 m = 100 cm
Mass	kilogram (kg), gram (g), milligram (mg) 1 kg = 1,000 g 1 g = 1,000 mg
Volume	cubic meter (m^3), cubic centimeter (cm^3) 1 m^3 = 1,000,000 cm^3
Density	kilogram per cubic meter (kg/m^3), gram per cubic centimeter (g/cm^3) 1,000 kg/m^3 = 1 g/cm^3
Temperature	degrees Celsius (°C), kelvin (K) 1°C = 273 K
Time	hour (h), minute (m), second (s)

Math Skills

Using numbers to collect and interpret data involves math skills that are essential in science. For example, you use math skills when you estimate the number of birds in an entire forest after counting the actual number of birds in ten trees.

Scientists evaluate measurements and estimates for their precision and accuracy. In science, an accurate measurement is very close to the actual value. Precise measurements are very close, or nearly equal, to each other. Reliable measurements are both accurate and precise. An imprecise value may be a sign of an error in data collection. This kind of anomalous data may be excluded to avoid skewing the data and harming the investigation.

Other math skills include performing specific calculations, such as finding the mean, or average, value in a data set. The mean can be calculated by adding up all of the values in the data set and then dividing that sum by the number of values.

Hour	Number of Ducks Observed at a Pond
1	12
2	10
3	2
4	14
5	13
6	10
7	11

SEP Use Mathematics The data table shows how many ducks were seen at a pond every hour over the course of seven hours. Is there a data point that seems anomalous? If so, cross out that data point. Then, calculate the mean number of ducks on the pond. Round the mean to the nearest whole number.

....

Graphs

Graphs help scientists to interpret data by helping them to find trends or patterns in the data. A line graph displays data that show how one variable (the dependent or outcome variable) changes in response to another (the independent or test variable). The slope and shape of a graph line can reveal patterns and help scientists to make predictions. For example, line graphs can help you to spot patterns of change over time.

Scientists use bar graphs to compare data across categories or subjects that may not affect each other. The heights of the bars make it easy to compare those quantities. A circle graph, also known as a pie chart, shows the proportions of different parts of a whole.

Write About It
You and a friend record the distance you travel every 15 minutes on a one-hour bike trip. Your friend wants to display the data as a circle graph. Explain whether or not this is the best type of graph to display your data. If not, suggest another graph to use.

SEP.1, SEP.2, SEP.3, SEP.6

The Engineering Design Process

Engineers are builders and problem solvers. Chemical engineers experiment with new fuels made from algae. Civil engineers design roadways and bridges. Bioengineers develop medical devices and prosthetics. The common trait among engineers is an ability to identify problems and design solutions to solve them. Engineers use a creative process that relies on scientific methods to help guide them from a concept or idea all the way to the final product.

Define the Problem

To identify or define a problem, different questions need to be asked: *What are the effects of the problem? What are the likely causes? What other factors could be involved?* Sometimes the obvious, immediate cause of a problem may be the result of another problem that may not be immediately apparent. For example, climate change results in different weather patterns, which in turn can affect organisms that live in certain habitats. So engineers must be aware of all the possible effects of potential solutions. Engineers must also take into account how well different solutions deal with the different causes of the problem.

Reflect Write about a problem that you encountered in your life that had both immediate, obvious causes as well as less-obvious and less-immediate ones.

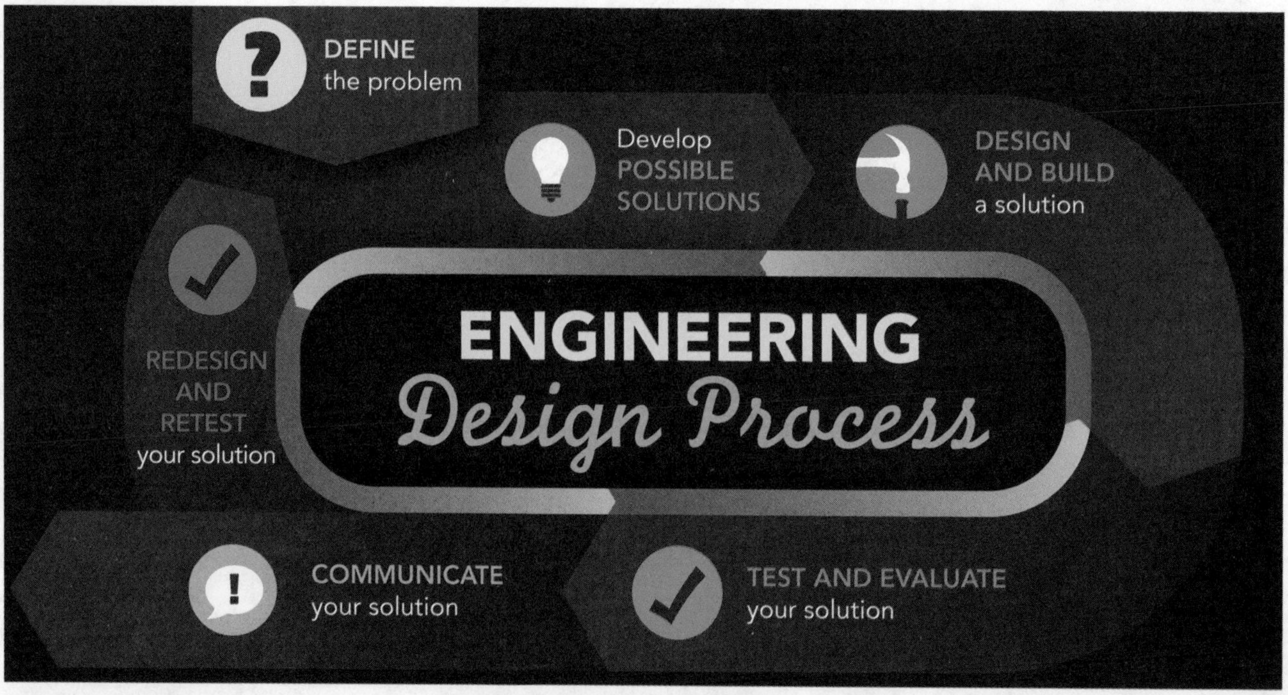

As engineers consider problems and design solutions, they must identify and categorize the criteria and constraints of the project.

Criteria are the factors that must be met or accomplished by the solution. For example, a gardener who wants to protect outdoor plants from deer and rabbits may say that the criteria for the solution are "plants are no longer eaten" and "plant growth is not inhibited in any way." The gardener then knows the plants cannot simply be sealed off from the environment, because the plants will not receive sunlight and water.

The same gardener will likely have constraints on his solution, such as budget for materials and time that is available for working on the project. By setting constraints, a solution can be designed that will be successful without introducing a new set of problems. No one wants to spend $500 on materials to protect $100 worth of tomatoes and cucumbers.

Develop Possible Solutions

After the problem has been identified, and the criteria and constraints identified, an engineer will consider possible solutions. This often involves working in teams with other engineers and designers to brainstorm ideas and research materials that can be used in the design.

It's important for engineers to think creatively and explore all potential solutions. If you wanted to design a bicycle that was safer and easier to ride than a traditional bicycle, then you would want more than just one or two solutions. Having multiple ideas to choose from increases the likelihood that you will develop a solution that meets the criteria and constraints. In addition, different ideas that result from brainstorming can often lead to new and better solutions to an existing problem.

Make Meaning
Using the example of a garden that is vulnerable to wild animals such as deer, make a list of likely constraints on an engineering solution to the problem you identified before. Determine if there are common traits among the constraints, and identify categories for them.

Design a Solution

Engineers then develop the idea that they feel best solves the problem. Once a solution has been chosen, engineers and designers get to work building a model or prototype of the solution. A model may involve sketching on paper or using computer software to construct a model of the solution. A prototype is a working model of the solution.

Building a model or prototype helps an engineer determine whether a solution meets the criteria and stays within the constraints. During this stage of the process, engineers must often deal with new problems and make any necessary adjustments to the model or prototype.

Test and Evaluate a Solution

Make Meaning Think about an aluminum beverage can. What would happen if the price or availability of aluminum changed so much that cans needed to be made of a new material? What would the criteria and constraints be on the development of a new can?

Whether testing a model or a prototype, engineers use scientific processes to evaluate their solutions. Multiple experiments, tests, or trials are conducted, data are evaluated, and results and analyses are communicated. New criteria or constraints may emerge as a result of testing. In most cases, a solution will require some refinement or revision, even if it has been through successful testing. Refining a solution is necessary if there are new constraints, such as less money or available materials. Additional testing may be done to ensure that a solution satisfies local, state, or federal laws or standards.

A naval architect sets up a model to test how the the hull's design responds to waves.

Communicate the Solution

Engineers need to communicate the final design to the people who will manufacture the product. This may include sketches, detailed drawings, computer simulations, and written text. Engineers often provide evidence that was collected during the testing stage. This evidence may include graphs and data tables that support the decisions made for the final design.

If there is feedback about the solution, then the engineers and designers must further refine the solution. This might involve making minor adjustments to the design, or it might mean bigger modifications to the design based on new criteria or constraints. Any changes in the design will require additional testing to make sure that the changes work as intended.

Redesign and Retest the Solution

At different steps in the engineering and design process, a solution usually must be revised and retested. Many designs fail to work perfectly, even after models and prototypes are built, tested, and evaluated. Engineers must be ready to analyze new results and deal with any new problems that arise. Troubleshooting, or fixing design problems, allows engineers to adjust the design to improve on how well the solution meets the need.

SEP Communicate Information Suppose you are an engineer at an aerospace company. Your team is designing a rover to be used on a future NASA space mission. A family member doesn't understand why so much of your team's time is taken up with testing and retesting the rover design. What are three things you would tell your relative to explain why testing and retesting are so important to the engineering and design process?

....

....

....

....

....

....

....

....

....

APPENDIX A

Safety Symbols

These symbols warn of possible dangers in the laboratory and remind you to work carefully.

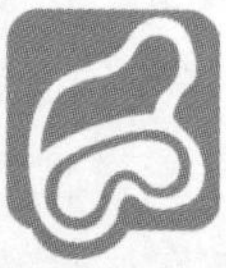

Safety Goggles Wear safety goggles to protect your eyes in any activity involving chemicals, flames or heating, or glassware.

Lab Apron Wear a laboratory apron to protect your skin and clothing from damage.

Breakage Handle breakable materials, such as glassware, with care. Do not touch broken glassware.

Heat-Resistant Gloves Use an oven mitt or other hand protection when handling hot materials, such as hot plates or hot glassware.

Plastic Gloves Wear disposable plastic gloves when working with harmful chemicals and organisms. Keep your hands away from your face, and dispose of the gloves according to your teacher's instructions.

Heating Use a clamp or tongs to pick up hot glassware. Do not touch hot objects with your bare hands.

Flames Before you work with flames, tie back loose hair and clothing. Follow your teacher's instructions about lighting and extinguishing flames.

No Flames When using flammable materials, make sure there are no flames, sparks, or other exposed heat sources present.

Corrosive Chemical Avoid getting acid or other corrosive chemicals on your skin or clothing or in your eyes. Do not inhale the vapors. Wash your hands after the activity.

Poison Do not let any poisonous chemical come into contact with your skin, and do not inhale its vapors. Wash your hands when you are finished with the activity.

Fumes Work in a well-ventilated area when harmful vapors may be involved. Avoid inhaling vapors directly. Test an odor only when directed to do so by your teacher, and use a wafting motion to direct the vapor toward your nose.

Sharp Object Scissors, scalpels, knives, needles, pins, and tacks can cut your skin. Always direct a sharp edge or point away from yourself and others.

Animal Safety Treat live or preserved animals or animal parts with care to avoid harming the animals or yourself. Wash your hands when you are finished with the activity.

Plant Safety Handle plants only as directed by your teacher. If you are allergic to certain plants, tell your teacher; do not do an activity involving those plants. Avoid touching harmful plants such as poison ivy. Wash your hands when you are finished with the activity.

Electric Shock To avoid electric shock, never use electrical equipment around water, when the equipment is wet, or when your hands are wet. Be sure cords are untangled and cannot trip anyone. Unplug equipment not in use.

Physical Safety When an experiment involves physical activity, avoid injuring yourself or others. Alert your teacher if there is any reason you should not participate.

Disposal Dispose of chemicals and other laboratory materials safely. Follow the instructions from your teacher.

Hand Washing Wash your hands thoroughly when finished with an activity. Use soap and warm water. Rinse well.

General Safety Awareness When this symbol appears, follow the instructions provided. When you are asked to develop your own procedure in a lab, have your teacher approve your plan.

APPENDIX B

Using a Laboratory Balance

The laboratory balance is an important tool in scientific investigations. Different kinds of balances are used in the laboratory to determine the masses and weights of objects. You can use a triple-beam balance to determine the masses of materials that you study or experiment with in the laboratory. An electronic balance, unlike a triple-beam balance, is used to measure the weights of materials.

The triple-beam balance that you may use in your science class is probably similar to the balance depicted in this Appendix. To use the balance properly, you should learn the name, location, and function of each part of the balance.

Triple-Beam Balance

The triple-beam balance is a single-pan balance with three beams calibrated in grams. The back, or 100-gram, beam is divided into ten units of 10 grams each. The middle, or 500-gram, beam is divided into five units of 100 grams each. The front, or 10-gram, beam is divided into ten units of 1 gram each. Each gram on the front beam is further divided into units of 0.1 gram.

Apply Concepts What is the greatest mass you could find with the triple-beam balance in the picture?

....

Calculate What is the mass of the apple in the picture?

....

The following procedure can be used to find the mass of an object with a triple-beam balance:

1. Place the object on the pan.
2. Move the rider on the middle beam notch by notch until the horizontal pointer on the right drops below zero. Move the rider back one notch.
3. Move the rider on the back beam notch by notch until the pointer again drops below zero. Move the rider back one notch.
4. Slowly slide the rider along the front beam until the pointer stops at the zero point.
5. The mass of the object is equal to the sum of the readings on the three beams.

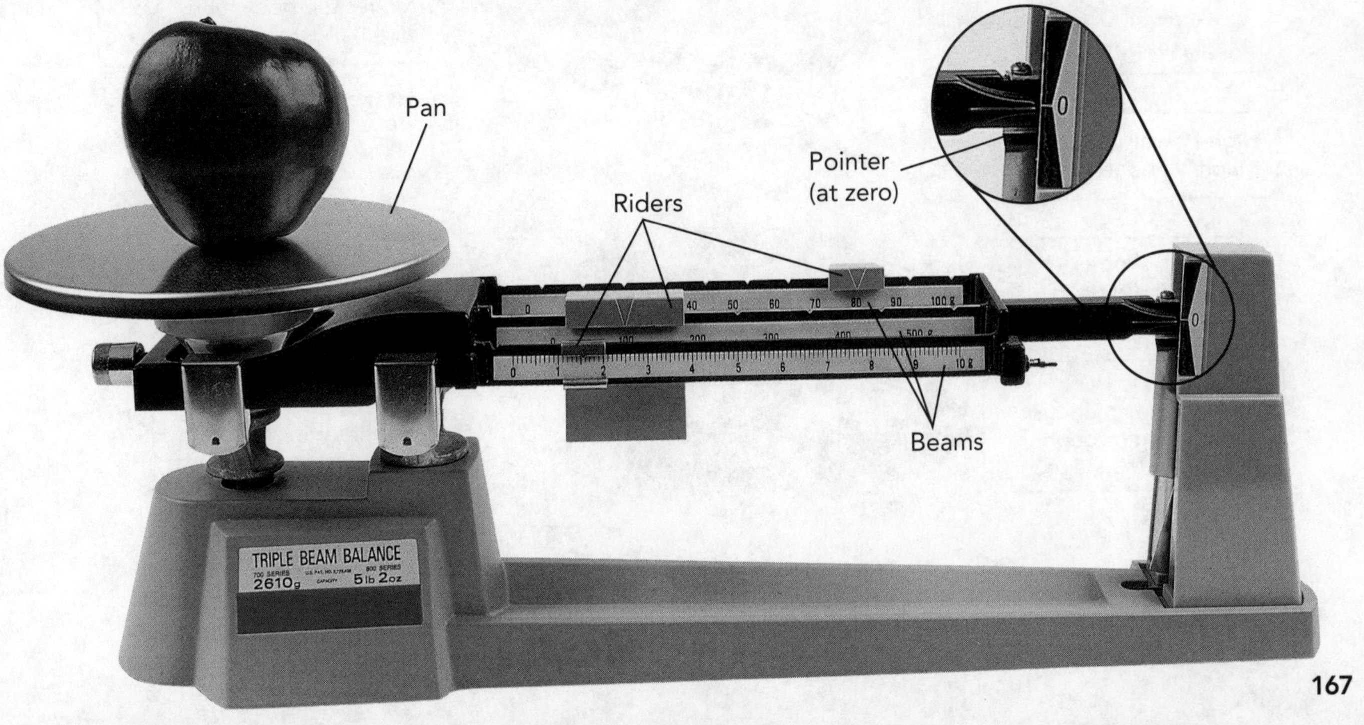

APPENDIX C

Using a Microscope

The microscope is an essential tool in the study of life science. It allows you to see things that are too small to be seen with the unaided eye.

You will probably use a compound microscope like the one you see here. The compound microscope has more than one lens that magnifies the object you view.

Typically, a compound microscope has one lens in the eyepiece (the part you look through). The eyepiece lens usually magnifies 10×. Any object you view through this lens will appear 10 times larger than it is.

A compound microscope may contain two or three other lenses called objective lenses. They are called the low-power and high-power objective lenses. The low-power objective lens usually magnifies 10×. The high-power objective lenses usually magnify 40× and 100×.

To calculate the total magnification with which you are viewing an object, multiply the magnification of the eyepiece lens by the magnification of the objective lens you are using. For example, the eyepiece's magnification of 10× multiplied by the low-power objective's magnification of 10× equals a total magnification of 100×.

Use the photo of the compound microscope to become familiar with the parts of the microscope and their functions.

The Parts of a Microscope

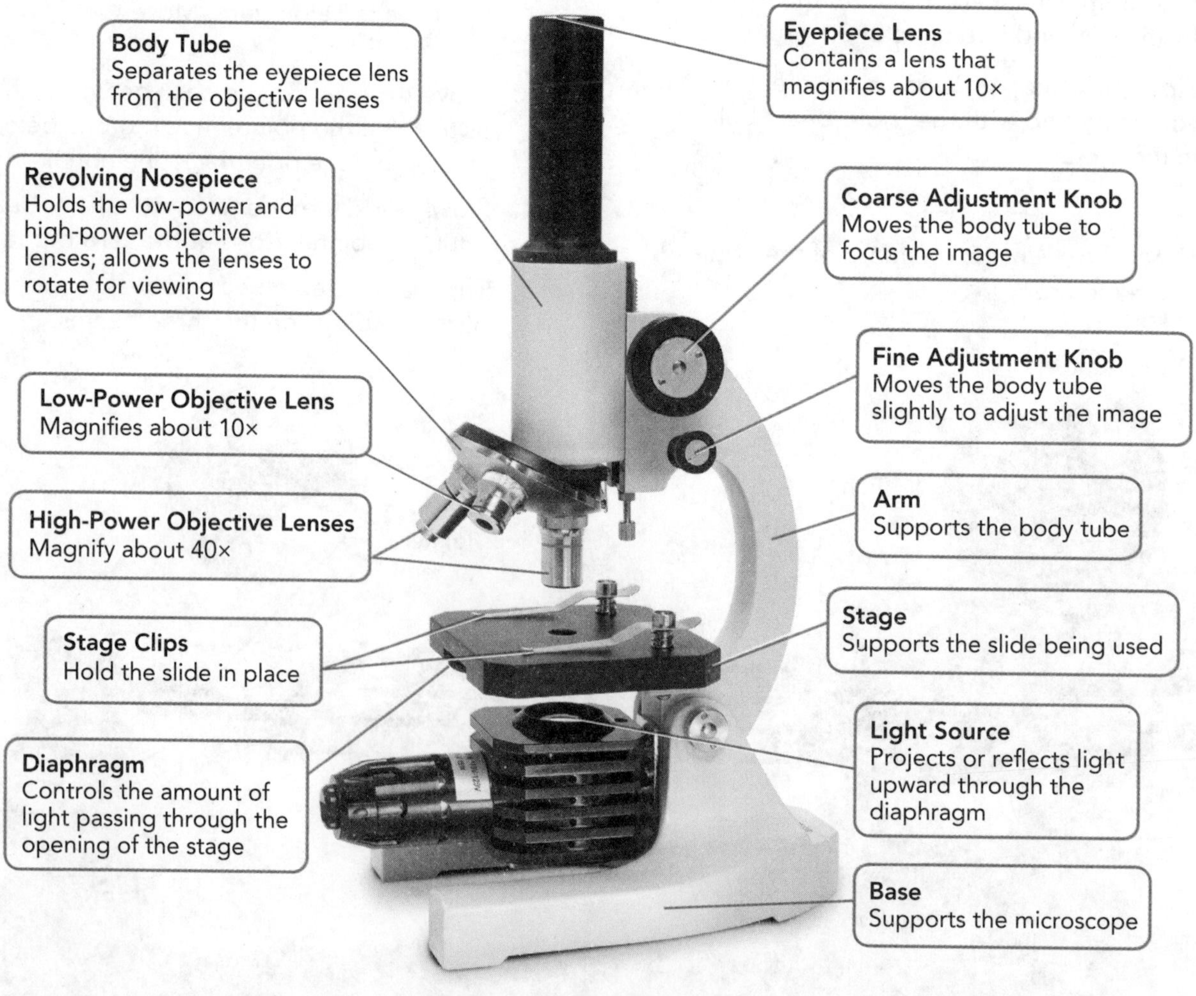

Body Tube
Separates the eyepiece lens from the objective lenses
Revolving Nosepiece
Holds the low-power and high-power objective lenses; allows the lenses to rotate for viewing
Low-Power Objective Lens
Magnifies about 10×
High-Power Objective Lenses
Magnify about 40×
Stage Clips
Hold the slide in place
Diaphragm
Controls the amount of light passing through the opening of the stage
Eyepiece Lens
Contains a lens that magnifies about 10×
Coarse Adjustment Knob
Moves the body tube to focus the image
Fine Adjustment Knob
Moves the body tube slightly to adjust the image
Arm
Supports the body tube
Stage
Supports the slide being used
Light Source
Projects or reflects light upward through the diaphragm
Base
Supports the microscope

Using the Microscope

Use the following procedures when you are working with a microscope.

1. To carry the microscope, grasp the microscope's arm with one hand. Place your other hand under the base.
2. Place the microscope on a table with the arm toward you.
3. Turn the coarse adjustment knob to raise the body tube.
4. Revolve the nosepiece until the low-power objective lens clicks into place.
5. Adjust the diaphragm. While looking through the eyepiece, adjust the mirror until you see a bright white circle of light. **CAUTION:** Never use direct sunlight as a light source.
6. Place a slide on the stage. Center the specimen over the opening on the stage. Use the stage clips to hold the slide in place. **CAUTION:** Glass slides are fragile.
7. Look at the stage from the side. Carefully turn the coarse adjustment knob to lower the body tube until the low-power objective almost touches the slide.
8. Looking through the eyepiece, very slowly turn the coarse adjustment knob until the specimen comes into focus.
9. To switch to the high-power objective lens, look at the microscope from the side. Carefully revolve the nosepiece until the high-power objective lens clicks into place. Make sure the lens does not hit the slide.
10. Looking through the eyepiece, turn the fine adjustment knob until the specimen comes into focus.

Making a Wet-Mount Slide

Use the following procedures to make a wet-mount slide of a specimen.

1. Obtain a clean microscope slide and a coverslip. **CAUTION:** Glass slides and coverslips are fragile.
2. Place the specimen on the center of the slide. The specimen must be thin enough for light to pass through it.
3. Using a plastic dropper, place a drop of water on the specimen.
4. Gently place one edge of the coverslip against the slide so that it touches the edge of the water drop at a 45° angle. Slowly lower the coverslip over the specimen. If you see air bubbles trapped beneath the coverslip, tap the coverslip gently with the eraser end of a pencil.
5. Remove any excess water at the edge of the coverslip with a paper towel.

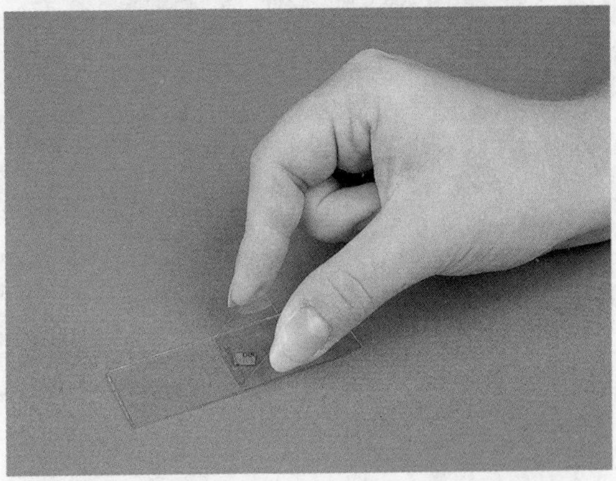

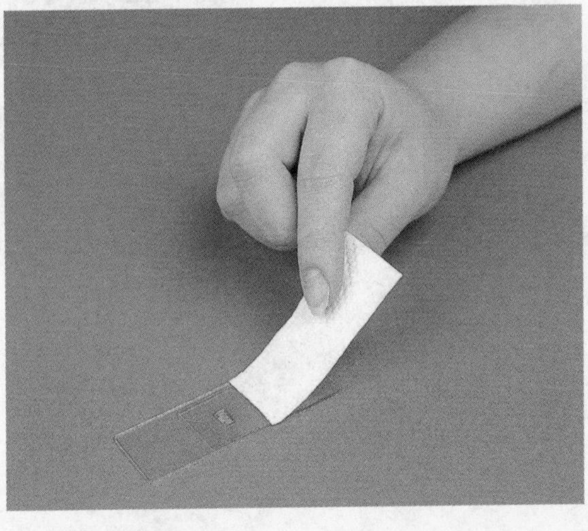

APPENDIX D

Periodic Table of Elements

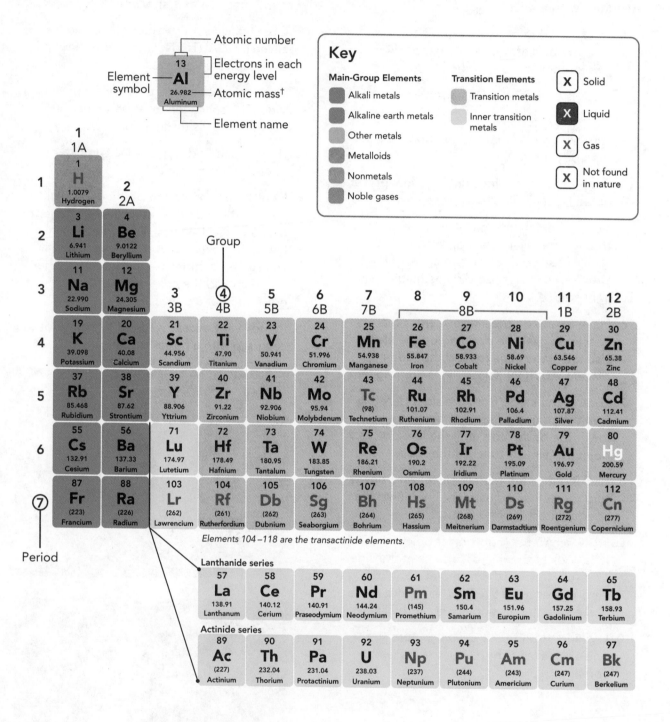

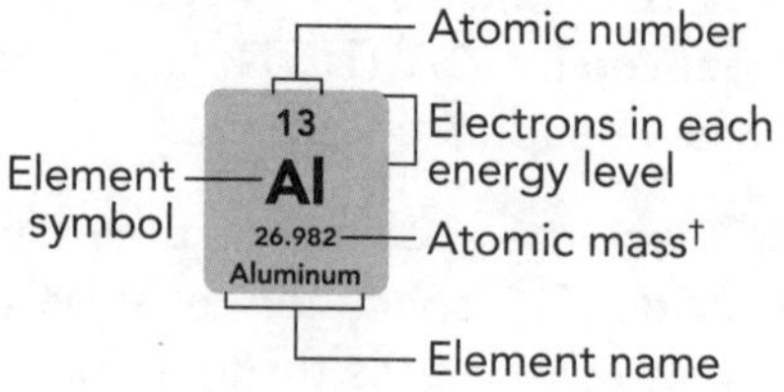

Key

Main-Group Elements
- Alkali metals
- Alkaline earth metals
- Other metals
- Metalloids
- Nonmetals
- Noble gases

Transition Elements
- Transition metals
- Inner transition metals

- X Solid
- X Liquid
- X Gas
- X Not found in nature

Period	1 1A	2 2A	3 3B	4 4B	5 5B	6 6B	7 7B	8	9 8B	10	11 1B	12 2B
1	1 H 1.0079 Hydrogen											
2	3 Li 6.941 Lithium	4 Be 9.0122 Beryllium										
3	11 Na 22.990 Sodium	12 Mg 24.305 Magnesium										
4	19 K 39.098 Potassium	20 Ca 40.08 Calcium	21 Sc 44.956 Scandium	22 Ti 47.90 Titanium	23 V 50.941 Vanadium	24 Cr 51.996 Chromium	25 Mn 54.938 Manganese	26 Fe 55.847 Iron	27 Co 58.933 Cobalt	28 Ni 58.69 Nickel	29 Cu 63.546 Copper	30 Zn 65.38 Zinc
5	37 Rb 85.468 Rubidium	38 Sr 87.62 Strontium	39 Y 88.906 Yttrium	40 Zr 91.22 Zirconium	41 Nb 92.906 Niobium	42 Mo 95.94 Molybdenum	43 Tc (98) Technetium	44 Ru 101.07 Ruthenium	45 Rh 102.91 Rhodium	46 Pd 106.4 Palladium	47 Ag 107.87 Silver	48 Cd 112.41 Cadmium
6	55 Cs 132.91 Cesium	56 Ba 137.33 Barium	71 Lu 174.97 Lutetium	72 Hf 178.49 Hafnium	73 Ta 180.95 Tantalum	74 W 183.85 Tungsten	75 Re 186.21 Rhenium	76 Os 190.2 Osmium	77 Ir 192.22 Iridium	78 Pt 195.09 Platinum	79 Au 196.97 Gold	80 Hg 200.59 Mercury
7	87 Fr (223) Francium	88 Ra (226) Radium	103 Lr (262) Lawrencium	104 Rf (261) Rutherfordium	105 Db (262) Dubnium	106 Sg (263) Seaborgium	107 Bh (264) Bohrium	108 Hs (265) Hassium	109 Mt (268) Meitnerium	110 Ds (269) Darmstadtium	111 Rg (272) Roentgenium	112 Cn (277) Copernicium

Elements 104–118 are the transactinide elements.

Lanthanide series

57 La 138.91 Lanthanum	58 Ce 140.12 Cerium	59 Pr 140.91 Praseodymium	60 Nd 144.24 Neodymium	61 Pm (145) Promethium	62 Sm 150.4 Samarium	63 Eu 151.96 Europium	64 Gd 157.25 Gadolinium	65 Tb 158.93 Terbium

Actinide series

89 Ac (227) Actinium	90 Th 232.04 Thorium	91 Pa 231.04 Protactinium	92 U 238.03 Uranium	93 Np (237) Neptunium	94 Pu (244) Plutonium	95 Am (243) Americium	96 Cm (247) Curium	97 Bk (247) Berkelium

†*The atomic masses in parentheses are the mass numbers of the longest-lived isotope of elements for which a standard atomic mass cannot be defined.*

13 3A	14 4A	15 5A	16 6A	17 7A	18 8A
					2 **He** 4.0026 Helium
5 **B** 10.81 Boron	6 **C** 12.011 Carbon	7 **N** 14.007 Nitrogen	8 **O** 15.999 Oxygen	9 **F** 18.998 Fluorine	10 **Ne** 20.179 Neon
13 **Al** 26.982 Aluminum	14 **Si** 28.086 Silicon	15 **P** 30.974 Phosphorus	16 **S** 32.06 Sulfur	17 **Cl** 35.453 Chlorine	18 **Ar** 39.948 Argon
31 **Ga** 69.72 Gallium	32 **Ge** 72.59 Germanium	33 **As** 74.922 Arsenic	34 **Se** 78.96 Selenium	35 **Br** 79.904 Bromine	36 **Kr** 83.80 Krypton
49 **In** 114.82 Indium	50 **Sn** 118.69 Tin	51 **Sb** 121.75 Antimony	52 **Te** 127.60 Tellurium	53 **I** 126.90 Iodine	54 **Xe** 131.30 Xenon
81 **Tl** 204.37 Thallium	82 **Pb** 207.2 Lead	83 **Bi** 208.98 Bismuth	84 **Po** (209) Polonium	85 **At** (210) Astatine	86 **Rn** (222) Radon
113 **Nh** (284) Nihonium	114 **Fl** (289) Flerovium	115 **Mc** (288) Moscovium	116 **Lv** (292) Livermorium	117 **Ts** (294) Tennessine	118 **Og** (294) Oganesson

66 **Dy** 162.50 Dysprosium	67 **Ho** 164.93 Holmium	68 **Er** 167.26 Erbium	69 **Tm** 168.93 Thulium	70 **Yb** 173.04 Ytterbium
98 **Cf** (251) Californium	99 **Es** (252) Einsteinium	100 **Fm** (257) Fermium	101 **Md** (258) Mendelevium	102 **No** (259) Nobelium

GLOSSARY

A

acid rain Rain or another form of precipitation that is more acidic than normal, caused by the release of molecules of sulfur dioxide and nitrogen oxide into the air. (116)

alluvial fan A wide, sloping deposit of sediment formed where a stream leaves a mountain range. (27)

B

birth rate The number of people born per 1,000 individuals for a certain period of time. (106)

C

chemical weathering The process that breaks down rock through chemical changes. (6)

conservation The practice of using less of a resource so that it can last longer. (110)

continental glacier A glacier that covers much of a continent or large island. (36)

crystallize To form a crystal structure. (77)

D

death rate The number of deaths per 1,000 individuals in a certain period of time. (106)

deflation The process by which wind removes surface materials. (18)

deforestation The removal of forests to use the land for other reasons. (124)

delta A landform made of sediment that is deposited where a river flows into an ocean or lake. (27)

deposition Process in which sediment is laid down in new locations. (15)

desalination A process that removes salt from sea water to make fresh water. (89)

desertification The advance of desert-like conditions into areas that previously were fertile; caused by overfarming, overgrazing, drought, and climate change. (127)

E

emissions Pollutants that are released into the air. (114)

erosion The process by which water, ice, wind, or gravity moves weathered particles of rock and soil. (5, 126)

exponential growth A rate of change that increases more and more rapidly over time. (107)

F

flood plain The flat, wide area of land along a river. (25)

fossil fuel Energy-rich substance formed from the remains of organisms. (58)

G

glacier Any large mass of ice that moves slowly over land. (35)

groundwater Water that fills the cracks and spaces in underground soil and rock layers. (29)

H

humus Dark-colored organic material in soil. (9)

I

ice age Time in Earth's history during which glaciers covered large parts of the surface. (36)

L

loess A wind-formed deposit made of fine particles of clay and silt. (19)

longshore drift The movement of water and sediment down a beach caused by waves coming in to shore at an angle. (42)

M

mass movement Any one of several processes by which gravity moves sediment downhill. (16)

mechanical weathering The type of weathering in which rock is physically broken into smaller pieces. (6)

N

natural resource Anything naturally occuring in the environment that humans use. (57, 123)

nonpoint source A widely spread source of pollution that is difficult to link to a specific point of origin. (113)

nonrenewable resource A natural resource that is not replaced in a useful time frame. (57, 123)

nuclear fission The splitting of an atom's nuclues into two nuclei, which releases a great deal of energy. (63)

O

ore A mineral deposit large enough and valuable enough for it to be extracted from the ground. (75)

overpopulation A condition in which the number of humans grows beyond what the available resources can support. (109)

ozone A form of oxygen that has three oxygen atoms in each molecule instead of the usual two; toxic to organisms where it forms near Earth's surface. (115)

P

petroleum Liquid fossil fuel; oil. (60)

plucking The process by which a glacier picks up rocks as it flows over the land. (37)

point source A specific source of pollution that can be identified. (113)

pollution Contamination of Earth's land, water, or air through the release of harmful substances into the environment. (109, 113)

R

renewable resource A resource that is either always available or is naturally replaced in a relatively short time. (67, 123)

runoff Water that flows over the ground surface rather than soaking into the ground. (23)

S

sand dune A deposit of wind-blown sand. (19)

sediment Small, solid pieces of material that come from rocks or the remains of organisms; earth materials deposited by erosion. (15, 139)

sewage The water and human wastes that are washed down sinks, toilets, and showers. (138)

soil The loose, weathered material on Earth's surface in which plants can grow. (9)

stream A channel through which water is continually flowing downhill. (24)

sustainable Using a resource in ways that maintain it at a certain quality for a certain period of time. (130)

sustainable use The practice of allowing renewable resources time to recover and replenish. (110)

T

thermal pollution A type of pollution caused by factories and power plants releasing superheated water into bodies of water. (139)

till The sediments deposited directly by a glacier. (38)

tributary A stream or river that flows into a larger river. (24)

U

uniformitarianism The geologic principle that the same geologic processes that operate today operated in the past to change Earth's surface. (5)

V

valley glacier A long, narrow glacier that forms when snow and ice build up in a mountain valley. (36)

INDEX

Page numbers for key terms are printed in boldface type.

A

Abrasion, 6, 7
- by glaciers, 37
- by waves, 40
- by wind, 18

Academic Vocabulary. *See* **Vocabulary, Academic**
Acid rain, 7–8, **116**
Agriculture
- and land management, 124–126
- and pollution, 138, 140, 143
- *See also* **Farming**

Air pollution, 113–121
- causes, 113–117
- indoor, 117
- outdoor, 114–116
- reducing, 118–119, 121

Allergens, 117
Alluvial fans, **27**
Anthracite, 59
Application of Skills. *See* **Connect It!; Design It!; Math Toolbox; Model It!; Plan It!; uDemonstrate Lab; uEngineer It!**
Aquaculture, 141
Aquifers, 87
Arêtes, 38
Assessment
- Evidence-Based Assessment, 46–47, 94–95, 148–149
- Review and Assess, 44–45, 92–93, 146–147

B

Balances, 167
Barrier islands, 42
Beach formation, 42
Bedrock, 9, 125
Bioenergy resources, 71
Biosolid recycling, 134
Birth rate, **106**
Bitumen, 59
Brooks, 24

C

Caltrans Highway Corridor Mapping project, 13
Car and truck pollution, 114–116
Carbon monoxide pollution, 114, 117
Carbonic acid, 7, 29
Careers
- Civil Engineer, 21

Case Studies
- Buyer Beware!, 32–33
- Nothing Goes to Waste, 134–135
- Phosphorus Fiasco, 82–83

Caves and caverns, 29–30
- sea caves, 41

Chemical weathering, **6**–7
Chlorofluorocarbons (CFCs), 119
Cirques, 38
Clear-cutting of forests, 131
Coal, 58–59
Compound microscopes, 168–169
Connect It!, 4, 14, 22, 34, 56, 66, 74, 84, 104, 112, 122, 136
Conservation, **110**
- habitat disruption and restoration, 124, 128–132

Continental glaciers, **36**
Creeks, 24
Creep (mass movement), 16–17
Crosscutting Concepts
- Cause and Effect, 62, 77, 88, 95, 99, 122, 125, 149
- Patterns, 16, 18, 33, 63, 79, 118
- Scale, Proportion, and Quantity, 4, 8, 10, 14, 17, 24, 66, 70, 112, 118, 122, 127, 136, 141
- Systems and System Models, 11, 12, 16, 26, 39, 40, 47, 51, 59, 63, 68, 79, 87, 99, 119

Cryosphere, 35
Crystallization (minerals), **77**

D

Death rate, **106**
Deflation (erosion), **18**
Deforestation, **124**
Deltas, **27**
Deposition, sedimentary, **15**
- and glacial erosion, 38
- and water erosion, 27–29
- and wave erosion, 42
- and wind erosion, 19

Desalination, **89**
Desert pavement, 18
Desertification, **127**
Design It!, 89
Digital Learning
- Assessment, 45, 93, 147
- Interactivity, 2, 8, 9, 10, 13, 15, 16, 19, 20, 23, 29, 30, 36, 38, 42, 43, 47, 54, 60, 64, 65, 67, 69, 71, 72, 73, 78, 80, 81, 85, 87, 89, 90, 95, 102, 106, 107, 110, 116, 119, 120, 126, 132, 133, 139, 140, 142, 143, 144, 149
- Video, 2, 21, 26, 54, 60, 68, 78, 102, 117, 128, 141, 145
- Virtual Lab, 5, 88
- Vocabulary App, 4, 14, 22, 34, 56, 66, 74, 84, 104, 112, 122, 136

Dowsing, 91
Drainage basin, 24
Drought, 127

E

Earthworms, 11
Ecological issues
- agriculture, mining, and land development, 124
- air pollution, 113–121
- forest management, 130–132
- habitat disruption and restoration, 124, 128–132
- mining, 82–83
- natural resources, 108–110, 123
- phosphorous cycle disruption, 82–83
- sinkholes, 32–33
- soil management, 125–128

waste management, 128, 134–135, 138
water management, 88–89
water pollution, 137–145
wetlands, 129
See also **Pollution**
Ecosystems
habitat disruption and restoration, 124, 128–132
wetlands, 129
Electronic balances, 167
Elements in periodic table, 170–171
Emissions, **114,** 116
reducing, 118
Engineering
Defining the Problem, 13
Impact on Society, 145
Sustainable Design, 73
See also **Science and Engineering Practices; uEngineer It!**
Engineering and design process, 162–165
communicating solutions, 165
defining problems, 162–163
designing, testing, and evaluating solutions, 164
developing solutions, 163
identifying criteria and constraints, 163
redesigning and retesting solutions, 165
See also **Science practices**
Environmental issues. *See* **Ecological issues**
Erosion, **5,** 15–19, **126**
and deposition, 15, 19, 27–29, 38, 42
by glacier, 35–39
and mass movement, 16–17
rate of, 6, 8, 15, 30, 37, 41
role of organisms in, 6
by water, 23–30
by waves, 40–42
and weathering, 5–8
of wetlands, 129
Exponential growth, **107**

F

Factories and pollution, 113, 114, 115, 138, 139, 143
Famine, 127
Farming
and land management, 124–126
and water pollution, 138, 140, 143
Features. *See* **Careers; Case Studies; Global to Local; It's All Connected; uDemonstrate Lab; uEngineer It!**
Fertilizers, 126
and pollution, 140
recycled, 134
Fjord, 38
Flood plains, **25**–26, 28
Flooding, 129
Forest management, 130–132
Fossil fuels, **58**
coal, 58–59
and global politics, 64
natural gas, 62
oil, 60–61
and pollution, 118, 139, 141
usage issues, 64, 67
and weathering, 7
Fracking, 62
Freshwater, 137–139, 145
Frost wedging, 6

G

Gas pollution, 117, 139, 141, 142
Geologic hazards, 32–33
Geothermal energy, 71
Glacial erosion, 35–39
Glaciers, **35**–36
continental and valley, 35
retreating, 39
Global to Local
Working Together to Reduce Air Pollution, 121
Groundwater, **29**–30, 85, 87
Growth, exponential, **107**
Growth of human population, 105–107
Gullies, 24

H

Habitats
disruption, preservation, and reclamation, 124, 128–132
See also **Ecosystems**
Headlands, 40, 41
Horns (landforms), 38
Humus, **9**–11
Hydroelectric power, 69, 73

I

Ice ages, **36**
Inquiry Skills. *See* **Science and Engineering Practices**
It's All Connected
The Pseudoscience of Water Dowsing, 91

K

Karst topography, 30
Kettles and kettle lakes, 39

L

Laboratory balances, 167
Labs
uConnect, xii, 52, 100
uDemonstrate
To Drill or Not to Drill, 96–99
Materials on a Slope, 48–51
Washing Away, 150–153
uInvestigate, 4, 6, 12, 14, 18, 20, 22, 24, 31, 34, 35, 40, 56, 57, 58, 66, 70, 74, 75, 84, 87, 104, 105, 108, 112, 113, 114, 122, 124, 136, 142
Lakes, 86
Land management, 123–132
and development, 124
and forests, 130–132
and natural resources, 123
and reclamation, 128

INDEX Page numbers for key terms are printed in boldface type.

and soil, 125–127
and wetlands, 129
Landfills, 128
Landforms
and glacial deposition, 38
and water erosion, 25, 27
and wave erosion, 41–42
weathering, erosion, and deposition cycle, 15
Landslides, 13, 16–17
Lenses (microscopes), 168
Lignite, 59
Limestone, 7, 29–30
Literacy Connection. *See* **Reading and Literacy Skills**
Lithosphere, 35
Litter (soil), 125
Loess deposits, **19**
Logging, 131
Longshore drift, **42**

M

Magnification (microscopes), 168
Mass movement, **16**
Math Connection
Analyze Proportional Relationships, 122, 136
Analyze Quantitative Relationships, 14, 112
Analyze Relationships, 56
Draw Comparative Inferences, 84, 104
Reason Abstractly, 34
Reason Quantitatively, 4
Represent Quantitative Relationships, 66
Math Toolbox
Causes of Land Degradation, 127
Comparing Glacier Thickness, 36
Comparing Weathered Limestone, 8
Distribution of Water Resources, 86
Energy Usage, 118
Major Landslides and Mudflows, 17
Natural Gas Consumption in the U.S., 62
Projected Growth Rates, 107
Sources of Oil Pollution, 141
Wind Power, 70
Meanders, 26
Mechanical weathering, **6**
Methane gas pollution, 114
Micro-hydro power, 73
Microscopes, 168–169
Mineral resources, 74–80
Minerals
distribution, 78–79
formation, 76–77
use, 80, 82–83
Mining, 80, 82–83, 109, 124
Model It!, 11, 26, 39, 68, 119
Moraines, 38
Mudflows, 16–17

N

Natural gas, 62
Natural hazards, mapping, 13, 16
Natural resources, 52–91
defined, **57, 123**
human consumption of, 108–110
mineral resources, 74–83
nonrenewable, 57–64
renewable, 67–73
water resources, 84–91
See also **Ecological issues; Forest management; Land management; Water pollution; Water resources**
Nonpoint-source pollution, **113**
Nonrenewable resources, **57**–64, **123**
fossil fuels, 58–62
nuclear power, 63
Nuclear fission, **63**

O

Oceans
dead zones, 140
and natural resources, 89
and pollution, 89, 140–143
Oil, 60–61
Oil pollution, 139, 141, 142
Ore, **75**
Overgrazing, 127
Overpopulation, **109**
Oxbow lakes, 26, 28
Ozone, **115**
Ozone layer, 119

P

Paris Agreement, 121
Peat, 59
Periodic table, 170–171
Permeable rocks, 8
Petroleum, **60**–61
Phosphorus, 82–83
Pipeline pollution, 139
Plan It!, 64, 125, 143
Plucking, glacial, **37**
Point-source pollution, **113**
Pollution, **109,** 113
of air, 113–121
from factories, 113, 114, 115, 138, 139, 143
and fossil fuels, 58–62, 64, 139, 141, 142
reducing, 118–119, 121, 128, 134–135, 142–143, 145
and waste management, 128, 134–135, 138, 140, 143, 145
of water, 88, 137–145
See also **Ecological issues**
Populations
births and deaths, 106
growth of, 105–107
and resource consumption, 108–110
Process Skills. *See* **Science and Engineering Practices**

Project-based Learning. *See* **Quest**

Q

Quest Check-In
Interactivity, 20, 43, 65, 72, 81, 90, 120, 133, 144
Lab, 12, 20, 31
Quest Findings, 47, 95, 149
Quest Kickoff
Ingenious Islands, 2
Predicting Boom or Bust, 54
Trash Backlash, 102
Question It!, 19, 78, 108

R

Radon, 117
Rapids, 25, 28
Reading and Literacy Skills
Analyze Text, 77
Ask Questions, 108
Cite Evidence, 57
Cite Textual Evidence, 19, 22, 23, 26, 56, 62, 63, 112, 115, 116, 122, 124, 129
Communicate, 165
Compare and Contrast, 158
Describe, 128
Determine Central Ideas, 58, 113
Determine Conclusions, 64, 104, 107, 109, 119, 141
Determine Differences, 58
Determine Meaning, 67, 74, 76, 78
Draw Evidence, 66, 71, 128, 132, 136, 137, 139
Explain, 19
Identify, 89, 136
Integrate Information, 28
Integrate with Visuals, 11, 14, 15, 16, 24, 28, 117, 129
Interpret Diagrams, 10, 18, 25, 30, 33, 37, 40
Interpret Graphs, 36
Interpret Photographs, 14, 27
Interpret Tables, 60
Summarize, 30, 68, 87
Summarize Text, 7, 80
Support Author's Claim, 84
Translate Information, 42, 127
Write Arguments, 116
Write Explanatory Texts, 4, 7, 9, 41, 143
Write Informative Texts, 34, 39, 41
Reading Check. *See* **Reading and Literacy Skills**
Recycling, 143
into biosolids, 134
Renewable resources, 67–73, **123**
biomass, 71
geothermal, 71
hydroelectric, 69, 73
solar, 68
wind, 70
Resources. *See* **Natural resources; Water resources**
Rills, 24
Rivers, 24, 86
and erosion, 26–28, 42
Runoff, 23
Rust formation, 7

S

Safety symbols, 166
Sand dunes, 19
Sandbars, 42
Sandstorms, 18
Science and Engineering Practices
Analyze Costs, 83
Analyze Costs and Benefits, 69
Analyze Data, 51
Analyze Proportional Relationships, 122, 127, 136
Analyze Quantitative Relationships, 14, 17, 70, 112, 118
Analyze Relationships, 56, 62
Analyze Systems, 47
Apply Concepts, 11, 28, 61, 76, 167
Apply Scientific Reasoning, 22, 34, 78, 84, 104, 153
Calculate, 60, 62, 83, 86, 135, 161, 167
Cause and Effect, 62, 77, 88, 95, 99, 122, 125, 149
Classify, 9, 38, 56
Compare Data, 153
Connect to Society, 80
Construct Arguments, 72, 135, 143
Construct Explanations, 4, 6, 18, 22, 29, 37, 51, 59, 74, 83, 99, 112
Construct Graphs, 8, 141
Define Problems, 19
Design Solutions, 89
Develop Arguments, 110
Develop Models, 11, 16, 26, 39, 68, 119
Develop Possible Solutions, 19
Draw Comparative Inferences, 84, 86, 104, 107
Engage in Argument, 135, 153
Evaluate, 65, 90, 120, 133, 144
Evaluate Change, 83
Evaluate Data, 8, 81, 107
Evaluate Quantity, 10
Evaluate Your Solution, 31, 43
Explain Phenomena, 86
Form Opinions, 33
Identify Limitations, 51, 99
Identify Patterns, 16
Infer, 66, 109
Make Observations, 77
Make Predictions, 112
Patterns, 18, 33, 63, 79, 118
Predict, 14, 19, 25, 40
Provide Evidence, 136
Reason Abstractly, 34, 36
Reason Quantitatively, 4, 8, 24
Refine Plans, 153
Refine Solutions, 20

INDEX

Page numbers for key terms are printed in boldface type.

Represent Quantitative Relationships, 66, 70
Synthesize Information, 11
Use Evidence, 51
Use Models, 11, 12, 40, 51, 59, 63, 79, 87, 99
Use Proportional Relationships, 17
Use Tables, 135

Science Notebook
Make Meaning, 5, 155, 159, 163, 164
Reflect, 57, 75, 85, 105, 123, 154, 156, 162
Write About It, 29, 113, 132, 137, 155, 156, 157, 158, 159, 160, 161

Science practices, 154–162
analyzing and evaluating, 154, 159, 164–165
classifying, inferring, observing, and predicting, 154
communicating, 157, 165
controlled variables, 157
curiosity, creativity, and skepticism, 155, 163
empirical evidence, 159
ethics and bias, 155, 157, 159
experiments and investigations, 154, 156–157, 162–164
explanations, theories, and laws, 158–159
math skills and graphs, 161
measurements, 160
models and prototypes, 154, 156, 164–165
objective and inductive reasoning, 155
scientific literacy, 159
See also **Engineering and design process**

Sea arches, 41
Sea caves, 41
Sea stacks, 41
Sediments, 15, 139
Sewage, 138
treating, 134–135, 143, 145
Sinkholes, 30, 32–33
Skills. *See* **Math Connection; Reading and Literacy Skills; Science and Engineering Practices**
Slides, wet-mount, 169
Slumps, 16–17
Smog, 115
Soil, 9
formation, 10–11
nutrient deposits, 10–11, 19, 25
Soil horizons, 10
Soil management, 125–128
Solar energy, 68
Stalactites and stalagmites, 29
Streams, 24
Strip mining, 7
Surface water, 85, 86
Sustainability, 130
Sustainable use, 110

T

Thermal pollution, 139
Till, glacial, 38
Tools
balances, 167
microscopes, 168–169
Topsoil, 125
Trees and forests, 130–132
Tributaries, 24, 28
Triple-beam balances, 167

U

uConnect Lab
Finding a Solution for Your Pollution, 103A–103B
How Does Gravity Affect Materials on a Slope?, 3A–3B
What's in a Piece of Coal?, 55A–55B
uDemonstrate Lab
Materials on a Slope, 48–51
To Drill or Not to Drill, 96–99
Washing Away, 150–153
uEngineer It!
Ground Shifting Advances: Maps Help Predict, 13
Micro-Hydro Power, 73
From Wastewater to Tap Water, 145
Uniformitarianism, 5
Units of measurement, 160
Uranium, 63

V

Valley formation, 25–26, 30, 37
Valley glaciers, 36
Vehicle pollution, 114–116
Vocabulary, Academic, 4, 5, 9, 14, 15, 18, 22, 26, 27, 34, 35, 40, 56, 66, 68, 74, 78, 84, 104, 106, 108, 112, 115, 122, 123, 136, 137

W

Waste management, 128, 134–135, 138, 140, 143, 145
Water erosion, 6–7, 23–30
by deposition, 27–29
by groundwater, 29–30
and karst topography, 30
by runoff, 23
and stream formation, 24
by stream movement, 25–26
Water pollution, 137–145
freshwater, 137–139, 145
marine, 140–142
and recycling, 135
and resource management, 137, 142–143
role of wetlands, 129, 142–145
Water resources, 84–89
and desalination, 89
distribution of, 85, 86, 87, 88
groundwater, 85, 87

human impact on, 88–89, 108, 137
oceans, 89
surface water, 85, 86
wetlands, 129, 142–145
Waterfalls, 25, 28
Watersheds, 24
Wave erosion, 40–42
Wave-cut cliff, 41
Weathering, 5–8
chemical, 7
mechanical, 6
rate of, 8
and soil formation, 9–11
See also **Erosion**
Wells, 87
Wetlands, 129
Wet-mount slides, 169
Wind energy, 70
Writing Skills. *See* **Science Notebook**

CREDITS

Photographs

Photo locators denoted as follows: Top (T), Center (C), Bottom (B), Left (L), Right (R), Background (Bkgd)

Covers

Front Cover: 35007/E+/Getty Images
Back Cover: LHF Graphics/Shutterstock

Front Matter

iv: Clari Massimiliano/Shutterstock; vi: Robert Harding/Alamy Stock Photo; vii: Panpilas L/Shutterstock; viii: Brian J. Skerry/ National Geographic/Getty Images; viii: KPG Payless2/ Shutterstock; ix: Gary Meszaros/Science Source/Getty Images.

Topic 1

xii: Robert Harding/Alamy Stock Photo;002: Maggie Steber/ Getty Images; 003: Xu Jian/Getty Images; 004: Russ Bishop/ Alamy Stock Photo; 006 TC: Thomas Mitchell/Alamy Stock Photo; 006 TL: Sean Kaufmann/Getty Images; 007 TC: Mironov/Shutterstock; 007 TL: IPics Photography/Alamy Stock Photo; 009: Madllen/123RF; 011 TCR: Sean Kaufmann/ Getty Images; 011 TR: Vinicius Tupinamba/Shutterstock; 013: Alejandro Zepeda/EPA/Newcom; 014: Macduff Everton/ National Geographic Magazines/Getty Images; 021 B: David Weintraub/Science Source; 021 TR: Roman Kadarjan/Alamy Stock Photo; 022: Songquan Deng/Shutterstock; 027 CL: Totajla/Shutterstock; 027 TL: Planet Observer/UIG/Getty Images; 029: Macduff Everton/Getty Images; 030: AP Images; 032 B: Cobalt88/Shutterstock; 032 BC: Spencer Grant/Getty Images; 034: Design Pics Inc/Alamy Stock Photo; 037: Pavel Svoboda Photography/Shutterstock; 041: Hemis/Alamy Stock Photo; 043: Mick Jack/Alamy Stock Photo;

Topic 2

052: Panpilas L/Shutterstock; 054: Philipus/Alamy Stock Photo; 058: Aleksandr Pobedimskiy/Shutterstock; 060: Louisiana Governors Office/Alamy Stock Photo; 062: National Geographic Creative/Alamy Stock Photo; 064: Everett Historical/Shutterstock; 066: Raulbaenacasado/Shutterstock; 070: Chris James/Alamy Stock Photo; 074: Henryk Sadura/ Shutterstock; 076: WaterFrame/Alamy Stock Photo; 077 B: Siim Sepp/Alamy Stock Photo; 077 T: Shu Hung Liu/ Shutterstock; 080: The Natural History Museum/Alamy Stock Photo; 082: Gabe Palmer/Alamy Stock Photo; 082: Pulsar Imagens/Alamy Stock Photo; 086: Larry Geddis/Alamy Stock Photo; 089: Bennyartist/Shutterstock; 091: World History Archive/Alamy Stock Photo; 096: Haizhen Du/Shutterstock; 097 B: Anton Starikov/Alamy Stock Photo; 097 TR: IStock/ Getty Images;

Topic 3

100: KPG Payless2/Shutterstock; 102: ThavornC/Shutterstock; 104: Justin Lambert/Getty Images; 109: Fotokostic/ Shutterstock; 110: Kletr/Shutterstock; 112: Por Nahorski Pavel/ Shutterstock; 116: Karol Kozlowski/Shutterstock; 118: Mark Kauzlarich/Bloomberg/Getty Images; 119: Science Source; 121: Vadim Petrakov/Shutterstock; 122: Brian A Jackson/ Shutterstock; 124 BCL: Chad Ehlers/Alamy Stock Photo; 124 BCR: Jiri Foltyn/Shutterstock; 124 BR: Rob Crandall/Alamy Stock Photo; 125: Perytskyy/iStock/Getty Images; 126 CL: Kletr/Shutterstock; 126 CR: Blickwinkel/Alamy Stock Photo; 127: JurgaR/iStock/Getty Images; 130: lowsun/Shutterstock; 132: George Clerk/Getty Images; 134: Philip Duff/Alamy Stock Photo; 136: iStock/Getty Images; 140: Rosanne Tackaberry/ Alamy Stock Photo; 142: US Navy Photo/Alamy Stock Photo; 143: ZUMA Press Inc/Alamy Stock Photo; 150: Philipp Dase/ Shutterstock;

End Matter

154 BCL: Philippe Plailly & Elisabeth Daynes/Science Source; 154 BL: EHStockphoto/Shutterstock; 154 TCL: Cyndi Monaghan/Getty Images; 154 TL: Javier Larrea/AGE Fotostock; 155: WaterFrame/Alamy Stock Photo; 156: Africa Studio/Shutterstock; 157: Jeff Rotman/Alamy Stock Photo; 158: Grant Faint/Getty Images; 159: Ross Armstrong/Alamy Stock Photo; 160: Geoz/Alamy Stock Photo; 163: Martin Shields/Alamy Stock Photo; 164: Nicola Tree/Getty Images; 165: Regan Geeseman/NASA; 167: Pearson Education Ltd.; 168: Pearson Education Ltd.; 169 BR: Pearson Education Ltd.; 169 TR: Pearson Education Ltd.

Program graphics: ArtMari/Shutterstock; BeatWalk/ Shutterstock; Irmun/Shutterstock; LHF Graphics/Shutterstock; Multigon/Shutterstock; Nikolaeva/Shutterstock; silm/ Shutterstock; Undrey/Shutterstock

Take Notes

Use this space for recording notes and sketching out ideas.

Take Notes

Use this space for recording notes and sketching out ideas.

Take Notes

Use this space for recording notes and sketching out ideas.

Take Notes

Use this space for recording notes and sketching out ideas.

Take Notes

Use this space for recording notes and sketching out ideas.

Take Notes

Use this space for recording notes and sketching out ideas.

Take Notes

Use this space for recording notes and sketching out ideas.

Take Notes

Use this space for recording notes and sketching out ideas.

Take Notes

Use this space for recording notes and sketching out ideas.

Take Notes

Use this space for recording notes and sketching out ideas.